A Superficial Reading of Henry James

A SUPERFICIAL READING OF HENRY JAMES
Preoccupations with the Material World

THOMAS J. OTTEN

The Ohio State University Press
Columbus

Library of Congress Cataloging-in-Publication Data

Otten, Thomas J.
  A superficial reading of Henry James : preoccupations with the material
world / Thomas J. Otten.
    p. cm.
  Includes bibliographical references and index.
  ISBN 0-8142-1026-0 (cloth : alk. paper) — ISBN 0-8142-9103-1 (cd-
rom) 1. James, Henry, 1843–1916—Criticism and interpretation. 2.
Material culture in literature. 3. Realism in literature. I. Title.
  PS2127.M37O88 2006
  813'.4—dc22
                                                    2006000595

Cover photograph: *Vase,* about 1897–1900. Object place: Boston, Massachusetts, United States. Grueby Faience Company, Boston, 1894–1909. Buff stoneware with applied decoration and matte glaze. 31.43 x 15.24 x 15.24 cm ($12^3/_8$ x 6 x 6 in.). Museum of Fine Arts, Boston. Anonymous gift in memory of John G. Pierce. 65.212.

Cover design by DesignSmith.
Type set in Adobe Garamond.
Printed by Thomson Shore, Inc.

The paper used in this publication meets the minimum requirements of
the American National Standard for Information Sciences—Permanence
of Paper for Printed Library Materials. ANSI Z39.48–1992.
9 8 7 6 5 4 3 2 1

FOR KELLY HAGER

Contents

ILLUSTRATIONS

ACKNOWLEDGMENTS

For reading some or all of the pages of this book, I thank Ian Baucom, Wai Chee Dimock, Kelly Hager, Victoria Hayne, Deidre Lynch, Michael Trask, Alexander Welsh, and Ruth Bernard Yeazell. Their praise and criticism have made this project much stronger than it would otherwise be. I also want to acknowledge a number of other people who have also contributed much to my intellectual life over the years I worked on this project: Lara Cohen, Kevis Goodman, Laura Green, Richard Kasemsarn, Thomas Kierstead, Vera Kutzinski, Jesse Matz, Christopher R. Miller, Pamela Sutton-Wallace, Stephen Trask, Maurice Wallace, and Lynn Wardley. Thanks as well to Gordon Hutner, who provided counsel at a crucial moment. Nancy Sommers and the late Richard Marius, both of the Expository Writing Program at Harvard University, gave me my first job along with much encouragement at the beginning of my career. And I am profoundly indebted to my colleagues in the Boston University English Department for their kindness and support as I was readying the manuscript for publication.

I am grateful to the Whitney Humanities Center at Yale University for providing an energizing forum for an early version of chapter 4, and I especially wish here to express my appreciation to Peter Brooks, the Center's director at that time. A Morse Fellowship from Yale University made possible the writing of much of the manuscript.

An early version of chapter 3 appeared in *American Literature* as "*The Spoils of Poynton* and the Properties of Touch" (1999); an early version of chapter 4 appeared in the *Yale Journal of Criticism* as "Slashing Henry James (On Painting and Political Economy, Circa 1900)" (2000). I thank the editors and referees of these journals for their challenging responses to my work. The two anonymous readers for The Ohio State University Press were exemplary for their generous intelligence. I am also indebted to my editors at Ohio State, Heather Lee Miller and Sandy Crooms, who have not lost their enthusiasm for publishing literary studies.

To Leslie Brisman, Wai Chee Dimock, and Joseph Roach—indispensable friends, guides, and examples—this unembroidered expression of my humble gratitude will have to suffice. This book began to take shape in my mind when I was writing a UCLA dissertation under the direction of Ruth Bernard Yeazell, with Alexander Welsh as second reader. Their extraordinary teaching seems to me an experience I am still learning from; their extraordinary range of knowledge is something I still seek to emulate.

My parents, Jewel T. Otten and James D. Otten, and my parents-in-law, Faye Paxson Hager and Lewis Hager, have been inspirations, each in her or his own way. My sister, Julia Anne Knier, who owns a boutique, knows a lot about accessories. I am also grateful to Brian Knier, Jennifer Hager, and Julian Bray, my in-laws and excellent friends, for their support. Kelly Hager is always my first reader.

A Note on Quotations

Unless otherwise noted, all references to Henry James's fiction are to *The Novels and Tales of Henry James,* The New York Edition, 24 vols. (New York: Scribner's, 1907–9). These references appear in the text by volume and page number.

References to Henry James's literary criticism, including the prefaces to the New York Edition, are to the two volumes *Literary Criticism: Essays on Literature, American Writers, English Writers* and *Literary Criticism: French Writers, Other European Writers, The Prefaces,* ed. Leon Edel and Mark Wilson (New York: Library of America, 1984); these references appear in the text with the respective abbreviations *LC* 1 and *LC* 2.

References to William James, *The Principles of Psychology,* ed. Frederick Burkhardt et al. (Cambridge: Harvard University Press, 1983) appear within the text, along with the abbreviation *PP* when context alone does not make clear the source of the quotation.

All emphases within quotations appear in the original; they are not my own.

INTRODUCTION

This book is about "the elaborate, copious emptiness of the whole Henry James exploit." That phrase is from H. G. Wells's notorious 1915 attack on James in *Boon,* the satiric miscellany in which Wells captures with perversely brilliant exactitude the dimensions and scale and governing ethos of the Jamesian novel, which is "like a church lit but without a congregation to distract you, with every light and line focused on the high altar. And on the altar, very reverently placed, intensely there, is a dead kitten, an egg-shell, a bit of string. . . ."[1] All of these images are precisely chosen (even if their fidelity to the Jamesian text is slightly grotesque); taken together, they map out both the properties of the material world in Henry James and the poetics, the rhetorical figures, to which those properties give rise. The egg-shell reflects those fragile collectables—often cracked ones— around which human relationships are so often arranged in James: objects like Madame Merle's teacup, and Poynton's spoils, and Maggie Verver's golden bowl. Then, too, the image literalizes Madame Merle's insistence, in her great speech on what she calls "appurtenances," that "every human being has his shell and that you must take the shell into account" (3:287). The carefully preserved string conjures up those collectors in James who, finding themselves in economically diminished circumstances, fulfill their acquisitive impulses by accumulating the ephemeral, focusing their finely tuned sensibilities on the lowest common denominator of the world of objects; it is the sort of thing that Fleda Vetch's father in *The Spoils of Poynton,* who collects pen-wipers, old calendars, and match-boxes, might pick up. (More slyly, Wells's string suggests the Jamesian concept of the *ficelle,* literally string or twine but also theatrical terminology James adopted in his comments in the New York Edition prefaces on the role of minor characters.) The dead kitten, suggestive of a morbid investment in a tiny body, outrageously exaggerates the immense amount of meaning carried in James's novels by vulnerable children (*The Turn of the Screw, What Maisie Knew*) and a diminutive and dying heroine (*The Wings of the Dove*).

The kitten, the shell, and the string add up to an "elaborate, copious emptiness," a cornucopia of insignificance, because for Wells the Jamesian novel focuses too much on too little of the material world: overly refined technique ("intensely there") is devoted to representing tiny bits of refuse. Indeed, the passage turns the characteristic materials of the Jamesian novel into trash; unlike the empty vessels of *The Portrait of a Lady* and *The Golden Bowl,* which serve to symbolize the ways in which forms, empty in themselves, can contain and focus human contents, this eggshell is permanently empty, nothing but rubbish. Like still-life paintings of dinner tables on the morning after, Wells's version of Jamesian materialism grotesquely magnifies the husks and rinds left in the wake of consumption. While the precious object in James's texts is often an antique splendidly toned by time, in Wells's account the Jamesian object is simply used up.

Wells's critique argues that James is both too materialist and not materialist enough, overly invested and invested in the wrong way in a material world he also largely effaces or ignores. If we consider Wells's argument not as an evaluation and instead as analysis, we are still faced with a textual problem, an inconsistency or even a paradox in James's narrative economy. Few things—and no material *things*—seem more characteristically Jamesian than the teacups and tapestries, the Limoges and Wedgwood and chinoiserie, the portraits and even the pagodas that at moments seem spotlit in the fiction. Such objects give the reader purchase on "the Jamesian"; they offer something like a cognitive handle (they are frequently objects that are meant to be grasped) on the highly, sometimes almost forbiddingly, nuanced surface of the texts and the highly, sometimes almost forbiddingly nuanced surface of the cultures the texts represent. In other words, the golden bowl is the most fungible thing a reader can find in *The Golden Bowl* because its represented material qualities, such as its hardness and its definite form, become cognitive ones the reader can keep in mind.

But if James's texts encourage a readerly overinvestment in their material surfaces, they also argue that these objects are ultimately inadequate as receptacles of meaning. The texts find closure by contesting the logic of their most central and material image (as in *The Portrait of a Lady*) or shattering that image (*The Golden Bowl*) or burning it (*The Spoils of Poynton*) or burying it ("The Last of the Valerii"). James's fictions end by largely and often flamboyantly divesting themselves of whatever acquisitions they've made along the way. They follow the pattern exemplified by *The Wings of the Dove,* which closes by reducing Milly's vast wealth to a check, dematerializing it into a slip of paper, one that Densher and Kate neither cash nor return.

Yet as that unresolved bit of almost-dematerialized matter suggests, texts never really *can* cancel images once they've introduced them; even a negated possibility must appear within a text in order to be negated, and so it makes its presence felt. Effaced objects in James's fictions leave behind a residue of shards and fragments; they remain present as a sort of afterimage that shapes our readings of the texts, even though the image itself has been crossed out. Like the infamous pagoda of *The Golden Bowl,* which exists only in the space of metaphor, such afterimages lend a sense of material immediacy to critical accounts of more serious topics—like consciousness or pragmatism or love—even as their ghostly quality means that questions of materialism need never be engaged. To put in one more way the large ambiguity I am attempting to capture here: spectacularly foregrounded but narrowly framed, finely detailed but ultimately expunged, the material world in James is governed by a variety of impulses that are difficult to read and rectify. Perhaps there is a kind of interdiction against reading that expunged world too closely, inasmuch as a matter like consciousness has been afforded a critical gravity denied to matters like curtains and coiffures.

Jamesian criticism has consequently had a difficult time catching hold of this indeterminate matter; James's critics tend to speak in their least nuanced voices and to shape their arguments into their most rigidly schematic patterns when taking up the work the material world performs in the fiction. Maxwell Geismar's outrageous assertion, in his hatchet job-cum-period piece *Henry James and the Jacobites* (1962), that "James thought the function of the artist was to teach the rich how to use their money better," might serve as an extreme example of that line of criticism that critiques James's commodifying vision, that holds, as Wells did, that James's fiction is overinvested in the material world or, to cast the point in a more contemporary critical idiom, continuously complicit with the strategies of capitalism and the leisure class. For Geismar, James's oeuvre is scandalous because it constitutes—and reduces to—"the Book of Good Taste," a vast manual for the economically prosperous but culturally insecure.[2] Laurence Holland's *The Expense of Vision* (1964)—as meditative and appreciative as Geismar is outspoken and cranky, and so a period piece of the opposite sort, almost Geismar's enemy twin—stands at the opposite extreme as it continually brings forward material particulars, only to evanesce these spoils away, taking them as symbols in a drama of Christlike sacrifice, allowing them to evaporate into a timeless realm of "memory and . . . art."[3] Because it works as a kind of foregrounded cancellation, the material world in James can generate exactly opposite critical views of itself, but in either case the position advanced keeps the things of James's texts from being read: matter disappears into the abstraction of commodity culture or into an equally abstract plot of what Holland calls "redemption." If for one kind of critic, a close reading of things runs the risk of recapitulating the commodity fetishism that governs the Jamesian text, then for another kind of critic, a close reading of things runs the risk of contaminating the reassuringly humanist ethos that lies at the center of the Jamesian project, repeating the failure of some of James's characters to draw a sufficiently bright line between their relations with persons and their relations to things. In either case, matter emerges as something to be purged, and what looked like an opposition in critical approaches eventually emerges as complementary varieties of antimaterialism, which is why Jean-Christophe Agnew can combine them in a single, highly influential essay, "The Consuming Vision of Henry James" (1983), an essay that argues first for a "visually acquisitive" James who is "wholly complicit" with the world of commodities, and then for a "wholly critical" James who in the late fiction "renounces" that commodity world he has presumably internalized.[4]

Even in more recent, more historicist, and considerably more nuanced studies by Martha Banta, Jonathan Freedman, and Mark Seltzer, the specific qualities of Jamesian material are ultimately abstracted away or treated anxiously and at a distance. In *Taylored Lives* (1993), her study of narrative and the rise of managerial systems, Banta considers Maud Lowder and Kate Croy in *The Wings of the Dove* and Charlotte Stant and Maggie Verver in *The Golden Bowl* as "efficiency experts and modern managers," female exemplars of the new culture of time-motion studies, employee supervision, and mechanized rationality.[5] Hence for Banta what is of interest is a deeper cultural structure that lies beneath Maud's "brilliant gloss," her "perpetual satin," her silk-covered sofas, her "huge heavy objects" that seem to Merton Densher both uniformly splendid and British, yet somehow various and so not containable within a single "rubric" (19:30, 76, 78). In Banta's brief analysis, all these materials disappear as a world of things and a text infamous for its ambiguity are breathtakingly abstracted into a parable of modern managerial systems. At least in this instance, ambiguities of the surface must yield to rationality for there to be a critical account at all.

Similarly, in the long reading of *The American* in Mark Seltzer's *Bodies and Machines* (1992), the materials of everyday life can enter into criticism so long as they serve a system of supervision, of disciplinary self-fashioning, of "determinations of the individual."[6] In the power-centered model of criticism that takes its conceptual core from Michel Foucault's *Discipline and Punish,* the sensory details represented in the literary text must ultimately be dematerialized into a diagram (Seltzer indicates that *The American* is "almost diagrammatic" as it "charts" the "relays" between bodies and objects and between persons and representations) or a "cultural logic" (a term that in Seltzer's usage is rephrased as "logistics" and so once again identifies materialist studies with the task of delineating a rationalized system).[7] In other words, the welter of objects and the endless moments of contact between bodies and things that make *The American* so materially rich that its wealth sometimes seems hard for a reader to manage must in the end give way to the abstraction of a set of logical proofs.

In *Professions of Taste* (1990), Jonathan Freedman begins his delineation of James's relation to aestheticism with a wide-ranging survey of the movement's distinguishing characteristics in Britain and its importation to America—a survey that examines changing ideals in home decor, the influence of Ruskin on the itinerary of the Grand Tour of Europe, and the bric-à-brac and cartoons that accompanied Wilde's lectures in America.[8] But as Freedman's study unfolds, and especially as it shifts its attention to James's fiction, this specificity about material objects and processes vanishes, blotted out by a critique of reification. In Freedman's hands, the concept of reification reduces various styles of ownership and use to an overly capacious category of "objectification" which itself effectively cancels the object *as* an object of scholarly inquiry. Hence the particular attributes of *The Portrait of a Lady*'s materialism are of little relevance to *Professions of Taste* because close engagement with that materialism is construed as a kind of ethical scandal, a repetition of Madame Merle and Gilbert Osmond's error of defining "the self as a mere collection of reified qualities"; thus the critic's task becomes one of neutralizing the novel's explicit, even extravagant, interest in "the shell," in "appurtenances," in "*things*," as Madame Merle calls them (3:287).[9] More specifically, the novel's complex idiom of surface and pliability, of opacity and polish, is in Freedman's reading sacrificed to the need to wrest a salutary ethics from a text so immoderately absorbed in the material world.

In making this critique of these three studies, I do not mean to be quarreling with their specific claims so much as I mean to be gaining some analytical distance from a convention that governs the genre of literary criticism, a protocol that ultimately hides from view the layers of the Jamesian text that will be my concern here. The disciplinary mandate I mean is the one that stipulates that material details need to be brought forward *but not for too long;* the grossly material, the sensing body, the space of touch and texture, the culture of the tabletop and the writing desk must lend their substance to scholarly writing's claims, but they must also in the end be effaced by the kind of abstraction through which critical writing achieves its own closure. I am suggesting, then, that some of the antimaterialism of earlier studies of James—those of the first wave of Jamesian criticism, which founded themselves on the relatively abstract thematics of "consciousness," "the imagination," and "renunciation"—persists in more recent, newly concretized critical practice. There is a micromaterialism of the Jamesian text that criticism has a hard time turning into criticism, an intimate interest in the world of objects and the life of the senses that readers register as a kind of signature for the Jamesian, yet that is ultimately disavowed, dismissed as peripheral to the work of making meaning, discarded like the refuse in Wells's caricature. A superficial reading of Henry James, it turns out, is not easy to maintain.

The present study is an attempt to make something of such surfaces and such traces of meaning; it is an attempt to capture in criticism the James who is "extremely preoccupied with the concrete," to employ *The Europeans'* description of its heroine.[10] By describing Gertrude Wentworth in that way, the novel underlines the fact that "she doesn't care for abstractions," that she critiques a style of life that cultivates a lack of style ("totally devoid of festoons," as she terms it), that she preempts a morality—an ethics of interpretation—that dispenses with the material world, finding surfaces a superficial obstruction of true significance (163, 79). The drama of *The Europeans* is the struggle to liberate surfaces from the abstractions that cancel them out, to pre-occupy thought accustomed to working with capacious terms of moral imperative ("self-control," "moral grounds") by waylaying it with material detail (75, 183). At many moments, the novel straightforwardly juxtaposes Puritan rectitude with a life lived according to the desires of the sensory imagination: the material pleasures of curtains and lace, imported by the European cousins Eugenia and Felix (they import both the things and the capacity for taking delight in those things), are in stark contrast to the Bostonian barrenness of the houses of the Wentworth and Acton families. But this opposition blurs considerably in *The Europeans'* more radical moments where the novel defines Puritanism as its ascetic but expensive, beautifully restrained material trappings: earnest New England Protestantism turns out in the novel to be the "clean, clear, faded" colors, the "small cylindrical stools in green and blue porcelain," the "highly-polished brass knocker" of the Wentworth's piazza (46–47). What might in the work of another writer be understood as articulated doctrine or formalized tenets of belief is instead in James understood as a style of thought, and that style of thought is in turn characterized as a style of things—even if that thought understands itself as inadequately expressed by the material practices that it can hardly avoid. "Extremely preoccupied with the concrete," James's cultural analysis in *The Europeans* defines history as the changing surfaces of the material world; his representation of the postbellum world of things in *The Bostonians,* with its rapidly expanding economy ("so many objects," "so many accessories," Basil Ransom will marvel) and its sharply different systems of taste, will differ enormously from the native asceticism and imported opulence of the pre-War novel.[11]

In rendering historical change and cultural difference as matters of material style, the Jamesian novel might quite accurately be seen as a forerunner to the new materialist criticism of our own time: like Susan Stewart in *On Longing*, it blurs the difference between philosophical abstraction and quotidian practice, finding in the objects of daily life figures that sustain and reiterate seemingly deeper cultural values; like Naomi Schor in *Reading in Detail*, it performs a "valorization of the minute, the partial, and the marginal"; like the later Raymond Williams of *Marxism and Literature*, it resists the "separation of 'culture' from material social life" and collapses the distinction—crucial to Williams's earlier work—between economic base and ideological superstructure.[12] For all of the theoretical differences and disciplinary distance that lie between them, these critics similarly presaged a turn to the material world in contemporary criticism; while they do not quite share a methodology, their versions of materialism are indeed united by certain habits of mind, especially a skepticism over the distinction between the superficial and the core, the empirical and the conceptual, the detail and the whole. As Williams notes, in commenting on a passage from *The German Ideology*, "'consciousness' and 'philosophy'" are no longer "separated . . . from 'real knowledge' and from 'the practical process,'" as new materialism resists the abstraction of ideology by pulling it into concrete practice.[13] As immoderately absorbed in the quotidian as he is in the consciousness that criticism has kept separate from that world of things, surfaces, and history, James might serve as a means of bringing more particular definition to new materialism even as new materialism provides a way of reading layers of the Jamesian text that have been smoothed out and rubbed away by idealist aesthetics.

This book has three purposes. The one that may seem the most straightforward is that of getting the right historical account of James and the material world, and so of showing how the texts change when the details of their surfaces are spotlit, conserved, collected, even obsessed over. Each of the chapters of Part II takes as its focus some small interchange between the sensing body and the world immediately adjacent to it, the world that forms the body's material edge. In chapter 3, the emphasis is on James's surprisingly strong preoccupation with touch and on his tendency to conceive of domestic spaces as tactile ones; the argument here is that through touch, the categories of social class are transformed into physical identities and so given a seemingly irrefutable bodily basis. Even when, as at the end of *The Spoils of Poynton*, the Jamesian narrative seems to flee from the world of things and all its contingencies and take refuge in the vagaries of isolate consciousness, a material grain and a stubborn physicality remain. Chapter 4 extends these emphases on materiality, interchange, and process into fin-de-siècle narratives of painting: James's "The Liar," "The Real Thing," and *The Tragic Muse*, Oscar Wilde's *Dorian Gray*, the aesthetics of Bernard Berenson and Giovanni Morelli, and the suffragist tactic of slashing paintings in public galleries, as well as the depiction of physical exchange within painting itself in the case of John Singer Sargent's *The Breakfast Table*. As it surveys these moments that dramatize the encounter between painted surface and viewing subject, this chapter argues that the space of viewership is a thoroughly dynamic one, rife with material consequences—a dynamism and a materiality that critiques of reification simply cannot account for or acknowledge. Like the chapter on painting, chapter 5, "Bodies, Papers, and Persons," reveals a set of social principles arranged around the materiality of representations: this chapter takes up the frequent fascination in James's texts with books, manuscripts, and newspapers, and shows how doctrines of privacy are given substance by a conflicted, unstable homology between writing and the body. In its readings of *The Aspern Papers* and "The Birthplace," this chapter shows how the melding of body and habitat comes to shape conceptions of the self's presence within the texts it produces and the printed matter—like newspapers or personal libraries—in which it invests itself. Chapter 6, "Adulterous Matter," brings the center of this book to its conclusion by testing its materialist approach on the abstractions of the late fiction. Beginning with the scene of adultery in the basement of the Soane Museum in *A London Life* and continuing with analyses of bodily and material metaphors in *The Sacred Fount* and *The Ambassadors,* this chapter argues that the displaced, largely occluded adultery plots of James's last major fictions reappear as an account of the material world. What is radical about the late fiction is that it evolves a materialism without reference, "promiscuous properties" that will not remain affixed to their bodily referents but instead come undone and circulate like museum pieces that are never in situ. Reading the late fiction in the context both of property theory and of fin-de-siècle museum handbooks and histories, this chapter argues that adultery becomes for James a cultural model, a way of conceiving artifacts that fully allows for flux, dynamism, and indeterminate boundaries.

The core of this book, then, limns in James's practical aesthetics; it charts the flow between persons and artifacts that, for James and his contemporaries, makes up everyday experience. In diagramming that interchange, this book makes several specific revisions to the usual way of understanding the role of the material world in James's writing: it argues that there is in James a significant interest in the sense of touch and hence in understanding the material world in terms of immediacy and reciprocity, as opposed to the distancing effects of vision; it argues that for James consumption is always reproduction and that stratifications of class are hence defined as various styles of use; it argues for the presence and importance of psychological and physiological theories—especially theories of empathy—which hold that objects become states of mind, and hence that consciousness always has a material grain, a physical character.

One way of generalizing on these claims is to say that this book offers a materialist and historicist rereading of Jamesian ambiguity; it identifies the ambiguity of the limits or edges of the body with grammatical patterns of *aporia* and indeterminacy both at the level of plot (an argument pursued in chapter 1) and at the level of prose style (chapter 2). Thus the second purpose of this book is to argue that James's narrative poetics presuppose— indeed, are made from—a specific set of material practices, customs, and objects. More broadly, I propose that the practical aesthetics of daily life detailed throughout this book shape the practices of close reading that compose narrative poetics and literary theory, poetics and theory decisively influenced by James's writing. In other words, critical ways of reading take a set of material conditions as a norm, an assumption that transcends the difference between critical schools. In chapter 7, I test and specify these claims by staging an encounter between materialist and rhetorical practice, arguing that a particular conception of the house and of the shaping of the body as fin-de-siècle culture conceives them becomes a myth buried deeply within the very opposite-seeming work of Paul de Man and Elaine Scarry. If this argument holds, then the stuff of the Jamesian text—the houses, the teacups, the ribbons, the Limoges—are still molding our conceptions of literary meanings, still giving material shape to our sense of texts.

This book's third purpose, practiced throughout and focused in the concluding chapter, is to bring clearer definition to new materialism, to make explicit the assumptions and methods that shape what has often seemed more of a critical sensibility than a school or movement guided by precepts and hypotheses. Much more particularly, my goal will be to contribute something to the understanding of the role literary language can play in the study of material culture. Here I would like to preview that closing argument so that the purposes of the approach adopted in the intervening chapters will be clear. In choosing James as the focal point for this work of theorizing, I choose a writer both closely identified with the material world and closely identified with the slippages of language that belie the sense of solidity and location that material world so often seems to promise in contemporary criticism. In the opening paragraph of *Bodies that Matter*, Judith Butler summarizes the purpose that inaugurated that book as one of trying to hone in on "the materiality of the body," a purpose that led to the realization that "the thought of materiality invariably moved me into other domains": ". . . I could not fix bodies as simple objects of thought. Not only did bodies tend to indicate a world beyond themselves, but this movement beyond their own boundaries, a movement of boundary itself, appeared to be quite central to what bodies 'are.' . . . perhaps this resistance to fixing the subject was essential to the matter at hand."[14] Butler's observations would, I think, be wholly intelligible to

Henry James, for a similar identification of materiality with movement is what governs Madame Merle's famous "analysis of the human personality" in *The Portrait of a Lady:* "What shall we call our 'self'? Where does it begin? where does it end? It overflows into everything that belongs to us— and then it flows back again" (3:287–88). "The body," William James writes in an almost equally famous passage in *The Principles of Psychology,* is "an abstraction," because "never is the body felt all alone, but always together with other things" (286).

"Together with other things," a "flow" back and forth, an "essential" "resistance to fixing": what I take from these quotations is that materialist criticism must be concerned with the linguistic operations by which substances of different orders—bodies and their objects—are forced together, assimilated, and inevitably split apart. This means not only that materialist criticism must be flexible, mobile, and heterogeneous as it constellates the histories of disparate realms, of incongruous domains of meaning: decor and costume, physiology and painting, philosophy and newspapers (or "a dead kitten, an egg-shell, a bit of string"). It also means that materialist criticism will have to be rhetorical criticism as well, will have to concern itself with the similes and metaphors that fold together disparate objects and substances, with the metonyms by which the perceptually ungraspable matter of the body takes on the impress of identity, even with the long paragraph of description that renders the body and its material milieu as indistinguishable (as will be demonstrated in chapter 2). In chapter 8, then, I will conclude with a frankly eclectic and frankly speculative exploration of the material history that lies within rhetoric by arguing that language is successively reconceptualized as a medium according to its analogues in a changing material world.

PART I

Turning to Matter in Henry James

CHAPTER ONE

REVOLVING HEROINES

In "Rose-Agathe" (1878), Henry James's most frankly fetishistic tale, a collector of bric-à-brac focuses his desires on a Parisian hairdresser's wife, a woman whom he finds "the most beautiful object" he has ever seen.[1] The connoisseur, named Sanguinetti, becomes a habitué of the shop, staring longingly through its plate-glass window, which displays "detached human tresses disposed in every variety of fashionable convolution," "ivory toilet-implements," and two rotating wax figures, "wig-wearing puppets" that display the newest styles; he invents little errands, purchases of cold cream and glycerin, that bring him closer to his beloved (121). Eventually he arranges to buy the hairdresser's wife, or so his friend, the tale's narrator, understands, ascribing this brazenly commodified approach to sexual relations to his friend's "Parisianized" morals (129). But when, in the tale's surprise ending, the narrator visits Sanguinetti's apartment, he finds he has been in error all along about which woman is the object of his friend's desires and even what sort of object-choice his friend has settled on. The woman in his friend's embrace is not the hairdresser's wife at all, but rather one of the wax manikins: as she "slowly turn[s] and gaze[s]" with her "beautiful brilliant face and large quiet eyes," the narrator discovers that she exists "only from the waist upward," "the skirt of her dress" is "a very neat pedestal covered with red velvet," and as she turns, her mechanical insides make a "creaking" sound (140).

If the story itself seems a creaky one—a contrivedness James perhaps puns on at the close—then all of its contrivances are ones James will render in far more convincing fashion two years later in *The Portrait of a Lady*. The diminutive connoisseur who lives in "a perfect little museum" will become "pretty" little Ned Rosier (both have a taste for Louis Quinze and Dresden shepherdesses). The creepy desire—both erotic and sterile—for a woman who is wholly tractable, whose body is decorative and manipulable even as it also lacks genitals and hence an autonomous sexuality, becomes not only Ned's desire for that "uncanny child" Pansy but also Gilbert's need for a wife who has "nothing of her own but her pretty appearance" (3:394, 4:195). The literal fact of buying another person in "Rose-Agathe" becomes only slightly more metaphorical in the way Gilbert and Isabel make each other's acquisition, and the acquisition of an effigy in the tale presages the ways in which the novel's lovers mistake each other's image for the real.

But "Rose-Agathe" might be most revealing for the way it exaggerates a certain Jamesian way of being interested in the material world, a Jamesian way of dwelling on the edges of the body and of aligning the body's malleable shape with the shape of a plot. Madame Merle's famous pronouncement in the *Portrait* that "we're each of us made up of some cluster of appurtenances" becomes literal truth as the story's heroine is made up of nothing but decorative materials, nothing but outer surfaces subject to endless reshaping, and a machine inside that is made to turn perpetually (as if it objectifies the restless minds of James's more celebrated heroines). As her compound name reflects, Rose-Agathe is made out of parts and serves to promote a line of commerce that sells accessories— "detached human tresses"—which, when worn, become indistinguishable from the body itself (so to speak) (121). In the oscillating logic with which we think of our bodies both as our possessions and as ourselves, hair is especially liminal, neither an appurtenance nor a body part, but somewhere in between. In this respect, hair might be said to embody a bodily ambiguity, epitomizing the uncertainty of the limits and logical status of our physical selves. As the tortured and hilarious debate in Melville's *Confidence-Man* over whether a bald man's wig can rightly be said to be "his own" hair suggests, the possessive pronoun itself blurs the distinction between essence and accident.[2]

The plot of "Rose-Agathe" is shaped by this equivocation between body and object as the narrator's perception shifts from thinking that a person is being treated as a thing (both because her beauty is assessed with a connoisseur's eye and because she is purchased) to realizing that a thing is being treated as a person (not only because the friend half-jokingly ascribes emotions and desires to her but also because his desire for her, almost frankly sexual, displaces onto a surrogate the needs and emotional investments usually reserved for persons). When at the story's end she turns toward the narrator as she revolves on her pedestal, she turns from a person into a manikin, turns into mere matter. Nor is this final turn of the plot the only kind of bodily transformation at work in "Rose-Agathe." As the display model of "Anatole, Coiffeur," the best hairdresser in Paris, Rose-Agathe's changing styles set the trend: "All the knowing people keep note of her successive coiffures" (136). Hence the uncanny effect Rose-Agathe has as a replica of the human figure is endlessly reenacted as Anatole's patrons successively restyle themselves, turning themselves into something strange yet simultaneously familiar. While the story of a manikin mistaken for a real person would seem a textbook case of the uncanny (that scenario is indeed one of Freud's examples), what is striking in James's story is how thoroughly the shock of the uncanny is tied to economy, linked to the commerce of the endless fashioning of the physical body.[3] More specifically, the unsettling effect of looking in the shop-window at a thing that resembles a human body repeats itself as one subsequently looks in the mirror and tries to take in the small collision of the familiar and the strange that characterizes the new haircut the model has prompted. As Mark Seltzer has argued in an essay centered on *The American,* the kind of confusion of body and thing epitomized in "Rose-Agathe" is a central operating principle both of the realist project in fiction and the economy of individuation that governs acts of consumption.[4] If the tale seems a trifle frivolous, then, this generalization of the uncanny into a broad model of economy, into a cultural model, suggests that following this text's twists and turns will be a critically productive enterprise.

At least in "Rose-Agathe," turning to matter in Henry James involves three kinds of turns that happen indistinguishably. The crucial turn of the story's plot (twisted like the "convolution" of a curl) and the turning or transforming of the human body (not just Rose-Agathe, but all Parisiennes who covet her "chic") coincide with and depend on the physical turning of the story's heroine (121, 128). At the coiffeur's, she is located behind plate-glass, is constantly in motion, and is successively restyled; hence she serves both as the embodiment of an ideal (the very "picture of a gracious lady," one might say in the language of the *Portrait*) that incites desire and as one that, for all its concreteness, remains inaccessible (4:105).[5] The text's narrative technique remains rigorously true to this ambivalence of emphatic embodiment that nonetheless cannot be grasped: James gets the body and its vicissitudes to center stage and then, in the last-minute transformation of human body into manikin, releases the referential hold the text has seemed to gain on the body, substituting artifice for the real thing. For all of the physical specificity of the narrator and Sanguinetti's conversations about Rose-Agathe—they have discussed her hair, her jewelry, how she looks from the rear—in the story's last paragraph it turns out the two have had in mind referents of wholly different orders as Sanguinetti has meant the coiffeur's manikin and the narrator has meant the coiffeur's wife. If at the end of the story the turning figure is associated with the emergence of a physical body, then it is also associated with something very much like the opposite: the failure of language to catch hold of the body and the emergence of a figure that, because it bears only a metaphorical resemblance to the body, gestures toward the fictive nature of language itself. In other words, the end of the story seems a matter of concrete materiality—Sanguinetti holds the beloved object in his arms—even as the figure Sanguinetti embraces is one that serves as a material emblem for language's inability to keep the body firmly within its grasp.

For James, then, the image of turning turns in its own right, oscillates between rhetorical figure, as in *The Turn of the Screw,* where it names a narrative effect, and bodily figure, as in the Jamesian *topos* of the turned back, the recurrent moment in which one character turns away from another, substituting the opacity of the body for the legibility of the face. "Turn" is the root meaning of trope, of course, and so by making the word serve double duty, James forces a link between language in its most explicitly figurative sense and the body at its highest degree of physical density: James's idiom blurs the difference between something as rhetorical as a story and something as impenetrably material as a body. More specifically and more significantly, a reading of "Rose-Agathe" begins to show that James's famously ambiguous style reflects a *material* ambiguity, as the turned back and the unnamed referent—familiar vehicles of Jamesian equivocation in the critical tradition—here emerge as hesitations about the nature of the body and its objects, as representations of a body that is itself equivocal. If this is more widely true within James's writings, then Jamesian ambiguity carries with it a history of the body and its objects that much criticism has failed to read; the syntactic reversals and hesitations, the inassimilable sentences, and the referentially unmoored pronouns circle around and reproduce a conception of bodies as densely material—inarguably real—and as endlessly protean—composed of shifting shapes and styles. In chapter 2, I will detail this identification between rhetorical and bodily styles by analyzing some peculiar features of Jamesian syntax. Here, I will begin to test the hypothesis that Jamesian ambiguity bespeaks an unstable bodily morphology—and begin to mark out the limits of that claim—by turning to a scene from the *Portrait* that is analogous to the closing scene of "Rose-Agathe."

The scene, from early on in the *Portrait,* is the one in which Lord Warburton presses his proposal of marriage to Isabel during an afternoon spent in the picture gallery at Gardencourt. Having turned away from Warburton and his probing of her motives, Isabel

> walked to the other side of the gallery and stood there showing him
> her charming back, her light slim figure, the length of her white neck
> as she bent her head, and the density of her dark braids. She stopped
> in front of a small picture as if for the purpose of examining it; and

there was something so young and free in her movement that her very
pliancy seemed to mock at him. (3:185)

This passage's description of the turned back is poised between "density" and
"pliancy." On the one hand, the "density," the solidity, of the body blocks
Warburton's drive to know Isabel and her motives for rejecting him; while
there is a long tradition of understanding faces as so legible that watching
them is comparable to the experience of reading, this passage takes the colors
of printed language—the whiteness of Isabel's neck, the darkness of her
braids—and transforms them into an unreadable blankness and a black abyss
where vision fails. But if the body here has a dense imperviousness, as if it
were an impenetrable statue, then it is also defined by "pliancy," as if it were
a manikin with the capacity for being refigured and reshaped or, perhaps, for
refiguring and reshaping itself. (Isabel is understood as having an autonomy a
figure like Rose-Agathe lacks, after all, but that autonomy proves more limit-
ed than it at first seems, and it seems even more attenuated if we think of the
manikin of the 1878 story as the predecessor of the heroine of the *Portrait* two
years later.) Bodily motion and flexibility become metaphors for the openness
to experience Isabel will name later in this scene as the state of "not . . . turning away," not "separating" herself from "life," from "the usual chances and
dangers" (3:187). Two different claims about the body—nearly opposed but
also mutually sustaining—are here tightly braided into a single conception
that is almost impossible to unweave: the body has both a solidity that resists
the incursions of others and a pliancy that allows it to change its shape. The
pause in front of the painting in this scene suggests both these implications
even as it leaves their relation unresolved, failing to indicate both whether
Isabel is to be seen as continuous with the painting or distinct from it, and
whether painting is here to be understood as the epitome of stasis (as it is so
often in the *Portrait*) or fluid (as is also the case in the *Portrait*).

Virtually all of the elements of "Rose-Agathe" find their way into this
segment of the novel. Their settings—the shop window and the portrait
gallery—are both devoted to the shaping and display of the human figure,
and much is made in both texts of the future setting a man can provide for
the object of his devotion—Sanguinetti's "perfect little museum" of a salon
where Rose-Agathe ultimately takes center stage and Warburton's numerous houses from which Isabel may choose if she will (140). Both plots are
frankly devoted to the effort to possess the embodiment of the ideal
woman: Sanguinetti finds Rose-Agathe "the most beautiful object [he has]
ever beheld" (125), while Warburton takes Isabel to be the realization of
his "ethereal" "idea of an interesting woman" (3:12). And both women
turn out to be the essence of "pliancy" (so to speak), open to endless refiguring, whether by the coiffeur or through experience.

It is just here, where the comparison begins to feel strained, that the territory of this book lies. The comparison between "Rose-Agathe" and the *Portrait* feels strained at this point because while the kinds of restylings of the self imposed by the hairdresser and by life's "usual chances and dangers" are conveyed through the same language—through a vocabulary that represents the pliancy of the human figure—the kinds of remakings at work in these texts (not to mention the kinds of bodies) seem to be of such different orders that comparing them amounts to a sort of mistake. Specifically, the mistake is one of taking a rhetorical resemblance for a denotative one, of mistaking a similarity of language for a similarity of what that language conveys. More specifically still, while a coiffure can be contained within—is even self-identical to—a body, it is not clear that the body is an adequate container for the meanings at work in the scene from the *Portrait*. Indeed, while the body is clearly at center stage in "Rose-Agathe," it is not altogether clear that the body is really the important issue in the passage from the *Portrait* just examined: perhaps matters like the inaccessibility of other minds or James's ironic handling of the conventions of the courtship plot would be the right things to stress instead. Finally, if the narrator of "Rose-Agathe" makes the mistake of taking a thing for a person, the reader of the *Portrait* makes something like the opposite mistake, understanding Isabel as a static and visible entity, only to be pulled up short in the novel's closing pages, where he is told what she would have looked like "if you had seen her," if she had been as static as the novel's title seems to promise, and so possible to hold in the field of vision (4:424).

Speaking very generally, this book will argue that James continually translates his interest in the concrete into figures that presuppose the body's presence, even as that body is nearly cancelled, effaced, fined down to the ontologically nebulous status of mere nuance, denied. James's writing traffics in matters that are difficult to conceive except in the bodily terms that that writing crosses out. James's figures for fiction itself presuppose a materiality that can never be grasped; their intuitive appeal (and so their enormous influence on subsequent criticism) depends on their making available the image of a world that has spatial coordinates, coordinates nowhere discoverable within or even logically applicable to fictional narrative. Just as the poetics of point of view presuppose a body located in space, so too does the psychological novel's devotion to tracing the ripples of cognition presuppose a center of consciousness lodged within some bodily locale.[6] Similarly, the figure of the "house of fiction" asserts solidity and illusiveness at the same time; what seems often unnoticed about this hugely quotable phrase is how it simultaneously promises and effaces a sense of physical location, splices together terms for the most and least

materially solid entities in a double gesture that has made the phrase equally amenable to the goals both of the most historicist critics and the most
deconstructive.[7] "The figure in the carpet" epitomizes this tendency of
James's narrative poetics, not only because the phrase brings together a
word that conjures up the highly decorated Jamesian interior with a
frankly rhetorical term and so links a sense of place with something
unplaceable, but also because "figure" itself wavers between a bodily figure
and a rhetorical one (15:217). The problem of the body is lodged within
the conceptual center of James's poetics, then; James folds a sense of
embodiment and physical location into the language with which we think
about novels even as his terminology also acknowledges the novel as a
purely rhetorical pattern. In other words, the turning that is flamboyantly
at work in "Rose-Agathe," and more quietly present in the *Portrait,* turns
into a formative critical idiom.

Still speaking very generally, this book will argue that there is in James a
powerful account of the material world, a deeply formative ontology that is
continually overwritten and obscured by James's epistemological concerns.
To move from "Rose-Agathe" to the moment I have identified in the *Portrait*
as a revision of the tale is to hear the same story told with a significantly different accent. While the body and its penumbra are emphatic, almost obsessive concerns in the tale, constituting a theme in their own right, matter's
role in the scene from the *Portrait* is to give grain and texture, a sense of compelling solidity, to the drama of knowledge which both depends on and
effaces that materiality. While it is not clear, as I noted earlier, that to take
the scene from the *Portrait* as being about the body is to take it in the right
way, it is certainly clear that the scene depends for its force on the invocation
of a substance—a body—that in fact makes substantial the scene's concern
with the opacity of persons. In his 1875 essay on Balzac, whom James simultaneously adopts as a model and poses himself against, James wrote of how
the "palpable world of houses and clothes . . . pressed upon" Balzac's "imagination": "There is nothing in all imaginative literature that in the least
resembles his mighty passion for *things*—for material objects, for furniture,
upholstery, bricks and mortar." Such a passion, for James, crowds out any
"moral life" (*LC* 2:48). The essay on Balzac is a partial rough draft here for
Madame Merle's speech in the *Portrait* professing her "great respect for
things," and in both the essay and the novel, James emphatically brings forward the material world and at the same time begins the process of its cancellation, implicitly marking it in the one as an artistic option he will not
exercise, and in the other as the philosophy of a liar.

If the body and its objects often become hard to see in the Jamesian
text, then in many ways this is true because James quite consciously
attempts to cover them up. As I indicated in the introduction, this book is

conceived as an attempt to work against the covering up and canceling of the material world in James, an attempt to highlight and dilate that side of James which, like Balzac, has "a might passion . . . for material objects." But much more exactly stated, this book's argument is that the delineation and the effacement of "*things*" are both materially specific processes in James and his culture. The very idiom with which we characterize those moments in which James turns away from matter—"effacement," "cancellation," "erasure," even "turn," as I have explained above—presupposes the concrete, identifies the expunging of the world of things as a concrete practice, suggests that such erasures are themselves a way of imagining matter.[8] To conceive of the effacement of matter (taking that word as carrying a dual sense of material stuff and of signification) is to conjure up the image of the tool—the brush, the pen, the chisel, the knife—in immediate contact with a substance that is made visible even as it is defaced.[9] Taking my cue from this idiom and the facts about creation it implies, I will argue that the body and its objects in James "embellish" and "disfigure" each other, to adapt a set of terms James opposes to each other in writing, in the preface to *Daisy Miller,* about his American girls (*LC* 2:1277). Objects obscure and overwhelm the body, sometimes to the point of making the body invisible, as we will see in the next chapter; the body takes on the characteristics of and absorbs the objects that surround it, sometimes to the point of eliminating objects' existence as independent entities, as I mentioned in the introduction. The material world in James and his culture is literally defined (that is, made representable) by this antithetical and edgy commitment both to material surfaces and to their effacement. This double process is a matter both of prose style and of material history, as the next chapter will detail.

CHAPTER TWO

A CULTURE OF
FAULTY PARALLELS

Two passages from novels adjacent to each other in James's career will focus the ambiguity at issue in this chapter. The first is from *The Spoils of Poynton,* that novel in which James gives freest play to his fascination with what he saw as Balzac's plot of materialist grasping. Having temporarily parted from her friend Mrs. Gereth, Fleda Vetch attempts to create a mental image of Poynton's mistress:

> The mind's eye could indeed see Mrs. Gereth only in her thick, coloured air; it took all the light of her treasures to make her concrete and distinct. She loomed for a moment, in any mere house of compartments and angles, gaunt and unnatural; then she vanished as if she had suddenly sunk into quicksand. (10:146)

The assumption that governs the passage is that Mrs. Gereth's visibility, almost her reality as a character, depends on the rarities she has amassed in her own house; thus, to think of her from any other vantage point ("any mere house") is to see her disappear. Objects make persons legible to others, then, an idea in keeping not only with the qualification in Madame Merle's appurtenances speech ("one's self—for other people—is one's expression of one's self"), but also with our critical sense of how objects within novels elaborate, fix, and locate character.[1]

What complicates this already complex relationship is that a closely analogous passage in James's next novel contradicts the implications of the passage from *Spoils,* drawing very nearly the opposite conclusion from the same phenomenon. The novel is *The Other House,* a title which signals this novel's status as a sort of pathological other, a dark double to James's more

orderly and subsequently much more canonized houses of fiction (in relation to *Spoils* its title is practically eponymous); the scene is one in which
a "showy" and "splendid" drawing room is so full of things that its occupant momentarily disappears. Overaccessorized with "many large pictures" and "many flowers" and dominated by "a huge French clock," "the
colour of the air, the frank floridity," and the "interposing objects" temporarily blot out Rose Armiger, one of the rivals for the hero's affections,
as Jean Martle, the other rival, enters the room.[2]

These two moments are almost exactly opposed because the one claims
that objects make the female body "distinct," articulating it as a figure,
while the other dramatizes the effacement of that figure by the objects
which surround it. But like any neatly opposed elements, these passages
share a conviction that allows them to be brought into relation with each
other. What the passages agree on is that the human (here specifically
female) figure is composed of the ground that the figure is typically understood as set off from. The accessories and furnishings usually expected to
confer upon the figure a location, a context, here constitute that figure
instead; the distinction between figure and ground wavers, and so, in
either passage, the lady vanishes. An oddly elaborated passage from *The
Other House* clarifies the point here (or, rather, crystallizes the confusion)
because it begins by making a fairly conventional observation on the influence of setting and then exaggerates that importance until the figure's
identity apart from the setting becomes questionable. As Jean Martle looks
at Mrs. Beever, the *grande dame* of the house that, in the scene quoted
above, obscures its lesser occupants, she

> perceive[s] once for all how the difference of the setting made anoth-
> er thing of the gem. Short and solid, with rounded corners and full
> supports, her hair very black and very flat, her eyes very small for the
> amount of expression they could show, Mrs. Beever was so "early
> Victorian" as to be almost prehistoric—was constructed to move
> amid massive mahogany and sit upon banks of Berlin-wool. . . . Jean
> knew that the great social event of her younger years had been her
> going to a fancy-ball in the character of an Andalusian, an incident
> of which she still carried a memento in the shape of a hideous fan.
> (14)

It is not just that Mrs. Beever's body has adapted itself to her furniture,
nor even that she has come to look like her furniture, that suggests how
amorphous the boundary between the body and its objects can become in
James; it is also that the defining moment of her life has been a triumph
of accessorizing, and that the fan, the visual focal point of her person,

appears against a ground made up of furnishings. If we push on this accessory a little harder, we can say that a large temporal unit (Mrs. Beever's life)
is compressed within a single, nonessential object, and so made part of a
continuous material surface.[3]

This continuity between the body and its things becomes for James
both a prose style and his theory of materialism; indeed, I ultimately want
to show how these two perspectives on this continuity themselves become
indistinguishable, and then to locate this continuity within American literary and cultural history. I will begin by considering a slip in the Jamesian
syntax, a slight wobble that functions as the grammatical equivalent of
what I have so far been treating only thematically. Consider, for example,
the opening sentence of "The Chaperon": "An old lady, in a high drawing-
room, had had her chair moved close to the fire, where she sat knitting and
warming her knees" (10:437). Very strictly speaking, this sentence contains
a small grammatical infelicity because it comes too close to suggesting that
the woman is knitting her knees as well as warming them; because the par-
ticiples "knitting" and "warming" are in parallel position and parallel form,
the object that follows should be governed by each. In a sense, this is just
the sense the passage wishes to convey, since sitting at a fire and knitting
an article of woolen clothing are both actions that keep a body warm.
Further, if it seems strained to suggest that the grammar of the sentence
blurs the distinction between body and appurtenance, then it is also a
nuance the paragraph goes on to embroider and to insist upon: "The old
lady sat motionless save for the regularity of her clicking needles, which
seemed as personal to her and as expressive as prolonged fingers." The simile here is an odd one, for the suggestion that the woman's tools seem "as
personal to her" as her fingers logically reduces to the statement that her
tools seem as personal to her as her person. In other words, the difference
that the trope of simile entails wavers even as, the sentence also suggests,
the animate body is "motionless" and the inanimate tools are animated. In
between the opening faulty parallel and the sentence on needles appears an
image of fluidity, of the London fog "ooz[ing]" into the room, which is
"full of dusky massive valuable things"; like the adjectives that in James's
New York Edition revisions habitually swim together unimpeded by punc-
tuation, the whole paragraph takes as its dominant impulse the fluid
exchange between elements.

Ultimately, I will argue that the faulty parallel and the pattern it introduces at the opening of "The Chaperon" constitute a cultural fault line,
that James's culture defines and locates its anxieties at the point where body
and object become each other's extensions. As I have begun to suggest, the
culture of the faulty parallel becomes in James a prose effect. The very
evenness of the prose surface—any prose, perhaps, but the long Jamesian

paragraph in particular—creates a medium in which persons and their appurtenances flow together, an unbroken expanse that makes no visual subordination or separation of body and object. In other words, prose must always blur the boundaries between person and object because there is no material difference or differentiation between what constitutes the self and what constitutes the objects that surround it. Unlike verse, which enforces its line-breaks, which often parcels things out in stanzas, and which consequently assimilates itself differently to material objects, prose creates a fluid surface in which the eye can mistake one kind of thing for another, a slippage the Jamesian syntax heightens and exploits. Prose is "the rhythm of continuity," as Northrop Frye defines it in *Anatomy of Criticism;* it is also the medium of exchange, enacting on a stylistic level the fluid transactions, the ceaseless turning, that characterize the Jamesian body.[4] Take for example the opening paragraph of "The Marriages," a passage in which nearly every sentence travels from the body to its objects or from objects to their body, a passage I will quote at length, since part of my point here is the visual impact of a mass of prose, a mass in which words for human and inanimate forms flow together:

> "Won't you stay a little longer?" the hostess asked while she held the girl's hand and smiled. "It's too early for every one to go—it's too absurd." Mrs. Churchley inclined her head to one side and looked gracious; she flourished about her face, in a vaguely protecting sheltering way, an enormous fan of red feathers. Everything in her composition, for Adela Chart, was enormous. She had big eyes, big teeth, big shoulders, big hands, big rings and bracelets, big jewels of every sort and many of them. The train of her crimson dress was longer than any other; her house was huge; her drawing-room, especially now that the company had left it, looked vast, and it offered to the girl's eyes a collection of the largest sofas and chairs, pictures, mirrors, clocks, that she had ever beheld. Was Mrs. Churchley's fortune also large, to account for so many immensities? Of this Adela could know nothing, but it struck her, while she smiled sweetly back at their entertainer, that she had better try to find out. Mrs. Churchley had at least a high-hung carriage drawn by the tallest horses, and in the Row she was to be seen perched on a mighty hunter. She was high and extensive herself, though not exactly fat; her bones were big, her limbs were long, and her loud hurrying voice resembled the bell of a steamboat. (18:257)

The confusion of bodily subject with material artifact in this passage begins with Mrs. Churchley holding Adela's hand, drawing this body part into her vast domain of matter, and then continues with the dissociative construction "Mrs. Churchley inclined her head," a phrase that grammatically turns her head into an object, almost an appurtenance (James applies that term to his heroine's beautiful head in "The Patagonia" [18:182]). The head therefore occupies a parallel position to the fan, mutually balancing objects in what is consequently understood as a "composition," a word that suggests that this body and its habitat have been constructed according to the dictates of portrait painting. In other words, an artifact that represents the person as a body situated within a characteristic environment has circled back, forming the basis for the person's shaping of herself. This blurring of the difference between the person and the objects that surround and represent her is carried forward by the syntactic parallels of the "big" items, which slide from the face to the shoulders and hands to Mrs. Churchley's jewelry. The lady herself (although the whole passage renders problematic that way of terming identity) almost vanishes; the paragraph's tendency to mix accessories with the body they accessorize creates prose that forms the stylistic equivalent of the passage from *The Other House* where a character's view of another is obstructed by an excess of things. By the time we reach the word "carriage," it is not even immediately clear whether this word refers to the way Mrs. Churchley carries her body or to the way her body is carried, a momentary ambiguity reinforced by the suggestion, in the last sentence quoted, that her voice is like a steamboat bell, a noise made by another mechanism of conveyance.

The Lady Vanishes effect in this passage is, then, not so much a theme the passage comments on as it is a technique of representation, a technique that fosters a particular way of imagining the body. The Jamesian paragraph carries with it a conception of the body as a continuous surface of parts; as in the opening paragraph of "The Marriages," the body and its objects are both atomized (into "big eyes, big teeth, big shoulders, big hands, big rings," for example) and fused into a single unbroken surface (as the parallel structure of the sentence listing the "big" items also exemplifies). In her appurtenances speech, Madame Merle precisely names this tension as she defines the "'self'" both in terms of a "cluster" ("we're each of us made up of some cluster of appurtenances") and of the process of "flowing" (the self "overflows into everything that belongs to us—and then it flows back again"). In a sense, what James remarks on through Madame Merle's vocabulary of cluster and flow here is a property of writing itself. On the one hand, writing can only represent the body with specificity by dismembering it, by breaking it down into its constituent pieces. As Susan Stewart remarks, "we know our body only in parts," a partitioning that writing is especially governed by, since it must unfold details in a temporal sequence; language can barely touch the body without dismantling it.[5]

On the other hand, the atomized bits with which writing reproduces the body and its habitat never *stay* atomized; they fuse with each other into new combinations, are drawn together as they find their places within an even, undifferentiated block of prose, acquire new and odd associations as the randomness of typesetting places them in unpredictable juxtapositions. To glance at the long Jamesian paragraph in the sort of half-reading, half-seeing mode with which we sometimes do look at novels is to glimpse a body coming apart as it comes together in new combinations with objects and accessories. The body and its objects seem never to appear apart, never to be held to discrete discursive spaces by a paragraph break but are always "paragraphed" together (the term is James's own, one meant in "The Papers" to capture how persons are assimilated into print).[6] In *The Golden Bowl*, Fanny Assingham is "covered and surrounded with 'things,' which were frankly toys and shams," coverings and surroundings that materialize the logic of the characteristic Jamesian paragraph (23:34). The sorts of matter that appear in the space between body and house, things like hair and its ornaments, fringes, draperies, brocaded sofas—mostly textiles—become a textual principle as they objectify the work of James's own prose, which itemizes and atomizes the objects it also stitches together, which makes the body visible by entangling it with alien matter.

    I have been discussing the long Jamesian paragraph as if it were a spatial construct (which it always literally is, of course), a concrete place that houses not so much a body as an indeterminacy; here I want to make those assumptions more explicit by bringing forward a passage that both exemplifies and illuminates the kind of paragraph I have been considering, a passage structured around an image that crystallizes the dimensions of the Jamesian paragraph itself. The scene is the one in *The Golden Bowl* where Amerigo is first reunited with Charlotte Stant; the image is that of the "cabinet," a word that first of all suggests a cupboard like the ones in the Bloomsbury shop where these two characters will soon see and not purchase the bowl itself. But "cabinet" also carries associations with the wonder-cabinets of Renaissance royals, collectors, and scientists, men like the Prince's fabled ancestors who loom so large in the novel's early pages. As Amerigo's long gaze takes in his former lover, the effect is one of recollecting and re-collecting (the passage is emphatic in its materialist take on memory) the bits and pieces of her body; her eyes and teeth and lips strike Amerigo "as a cluster of possessions of his own," "items in a full list, items recognised, each of them, as if, for the long interval, they had been 'stored'—wrapped up, numbered, put away in a cabinet. While she faced Mrs. Assingham the door of the cabinet had opened of itself; he took the relics out one by one" (23:46). As the paragraph moves forward, its progress replicates the structure of the cabinet in several ways, first of all

because, like the cabinet, it contains the details of Charlotte's body in separate compartments, small rhetorical spaces that house her hair, her arms,
her fingernails. And like the rare objects of the Renaissance cabinet, which
were often chosen and arranged so as to blur the division between art and
nature and hence to appeal to a poetics permeated by Ovidian metamorphosis, the fragments that compose Charlotte's body hover on the edge
between nature and culture.[7] There is, for example, her hair, brown but
with "a shade of tawny autumn leaf" added to it "for 'appreciation,'" a tone
the passage identifies neither as natural nor as artificial, and so which hovers in between. There are "the sleeves of her jacket," parts of her clothing
syntactically parallel to and hence equated with body parts like her hands,
and which almost hide from view "free arms" that have "the polished slim-
ness" of Renaissance Florentine sculptures done in "old silver and old
bronze." There is "her special beauty of movement and line when she
turned her back, and the perfect working of all her main attachments, that
of some wonderful finished instrument, something intently made for exhibition, for a prize." Nothing in that last sentence tells the reader whether
"main attachments" refers to the body or its accessories; indeed, the whole
paragraph has rendered that relation undecidable, with arms that take on
the qualities of sculpture and a body with a generally "finished" quality
that suggests a seamlessness between itself and its objects. The passage has
an extraordinarily material specificity, then, but its governing conception
of matter is as something that metamorphoses, that turns.

Given the passage's obsessive focus on such oscillations and metamorphoses, it is no wonder that the paragraph finds its climax and conceptual
center in the center of Charlotte's body: after a long series of balanced sentences listing the items the Prince "knew," we read, "He knew above all the
extraordinary fineness of her flexible waist, the stem of an expanded flower,
which gave her a likeness also to some long loose silk purse, well filled with
gold-pieces." The "flexible waist" is the pivot and driving motor of the passage because it is here, at the body's center of gravity and its least fungible
part, that the turning figure of the body and the turning of rhetorical figures become clearly inseparable. The waist is a body part made to turn, one
defined less by its structure than by its motion. It is also a part, in the
corset-wearing nineteenth century, that is made for shaping; it epitomizes
the malleability of the female body. Its comparison to a flower signals its
alliance with the flowers of rhetoric and, further, with the way in Western
poetics that image serves as figure both for the female body and for language itself. Similarly, the purse and gold pieces reflect an economy of
exchange, an endless transaction of metaphors and of matter: money facilitates the exchange of material goods, compresses material values into
itself, into something so physically small it can seem almost immaterial, yet

that also epitomizes the various qualities of matter, whether it be purity, as in gold, or filthiness, as in paper currency. At the center of Charlotte's body lie all the arch-symbols of exchange and transformation, then, because that body keeps turning into shapes of a different kind; as malleable as language itself, the body is understood as metaphor made literal and material. As in "Rose-Agathe," which ends with Sanguinetti holding the turning figure "round her waist" (140)—which ends, that is, both by representing the body as firmly grasped and by dramatizing language's inability to maintain a firm referential hold on that body—this passage from *The Golden Bowl* forces together nearly contradictory claims about the body, wedges together a claim for a dense materiality with a series of images for rhetoric.

From this passage I will draw two hypotheses about the Jamesian body, ones that the rest of this book will test and refine. First, the Jamesian body is defined by a wavering distinction between center and periphery. In this passage from *The Golden Bowl*, the extremities of Charlotte's body are characterized by a metamorphosis that the passage also finds operating at the body's center; what is central about this body is what happens at its edges. The Jamesian text overloads the bodily periphery with significance, making heavy investments in a coiffure or an Andalusian fan, and then denies the separability of outside and inside. Peripheral matter—which is to say both things that exist along the body's edges and things usually held as marginal in importance—becomes central.

The term "periphery" here carries with it the word "paraphernalia": both words contain the root for the verb "to bear," to carry, transport, or hold. These terms are not really James's (in fact, he rarely uses them); I choose them because together they convey in compact form the way in which the accessory defines the Jamesian body, marking out its edges, even as that accessory also recedes to the periphery of readerly attention. "Paraphernalia" also brings to bear the gender of this formative tension because it contains the now-obsolete legal meaning of a woman's personal property, the objects of her person, like her jewels and clothing, property beyond her dowry, which the law allows her to claim as her own, apart from her husband, in certain highly circumscribed situations.[8] The image of the periphery in James is a matter of the body, of objects (especially ones from the realm of women's fashion), of matter.

This point about peripheral matter is worth making because the structure composed of center and circumference is so basic to James's theory of composition and becomes so influential in subsequent criticism. Few sentences in the New York Edition prefaces have been so overquoted as the assertion, from the preface to *Roderick Hudson,* that "Really, universally, relations stop nowhere, and the exquisite problem of the artist is eternally but to draw, by a geometry of his own, the circle within which they shall happily *appear* to do so" (*LC* 2:1041). But while later critics abstract that sentence into a statement of general aesthetic truth, James does not.[9] For the example that develops this philosophy of "the continuity of things" is that of the embroidery canvas, with its "vast expanse" of "little holes" to be covered with the "flowers and figures" produced by the embroiderer's needle. James thus construes the problem of peripheries in the terms of women's art and labor, in terms of the production of an object of decor or an article of clothing. In the preface to the New York Edition volume that contains *Daisy Miller,* James makes particular this concrete grounding I am arguing for this recurrent image of the periphery he elsewhere calls "the sharp black line," "the neat figure of a circle consisting of a number of small rounds disposed at equal distance about a central object" (*LC* 2:1123, 1130). Thinking back to a brief visit to New York early in his career, James recalls his sense of alienated distance from the "down-town" world of business, male territory he can only "hov[er]" about "superficially, circumferentially," while the "up-town" world of "the music-masters and French pastry-cooks, the ladies and children" is his native habitat (*LC* 2:1273–74). Like all metaphors in the prefaces, this image of the circumference slips and slides, but it slips and slides in a specific direction: into accounts of consciousness itself, as when in the *Wings of the Dove* preface James writes of Millie as his "centre" and the secondary characters as her "circumference" (*LC* 2:1292). James understands his interest in consciousness, then, in the same language with which he conceives a broader social world of concrete making; the image of the periphery that defines consciousness carries with it—is in fact inseparable from—a concern for the body and its passages through a world of matter.[10]

The center of consciousness thus entails as it displaces a periphery of matter, which is to say that the center of consciousness is literally inconceivable or at least very hard to conceptualize without a material outline that hovers at its edges and defines its furthest reaches. This is to say that the center of consciousness presupposes a materialism without ever specifying the nature of the matter involved. In other words, James's way of imagining consciousness both necessitates and effaces a concern for matter because consciousness is first conceived along the lines of material structures and processes and then given a name which abstracts it from those structures, which insinuates for the mind a self-sufficiency, an isolation only quietly undermined by the suffix (the "con" in "consciousness" means "with"). But as I have begun to show with *The Golden Bowl*'s portrait of Charlotte and with moments from the prefaces, center and periphery prove as inseparable in James's poetics as they are in the geometry James uses to illustrate this structure in the famous passage from the preface to

Roderick Hudson. While this book attempts to read James with peripheral vision—to fix and hold in view matter like old brocades and old bronzes—it also argues that James and his culture disrupt the routine economy of significance that weights the center with overwhelming significance and holds the margin to its marginal status.

The second hypothesis I will draw from Amerigo's vision of Charlotte concerns the tension in the passage between an extreme physical specificity (the parts of Charlotte's body are itemized, catalogued) and an ostentatiously metaphorical character (Charlotte is compared to a sculpture, a huntress, a flower, a purse, and in the end of the passage, a muse). The body parts the passage itemizes turn out to be so endlessly indeterminate as they swing between the natural and the artificial, between the contained and the uncontainable and ungraspable, and between the exhibited (Charlotte's "special beauty" is "something intently made for exhibition") and that which cannot be held in the field of vision (Charlotte's "turned . . . back" is remarked upon at almost the same moment she's said to be made for display) that twice in the passage James's language comments on its own inadequacy, calling its own terms "clumsy" at the opening and then, in the middle of the passage, describing Charlotte's hair as "indescribable." But while this passage keeps spinning, it does not quite spin in random directions; rather, its oscillations between the materially specific and the rhetorically figurative recreate the body as malleable, protean, made up of parts that may be transformed or exchanged. What the passage unwraps and displays is the figurative potential of the physical body: the indecision between metaphor and materiality that characterizes the passage is anchored in the relation between body and appurtenance.

This argument is, as it stands, highly schematic, and many of the ensuing pages will be devoted to clarifying and nuancing it. Here I would like to indicate more fully what I mean it to accomplish. My purpose has been to draw a set of lines between our readerly response to James's style and the status of the body in James's culture, to find an account of matter in the effacement of reference, to argue that Jamesian ambiguity itself presupposes and advances a set of assumptions about the material world. If we as readers can't quite decide where the bodies are in James—and I mean here both that matters of consciousness and epistemology deflect our attention away from bodies and that James's novels (especially the late ones) complicate or frustrate our sense of reference to a world outside the text—then this is because James and his culture can't decide where or what bodies are either, can't decide where to draw the line between bodies and objects, and can't decide whether the point of contact between them is seamless or fissured. "Just look there: is that a person or a thing?" asks the heroine of *A London Life,* at the climactic moment of that novel (10:357–58). Jamesian syntax and plot represent a culture in which that question becomes ask-able, a culture in which in the blink of an eye or the progress of a sentence the difference between persons and things becomes a matter of suspense, matter held in suspension.[11]

This moment of suspension in *A London Life,* like the confusion over the object of Sanguinetti's devotion in "Rose-Agathe" or the Vanishing Lady passages discussed above, recapitulates a fairly particularized conven-tion of James's American-Renaissance forebears: instances in which a thing is mistaken for a person or a person mistaken for a thing, instances in which a sudden and fleeting visual confusion compresses into a single moment the larger cultural tensions that make up antebellum culture's cor-poreal economy, its understanding of the relation between bodies and objects. For example, in Rebecca Harding Davis's *Life in the Iron Mills* (1861), "the white figure of a woman" flashes "in bold relief" out of the "heavy shadows" of the mill, a woman who seems at first glance "alive" and then visually resolves into a sculpture made by one of the workers from the dross left over by the smelting process.[12] In Poe's "The Man That Was Used Up" (1839), a story set in as leisured a milieu as Davis's is industrial, the astoundingly handsome, "truly fine-looking" Brevet Brigadier General John A. B. C. Smith turns out to be little more than a torso adorned with exquisite prostheses; as the story's narrator discovers, Smith has been so scalped and dismembered in the Indian Wars that without his appurte-nances he is nothing but an "exceedingly odd looking bundle," a bundle that can pass for a whole man only when he has lurched back into his numerous falsies, which he does before the narrator's "staring eyes," dis-pensing while he does bits of advice on where to get "the best" "cork leg," the finest shoulders, and the best wig.[13] In Hawthorne's "Drowne's Wooden Image" (1844), the people of Boston "r[ub] their eyes" in confu-sion as a sculpted figure of a lady, bedecked in lace, jewelry, and a fan, seems to come to life and take a stroll in the streets, while in his "Mrs. Bullfrog" (1837), a stage-coach accident momentarily reveals the narrator's new wife to be a "fearful apparition," a "hobgoblin" "of grisly aspect, with a head almost bald, and sunken cheeks" when deprived of her wig and false teeth.[14] In these examples, the turning figure links the commerce of appur-tenances with allegories of artistic creation as the figures at these tales' cen-ters shift back and forth between artifice and nature in a vision that blurs the difference between—or rather comprehends the inseparability of—the body and its objects.[15]

To appoint these moments as exemplary and to characterize them as I have done is at once to argue for a specific view of American-Renaissance romance, to argue for the existence of a specifically American-Renaissance body, and to argue for a specific relation between that genre and that body.

In "The Custom-House," the long essay that introduces *The Scarlet Letter*, Hawthorne famously defines romance in terms of objects that oscillate in the field of vision, that hover in the indeterminate half-lit zone between "the Actual and the Imaginary."[16] The setting that illustrates this definition—the setting that materializes this hazy materiality, in other words—is the chambers of a house glimpsed in moonlight, "the little domestic scenery of the well-known apartment" with its familiar objects, like books, chairs, a doll, or a "child's shoe." In the glow of moonlight, such objects simultaneously retain the intimate familiarity of human touch (the chairs each retain their "separate individuality," for instance) and appear estranged from their user: "whatever . . . has been used or played with, during the day, is now invested with a quality of strangeness and remoteness, though still almost as vividly present as by daylight" (35).

This is the scene, then, that Hawthorne employs to generate those capaciously abstract categories, "the Actual and the Imaginary." But what produces those endlessly flexible terms that define the endlessly flexible genre of romance is something a lot less abstract: romance is epitomized by the tension that characterizes the body's objects, a tension between the feeling that such objects are part of one's person and the realization that such objects are wholly alienable.[17] The hazy visionary glimmer of romance—the optical illusions, the shadows and apparitions of the tales by Hawthorne and Poe and Davis described above—is a vision that matches and hence perceives the vicissitudes of corporeal identity.

When Hawthorne is practicing instead of theorizing romance, his categories of the actual and the imaginary become still more materially specific as they are played out in the bodily ambiguities of accessories, ornaments, wounds, and prostheses. *The Marble Faun* (1860), a novel published in England under the title *Transformation,* closes on what may seem a very odd question: "Did Donatello's ears resemble those of the Faun of Praxiteles?"[18] For all of its oddity, the question, which remains emphatically unanswered and unanswerable, is absolutely characteristic of Hawthorne's tendency to construe romance in terms of a wavering tension and a wavering continuity between physiology and artifice, and his tendency to treat that relation as one that precludes closure. The *A* that may or may not be revealed on Dimmesdale's chest at the conclusion of *The Scarlet Letter,* the *A* that may or may not be the result of self-mutilation or necromantic drugs or the spontaneous physical manifestation of guilt, works in much the same way as it literally embodies the textual principle of indeterminacy, turns the instability of writing (it is a letter, after all) into a matter of physiology. In *The Blithedale Romance,* Hawthorne construes in terms of fashion this sense of ontologically fuzzy embodment, a fuzziness that in turn contributes to the instability of this notoriously incoherent novel. What the novel cannot decide is how deeply fashion permeates the body or how much of personal identity is lodged within and sustained by the superficial drape of, say, a veil like the one that covers Priscilla during her mesmerist performances; at moments, the text entertains the possibility that all of this woman's existence is "comprehended within that mysterious veil."[19] In its portrait of Westervelt, the Veiled Lady's mesmerizing wizard and manager, the novel follows the same pattern of thought in a series of fine delineations, moving from his overly elegant clothing—his blindingly white shirt, his "exquisitely wrought" watch chain—to the barely visible "gold band around the upper part of his teeth," which reveals them to be prosthetic, to the supposition that there is "nothing genuine about him," that "his semblance of a human body [is] only a necromantic, or perhaps a mechanical contrivance" (86, 88, 174).

In his 1879 book on Hawthorne, James reproduces this wavering embodiment as an indecision about Hawthorne's claims to realism. Commenting on Hawthorne's notebooks, James writes that "outward objects play much the larger part in" them; Hawthorne pays an almost radical allegiance to the "minute" and the "trivial," to the concrete instead of "convictions" and "ideas" (*LC* 1:350). Commenting on *The Scarlet Letter,* James writes that the book's "faults" are "a want of reality and an abuse of the fanciful element . . . the people strike me not as characters, but as representatives, very picturesquely arranged, of a single state of mind" (404). James knows that these two claims don't really accord with each other, knows that the excessively objective cannot also suffer from "a want of reality," and so in the middle of his commentary on *The House of the Seven Gables,* he tries to repair the contradiction. While Hawthorne "had a high sense of reality," he "never attempted to render exactly or closely the actual facts of the society that surrounded him"; while *Seven Gables* has "more literal actuality than" the other novels, its characters "are all figures rather than characters—they are all pictures rather than persons" (412, 413). James comes very, very close here to defining the actual as the figurative—in large part, I am suggesting, because he finds in Hawthorne both a commitment to representing the body with precision and to representing that body as continually "embellished" and "disfigured," to adopt the terms James will give to this wavering ontology much later in his New York Edition prefaces (*LC* 2:1277).

Thus it makes curious sense that the most realistic character for James— "the nearest approach that Hawthorne has made to the complete creation of a *person*"—is Zenobia in *Blithedale,* a character deeply and heavily identified with artifice (*LC* 1:420). James comes to terms with his contrary intuitions about Hawthorne's realism by grounding those opposed claims within one body. Even in the case of Zenobia, James cannot quite manage a coherent account, suggesting early on in *Hawthorne* that her portrait attains "a greater reality" than those of the other characters in spite of being "full of alteration and embellishment"; later on he indicates that Zenobia is "more concrete," "a more definite image" *because* she is "produced by a greater multiplicity of touches" (379, 420). Uneasily, then, James identifies the continuously refigured body as the real thing. And what sort of body is it that qualifies as real, as "concrete"? (420). Zenobia is ample, fleshy, and very much contrived, covered over with layers of artifice. Her clothing, of which so much is made in the text, is perfectly calculated in its effects, even when it is at its simplest, as when Miles Coverdale first meets her at Blithedale: "She was dressed as simply as possible, in an American print . . . but with a silken kerchief, between which and her gown there was one glimpse of a white shoulder. It struck me," Coverdale says, "as a great piece of good-fortune that there should be just that glimpse" (15). When she returns to Boston at the midpoint of the novel, she changes her couture accordingly, setting off her beauty with a "redundance of personal ornament" so that she is "transformed" into "a work of art" (152, 151). Her perpetual, impossibly tropical, flower, which serves as a chic sort of sartorial trademark, focuses how thoroughly Zenobia's body is registered as made for display and identified with the accessory; and when she exchanges the real flower for a "cold and bright transfiguration," "a flower exquisitely imitated in jeweller's work," her body becomes a figure for the metamorphosis of nature into artifice (151).

The epitome of artifice and transformation and accessory, Zenobia also becomes, as *Blithedale's* plot unfolds, a figure for the wounded and dismembered body, the body that falls apart. Her death is narrated as the dismantling of her highly elaborated surfaces: she removes her flower first and then, before finding her body, the Blithedalers find her handkerchief and then one of her shoes, a French-made shoe of kid (the text is almost immoderately detailed here) that Coverdale preserves as a keepsake or fetish. Finally, the body itself is skewered, pierced by the long hooked pole used to draw her corpse out of the pond in which she has drowned herself, as if the illusions that throughout the novel define Zenobia's physical presence are finally pierced.

James locates the real in the emphatically vicissitudinous body; he recognizes, even if at times conflictedly, that the American Renaissance body that matters to his own poetics is the prosthetic one, the body that clusters accessories around itself and that flows into them in a seemingly unbroken continuum of physiology and artifice. In midcentury American literature, appurtenances flesh out the body, serve as extensions of or substitutions for its corporeal essence, an essence that in turn no longer seems quite essential. It is just here, at the point where Zenobia's flower and shoe come to seem like body parts, or where Westervelt's teeth substitute for the real things, or Poe's used-up man turns into a cluster of boutique purchases, that the concerns of the philosophy of personal identity and of fashion become indistinguishable. As readers of Sharon Cameron's *The Corporeal Self* will recognize, the perspective offered here owes much to that book's emphasis on the way that American-Renaissance texts investigate identity by almost literally putting pressure on the body, by dismembering it, denying it, supplementing it, and confusing its literal fact with its allegorical significance.[20] It is this confusion that fascinates Hawthorne in such characters as Zenobia and that in turn fascinates James, a confusion between fashion and philosophy, between material accident and metaphysical essence. This confusion is also what moves Melville to turn a haircut into a heated philosophical debate on the corporeal basis of possessive individualism in *The Confidence-Man,* or to observe, in *Moby-Dick,* that Ahab "wears" his whale-bone leg "like a gentleman."[21]

Moby-Dick is the full-scale anatomy of anatomy in American-Renaissance literature; it is also and consequently the text that most thoroughly confuses material periphery with conceptual or psychological center and the physiologically given with the culturally shaped. As Samuel Otter has demonstrated, Melville writes so as to generate "material analyses of consciousness"; his prose "give[s] heft to thought" through the "restless dissecting of all kinds of bodies."[22] Much more specifically, Melville gains purchase on the material world and its economy by envisioning it as a vast, perpetual, chiastic relation between wound and prosthesis, a bodily ebb and flow that is the novel's anatomy and its political economy. The novel's obsession with amputation and dismemberment—with amputated legs and chopped-off toes and unscrewed navels—seamlessly shades into its description of material making, as butchered whale parts become food, fuel, coats, fiddle bows, skirt hoops, umbrella handles, and canes. With Ahab's leg, the whale heals the wound it causes, fills in the hole in the human world that it has made, as the leg is lost to Moby Dick's jaws and then replaced with a prosthesis fashioned from another whale's bone. More generally, the whale has a "compacted collectedness" that culture undoes, that culture *becomes* culture by undoing; the whale is a "monstrous cabinet" of "marvels," one that yields all manner of "specialties," of human accessories, whether they be legs, canes, or skirt hoops (284, 302, 285).

One reason for summarizing here the economy of *Moby-Dick* (a novel James perhaps never read) is that its image of the prosthesis lies at the emotional core of the James family, serves as a metaphor by which William and Henry theorize the matter of the body, conceptualize their own physicality, and negotiate the slippery relation between psychological and corporeal accounts of the interior of persons. One of the better-known pieces of

Jamesian minutiae is that Henry, Sr., burned his left leg in a fire, probably at the age of 13, a wound so serious that the leg was amputated, probably several years later, and replaced with a wooden one, which was itself replaced periodically throughout the philosopher's life.[23] Henry James, Sr., embodied the American-Renaissance body, which is to say his physique follows the contours of and replicates the problems posed by the fictional bodies of Captain Ahab, General John A. B. C. Smith, and Zenobia. It is as if Henry, Jr., were named after and bred by a trope that took on flesh, by a metaphor that forged an imperfect link between that flesh and the sort of sculpted matter that figures so prominently in the fictions of Hawthorne, Melville, and Poe. As several moments from his children's lives and writings will suggest, Henry, Sr., was a walking object lesson in the nuances of corporeal and personal identity. While my emphasis here may occasion the worry that I am relying too much on something that is literally accidental, my argument is that this physical detail reflects and fosters a disruption of the difference between essence and accident, suspends the distinction between what is central and what is superficial.

In an *Atlantic Monthly* essay on the physiology of walking and the evolving technology of shoes and prostheses, Oliver Wendell Holmes clarifies some of the assumptions that hovered about the body part at issue here. Published in 1863, when the Civil War had made healthy, efficient walking—or marching—a matter of political urgency and the replacement of lost limbs seem like a matter of national healing, the essay takes improvements in artificial-limb technology as "one of the signs of our advancing American civilization," an advance that might repair the bodies that civilization has torn apart: "War unmakes legs, and human skill must supply their places."[24] The essay thus understands the human body as wide-open to fabrication and the technological and the physiological as almost indistinguishable. Indeed, while watching recent amputees learn to use the newly improved prostheses made by B. Franklin Palmer, Holmes professes that he was so wholly uncertain "which was Nature's leg and which was Mr. Palmer's" that he "selected *the wrong leg*. No victim of the thimble-rigger's trickery was ever more completely taken in than we were by the contrivance of the ingenious Surgeon-Artist" (577). As in the moments of confusion in Poe, Hawthorne, and Davis, and as in the Jamesian passages where persons disappear into a welter of things, the body wavers in the field of vision in a *trompe l'oeil* effect, which reproduces in a glance the continuity between person and appurtenance. (A thimble-rig is a shell game, a reference with which Holmes suggests that the "trickery" and disguise formerly assigned to the midcentury confidence-man now style the body at large.) Holmes understands this continuity as more than just a visual illusion, however, for in his explanation of how amputees

adjust to their new legs, the connection between person and thing is figured as a matter of neurology: "gradually the wooden limb seems to
become, as it were, penetrated by the nerves, and the intelligence to run
downwards until it reaches the last joint of the member." Similarly, "the leg
is stupid until practice has taught it just what is expected from its various
parts," a remark that suggests that intelligence and consciousness are
lodged within this appurtenance, "the half-reasoning willow" wood from
which the best legs are made (576–77, 578). The finest wooden leg is
"shaped very much as a sculptor finishes marble, with an eye to artistic
effect," and its wearer is "solaced with the consciousness that he carries so
much beauty and symmetry about with him" (577).

Holmes's sense of the prosthesis as a luxuriously refined extension of the
body that also renders ambiguous the matter of bodily integrity is one
William and Henry James share; it is an image that focuses their contradictory intuitions about the physicality of selves and the relation between
that physicality and the world of objects. Hence a famous passage in *The
Spoils of Poynton* imagines the loss of a house and its furnishings as an
"amputation" and the new house as a "lovely wooden substitute" (10:69).
And as in Holmes's account of the wooden leg as "half-reasoning," James
figures the "chopped limbs" as seemingly conscious, as having the ability
to "suffer"; in both texts, the prosthesis leads to a blurring of the difference
between the objects of consciousness and consciousness itself (10:78). In
his essay on "The Consciousness of Lost Limbs" (1887), William James
blurs this same difference—even after one reads the essay, it remains questionable whether the title means that limbs have or rather are the objects
of consciousness—while also grounding this metaphorical substitution in
the psychology of neuroanatomy.[25] While sensation only becomes a matter
of consciousness at the center of the nervous system, the mind locates that
sensation at its physical source, a habit amputees haven't unlearned. James
explains the psychology of sensation as a confusion between center and
periphery so that what really happens inside is experienced as something
that happens along the edges of the body, even when those edges are no
longer there.

This metonymic confusion of cause and effect is important because
James keeps generalizing it, extending it far past the case of the partially
dismembered body to the psychology of the relation persons with intact
bodies have to the material world. This confusion pertains, first of all, to
the relation between hand and tool as "we project to the extremity of any
instrument with which we are probing, tracing" or "cutting" "the sensations which the instrument communicates to our hand when it presses the
foreign matter with which it is in contact."[26] That sentence appears within
a footnote to the lost-limbs essay; a few years later, in the *Principles of*

Psychology, James places phantom limbs and prostheses in a still wider context, using the axiom that sensations "migrate from their *original locality*" to explain how hair, teeth and fingernails, canes, pencils, knives, elbows, lost and whole and replaced limbs become extensions of and so parts of the sensing body (685, 682–88). (The fact that James feels the need to explain how something like an elbow becomes part of—and sometimes detached from—the sensing body is perhaps evidence enough for the claim that the subjective body is for James a highly malleable one; that the elbow is obviously a part of the body is anything but self-evident in the chapter on sensation, in other words.) For James, considering the psychology of the sensing body means considering a body which perpetually shifts its shape; the *Principles'* famously protean conception of consciousness extends to, and is in large part experienced through, the self's material life.

Body parts and objects around the body are hence defined by James as detachable extensions of consciousness; consequently they are turning figures, ones that endlessly waver in what James calls "*vicissitudes in the me*" (*PP,* 351). A scene in the *Principles'* chapter on the perception of objects will suggest the extent to which Jamesian psychology takes as its subject matter the material world of the body's periphery and the extent to which Jamesian psychology follows and reworks the material structure of American-Renaissance romance. Presented by James as an example of optical illusions, the anecdote takes place on a steamer; it thus associates visual disorientation with the mobility of transatlantic culture, with a journey that, in the second half of the nineteenth century, is coded as a mission in the acquisition of European refinement and its fungible objects. James is lying on his berth while listening to the sailors work on deck, when, "on turning [his] eyes" he "perceived with perfect distinctness that the chief-engineer of the vessel had entered [James's] state-room, and was standing looking through the window" at his men scouring the deck. "Surprised at his intrusion, and also at his intentness and immobility," James watches the figure for a time before he eventually sits up in his berth and discovers that "what [he] had taken for the engineer was [his] own cap and coat hanging on a peg beside the window" (745–46). The vagaries of romance, its corporeal oscillations, here become the stuff of psychology as the shifting shapes of the body in daily life hover and switch back and forth between constituting the self and becoming physically and perceptually alienated from it. In an early and highly Hawthornesque story called "The Romance of Certain Old Clothes" (1868), a story that holds true to its title by detailing the accoutrements of female dress on every single page, Henry James had brought his plot to a close by imagining a collection of dresses and accessories as haunted by their previous owner. Here in the *Principles,* this sense of phantasm constitutes the perceptual pathology of everyday life, as the clothing and accessories that William had earlier in his psychology defined as part of "*the material Self*" become detachable in an economy conceived along the lines of lost limbs and their prosthetic replacements (*PP,* 280).

A scene in the *Principles'* chapter on association complements this one by substituting the deep familiarity of the parlor for the jarring estrangements of a stateroom in transit. James designs this scene to show how one kind of sense impression, like touch, can awaken through association other types of sensations, like vision; one sense "reproduce[s]" another as the self travels through an environment full of objects "tinged with the egoistic interest of possession" (524, 540). In its locale of the parlor, its darkened lighting, its focus on accessories, and its interest in the tension between the actual and the imaginary, the scene almost explicitly revisits the scene of romance as Hawthorne represented it at the beginning of *The Scarlet Letter;* the passage uses the tension between the finely detailed concrete object and the ghostly phantasm, a tension that for Hawthorne defined the technique of romance, to represent the smallest perceptual acts of daily life. Perhaps it is because it manages so convincingly to pull together the concrete and the phantasmic that the passage is also one of the most beautiful William James ever wrote:

> Let a person enter his room in the dark and grope among the objects there. The touch of the matches will instantaneously recall their appearance. If his hand comes in contact with an orange on the table, the golden yellow of the fruit, its savor and its perfume will forthwith shoot through his mind. In passing the hand over the sideboard or in jogging the coal-scuttle with the foot, the large glossy dark shape of the one and the irregular blackness of the other awaken like a flash and constitute what we call the recognition of the objects. The voice of the violin faintly echoes through the mind as the hand is laid upon it in the dark. . . . (524)

With its fruit and violin, its smoking-implements and sideboard, the space of this passage is the space of still life; it gathers together the accessories of the genre of painting that takes the most intimate and unremarked material layer of everyday life as its subject.[27] Perhaps still life is always the meeting ground of the epistemological and the economic as its interests in material and cognitive acquisitions coalesce into a single picture; it is certainly the case that these two become indistinguishable in James's shadowy parlor. Perception here becomes an incessant "reproduc[tion]" of the object, as William James calls it here in the *Principles* and as Michel de Certeau characterizes it in *The Practice of*

Everyday Life; the acts of consumption that the latter describes as *"another* production," a "re-use of products" that "insinuates itself everywhere, silently and almost invisibly," work in James's text at the most basic level, as the sensing body travels through a cluster of things that painting has coded as the epitome of the consumed object.[28] As prosthesis is to stump, so the matches and orange are to the sensing hand and to the imagination which guides it and fills out its perceptions: what happens at the edge of the body is a perpetual act of extension and completion.

If that analogy seems somewhat exaggerated, then there is also something exaggerated about the Jameses' tendency to define the body as both wounded and accessorized, to think of the body as suffering a disorder or lack that the accessory might heal. In *Moby-Dick,* Melville lingers over an anecdote about an English beggar, a sailor whose leg has been torn off by a whale's jaws and who now stands by the London docks, "holding a painted board before him, representing the tragic scene in which he lost his leg" (231–32). "Ruefully contemplating his own amputation," the sailor stands with "downcast eyes" focused on a scene that is both his story and his portrait, a seascape depicting a whale demolishing the beggar's ship. The picture functions as a portrait inasmuch as it captures the origins of the lack that is the sailor's identity; it fulfills the role of portraiture to convey what is most essential, even as it resists the tendency of portraiture to present its subject as freestanding, standing apart from the conditions that have made him what he is. Melville's image is complex because the sign (it is literally a sign) of dismemberment, absence, and lack serves as an appurtenance (something added to the body) at the same time that it solicits passersby for a donation which would somehow ameliorate the loss (of the limb) that it depicts.

Something very much like this sense of wounded body and compensating paraphernalia lies at the center of Henry James's conception of himself, while it also emerges, in passages like the ones I have earlier canvassed from his fiction, as James's model for imagining the structure of culture. One of the more notorious facts of James's biography—a fact James himself *made* notorious in *Notes of a Son and Brother,* the volume of autobiography he published in 1914—is what he called the "horrid even if . . . obscure hurt" he suffered while helping to put out a fire, an injury that coincided with the outbreak of the Civil War, an injury which James generally phrased in terms that manage to maintain a stubborn sense of physicality even as they avoid a sense of physical particularity, avoid giving the injury a specific bodily location.[29] The story of the actual mishap in *Notes,* for example, has an almost clinical detachment as James described himself "jammed into the acute angle between two high fences, where the rhythmic play of [his] arms, in tune with that of several other pairs" coaxed an old fire engine to do its work, but this detailedness is suspended at the very point where James is left with an unspecified injury, a wound that will not heal (415). Many critics have noted that James gives schematic pattern to his life by reworking the story of his father's injury, working the trauma of an incurable burn into his own autobiography; what goes unnoticed in such accounts is how James shapes his life around the ambiguities of bodily shape, around an image that blurs the difference between physique and artifice.[30] My interest in this well-worn image—more or less a cliché of Jamesian commentary—is not in whether this is part of a reliable narrative, and it is not in what the never-quite-specified hurt really is (most readers have assumed a bad back, the classic unverifiable symptom). Rather, my interest is in what has allowed this cliché to become so notorious and so over-cited, in what makes it seem, to James in 1914 and to many critics since, a resonant and convincing summation of both James's art and his subjective life. My purpose is to limn in the conceptions and predispositions this image brings with it yet never clarifies. Giving in to the force of this cliché citation for a moment while also seeking to gain some critical distance on it, I will sum up the argument of this chapter by considering three nuances of James's career as a body, three strands of his complex corporeal biography.

In the first place, James defines the "obscure hurt" as a matter of neither psyche nor soma but as something that hovers in between. The "catastrophe" is "private," "physical" but "extraordinarily intimate"; it is an "injury," an "interest," and a "bewilderment" (414–16). As it describes his wound, James's language shifts back and forth between the association of pain with the visible reality of the mutilated body and the contrary recognition that pain must ultimately be experienced in (and as) overwhelming solitude. Indeed, the narrative in *Notes of a Son and Brother* exaggerates to an extreme that paradox that governs the epistemology of injury, its association with both the violently visible and the wholly unshareable, because as the story unfolds, it intertwines, in "queer fusion or confusion," with the outbreak of the Civil War (414). As James makes explicit, his "huge comprehensive ache" locates itself neither in his "own poor organism" nor in "the enclosing social body," but instead in some place between. Hence the narrative of consciousness becomes indistinguishable from a tale of maimed bodies, of a national "body rent with a thousand wounds," in this very late Jamesian fiction that implicitly claims to sum up and contain all the rest (415). Inasmuch as the narrative of consciousness and the tale of the body *do* take their shapes from each other, Jamesian criticism is in turn generated and molded by a body it never reads.

Second, the hurt is continually reworked as James incessantly re-produces his bodily complaints, and third (it will be part of my point that these two points are inseparable), the body is continually retrofitted, appurtenanced, accessorized, and supplemented. At key points in his life, James focuses a moment *as* a crucial instance by centering it in a bodily disorder or change, constituting his own biography as a matter of disordered digestion (there are many letters to William in the 1860s about constipation), or chewing (both the adoption of Fletcherizing and its abandonment are conceived as turning points), or obesity, or having his teeth pulled, or shaving his beard. As this range of disparate-seeming examples suggests, the discourse of illness for James blends into that of fashion and accessories as the styling of the body's surfaces and the cure of deeper matter are conceptualized by means of each others' terms. Writing to a profoundly depressed William in 1870, James recommends a therapy of weight-lifting, an experience that is "worth" "the trouble" "for the joy of hugging to your heart that deep & solid conviction which you wring from those iron weights."[31] What is striking here is how a medical treatment blurs into something like a fashionable trend—the weights were part of the slightly gimmicky program of one Dr. Butler—and how the weights outside the body strengthen the body's insides, a strengthening that in turn is registered as the psychological state of "conviction." The same kind of economy governs a letter of a year earlier from William to Henry, a letter that begins with specific instructions for preparing a home remedy for constipation, goes on to suggest Henry see the London doctor Thomas King Chambers ("a first rate man for the digestive canal, but also rather fashionable & busy"), mentions that Alice James is trying the "lifting cure," and ends by reporting that "Father is gone off to [New York] this m[or]n[in]g . . . to get a new leg."[32] As a composition, the letter might be said to pivot on this leg, to be grounded in the prosthesis. Like virtually every other passage I have surveyed in this chapter, this letter doesn't even maintain a notion of bodily wholeness as something lost and perhaps recoverable; rather, it so generalizes the relation between artificial part and incomplete whole that the body is in perpetual question, ceaselessly turning.

The concerns of William's letter are completely quotidian; it portrays the James family going about the business of daily life. Alice "goes . . . to the lifting cure 3 times a week, and walks & pays evening visits" "on the off nights." William's own bad "back remains in status quo—or if anything, better"; he is "going to start galvanism this week." In the meantime, he writes, "the days . . . pass easily and rapidly, altho' I do exceedingly little work of any sort."[33] It is just here, with this quiet sketch of ordinary life in Cambridge in 1869, a life in which the leisurely work of self-maintenance has replaced other kinds of work, that we can mark the difference between the Jamesian body and the American-Renaissance bodies that prefigure it.

For it is not quite true, as I have come close to implying above, that the

American-Renaissance body is a perpetually turning figure like these later ones are; the prosthetic bodies of Ahab and Zenobia and General Smith are fatally wounded, and their supplements of ornament and artifice can forestall death only for a time before they are rent into pieces (like Ahab and General Smith), or before they stop turning and assume the hard immobility of sculpture (like Zenobia). American-Renaissance writers are uncomfortable with the compensations of prosthetics, a discomfort evident in the frequency with which they deny their efficacy, their compensatory powers, in the end. Zenobia's attractions are many, but because they *are* so many and her body is so overly elaborated, it is equated with a falseness for which she must die; and her drowning herself in the pond recapitulates the fact that she has earlier drowned herself in ornament. Early James still appreciates this principle of death by fashion; Daisy Miller's death, by miasma, is figured over and over in that story by images of how fluid and mobile her accoutrements are: she shares her clothes with her mother, she's defined by her shawl, she became the name of a sartorial style in addition to becoming the name of a behavioral type.

But in *The Europeans,* published the same year as *Daisy Miller* (1878), James begins to move away from associating prosthesis and ornament with death and to think of daily life as itself a process of perpetual bodily refiguration. While the novel equates Eugenia's malleable view of the truth with her flair for draperies and accessories that obscure true vision, and while she is banished from the novel because of them, she leaves behind her a taste for the supplemental appurtenance. "What is life, indeed, without curtains," Gertrude, the newly fashion-conscious heroine, asks as she realizes she has been leading an existence of harsh light, a life "totally devoid of festoons."[34] The consequences of redefining "life" as a matter of "festoons" are what the present study seeks to trace.

That redefinition can be further demonstrated by considering how the representation of race and slavery shifts from the time of some classic texts of the American Renaissance to some moments in James's own writings of the late 1870s and 1880s. I have delayed bringing up this context—one of the real and current controversies in James studies—because considering it will bring my own argument to completion by demonstrating how much meaning, how much history, James compresses within the supplemental ornament. Underlying the American-Renaissance symbolic economy of the transformation of persons into things and things into persons is a specific political economy, that of chattel slavery; indeed, it would be possible to revisit virtually all of the examples discussed above and find in them moments where the slave supports the remade white body (as in the moment where Pip implores Ahab to "use poor me for your one lost leg" in *Moby-Dick*) or where the slave's body fuses with the material goods that constitute white privilege (as in the moment where *Life in the Iron-Mills* details the appearance of a "mulatto girl," following her mistress, carrying a basket of fruit and flowers on her head).[35] To choose one further—and unusually clear—example: while it is true that Poe's General John A. B. C. Smith has purchased his prostheses with a connoisseur's care, it is also true that he is powerless to keep himself together on his own. Rather, he relies on his slave, "the black rascal" Pompey, to reassemble him each morning: the wholly commodified body, which is never more than momentarily finished, relies on another kind of human property for its incessant manufacture.[36] Even when, as in Hawthorne's images of the disassembled and remade body, the work slaves do is ostensibly absent, one senses that it is underwriting the material and bodily transformations at work in the literary texts of mid-nineteenth-century America. For it is hard to imagine nineteenth-century Americans finding those metamorphoses so *easy* to imagine if slavery had not conditioned their conceptions of persons and property.

Hence it follows that the baldest statement of the reversible identities of persons and things is not any formulation of Melville's or Hawthorne's or Davis's or Poe's; rather, it is Frederick Douglass's statement to his reader, at the midpoint of his 1845 autobiography, "You have seen how a man was made a slave; you shall see how a slave was made a man."[37] When Douglass's owner, Mrs. Lucretia, dies, Douglass observes that "all the property of my old master, slaves included, was in the hands of strangers,—strangers who had had nothing to do with accumulating it" (91). Human beings thus take on the characteristic of alienability, the characteristic definitive of property. At the same time, slaves lack the insensate nature that makes property an object easy to control, that makes it subject to its owner's projected desires. Much of the conflict of Douglass's narrative is generated by his anomalous status as property that is self-conscious: "Any thing, no matter what, to get rid of thinking!" he exclaims shortly after he learns to read and thus to reflect on his own feelings by finding them mirrored in his reading (84). This tension between property and persons is what drives much abolitionist writing, as two of Harriet Beecher Stowe's chapter titles in *Uncle Tom's Cabin* suggest: "Showing the Feelings of Living Property on Changing Owners" and "In Which Property Gets into an Improper State of Mind."[38]

Take it as an axiom of our current conception of the American Renaissance, then, that the relation between persons and property is crucially entangled with the political and symbolic economies of slavery, as important studies by Walter Benn Michaels, Mark Seltzer, and Lori Merish have demonstrated.[39] But how do these economies work when they work their way into the fictions of Henry James? Answers have been various and contradictory: that James identifies with the segregation of Jim Crow America (Kenneth Warren), that he doesn't (Walter Michaels), that he replicates racist stereotypes even as he also makes his racial representations suggestive of a modern and mobile conception of identity (John Carlos Rowe).[40] None of these arguments mentions one of the few (the only?) African American characters in James's fiction to receive a proper name, however. When Eugenia takes possession of the little house the Wentworths loan her in *The Europeans,* she relieves its severity with "anomalous draperies," "pink silk blinds," "India shawls"—all pieces of the "copious provision of the element of costume" she has "brought with her to the New World" (79). One element of this decor, however, is not imported, but native, an element Eugenia asks the Wentworths to supply: "I must have a cook! . . . An old negress in a yellow turban. I have set my heart upon that. I want to look out of my window and see her sitting there on the grass, against the background of those crooked, dusky little apple trees, pulling the husks off a lapful of Indian corn. That will be local colour, you know" (83–84). In the next chapter, a page later, the narrator notes that Eugenia is indeed "enjoy[ing] . . . whatever satisfaction was to be derived from the spectacle of an old negress in a crimson turban shelling peas under the apple trees" (85). Still later, we learn the name of this woman in the turban: Azarina (151).

Far from the segregationist, revulsed, and openly racist perspective Kenneth Warren discovers in James's story "The Point of View," the vision of racial difference James develops here is emphatically Orientalist. Azarina's "polished ebony," which "contrast[s]" so effectively with her crimson turban, links her to the other objects in the novel which have been given a wonderful sheen—like the "highly-polished brass knocker" on the Wentworth's front door—and to the objects that bespeak "Eastern trade"—like the "green and blue porcelain" stools of the Wentworths' and the "most delightful *chinoiseries*" of Robert Acton's, such as his "pagodas of ebony" (151, 47, 46, 107). Writing in 1878 about a free black woman in the antebellum North, James encapsulates the national trauma of race within one of the tropes of aestheticism, capturing both the issue of emancipation and his own artistic principles within this person who functions for Eugenia as an element of landscape, an outdoor appurtenance. For while Azarina is indeed pressed into serving as an element of composition that meets Eugenia's expectation of "local colour," she also resists fulfilling Eugenia's fantasies, remaining "dry and prim" whereas Eugenia had hoped for "a savoury wildness in her talk," something that would sound distinctively "African" (151). The last appurtenance the present chapter considers is a human being, then, one who maintains a stubborn independence even as she is also made to serve the ends of a specific artistic program.

Considered as such, Eugenia's manipulation of Azarina is neither wholly scouted by *The Europeans* nor wholly adopted; that manipulation ultimately fails, but it also resembles the new and pleasurable power the novel's heroine, Gertrude, finds in "mak[ing]" other characters conform to her own desires (125).

This chapter has begun its work with a most superficial reading of the Jamesian text, considering the physical appearance of a long paragraph of descriptive prose; it has ended with a heroine whose growth can be measured by her ability to manipulate accessories (at the start of *The Europeans*, Gertrude becomes confused when she tries to explain how to wear a scarf; by the novel's midpoint, she is adept at mixing and matching other people as she works with Felix to wed her sister to her own unwanted suitor, Mr. Brand [48, 125]). In between has come consciousness with its accompanying poetics of point of view, a disembodied shape that, this chapter has argued, emerges from historically specific patterns of consumption and reproduction, from a set of material practices, from a lifestyle that cultivates the body. Those patterns, practices, and lifestyles are what Part II of this book will detail.

PART II

Practical Aesthetics

CHAPTER THREE

THE PROPERTIES
OF TOUCH

In taking up *The Spoils of Poynton* (1897), my purpose is to get at some
meanings in Henry James that criticism's obsession with vision has made
hard to see. Rather than gazing at a spectacle or diagramming a system of
surveillance, this chapter seeks to dwell within the most intimate spaces of
the material world—spaces in which the distance that vision inevitably
implies narrows and the sense of touch takes over. Only through what we
might think of as a tactile reading of this novel can we begin to uncover
the meanings it holds for a history of the body and the body's objects.

At first glance, it seems *The Spoils* would more profitably be discussed
in terms of vision; whether we think of it as point of view or display or surveillance or voyeurism, that's the sense we talk about when we talk about
Henry James. Then, too, the objects the novel's title names—the Limoges
and Wedgewood, the cabinets and tapestries—may seem to fulfill in a
straightforward way the code of conspicuous consumption. In Thorstein
Veblen's *Theory of the Leisure Class,* commodities are primarily visual: the
purpose of acquisition is to produce a "spectacular effect," a "studious exhibition of expensiveness" that demonstrates to others one's exemption from
useful activity.[1] And so it is a matter of some interest that *The Spoils* repeatedly focuses on the sense of touch, rather than vision, and that while the
habits of the eye are not exactly slighted, they figure most frequently in
their coordination with the hand. The movements most characteristic of
the novel are ones like fingering, handling, fondling, arranging, gathering,
rubbing one's hands together (as Mrs. Gereth continually does, sometimes
in delight and sometimes in nervous agitation); with *The Spoils,* James's
famously "grasping imagination" turns to the literal act of grasping.
Indeed, Mrs. Gereth specifically privileges touch over vision, casting in

tactile terms the intimate knowledge she has of her objects: "Blindfold, in the dark, with the brush of a finger, I could tell one from another" (10:31). Likewise, when Fleda Vetch becomes reacquainted with the objects after their translation to Ricks, the site of Mrs. Gereth's widowed banishment, her recognition seems wholly a matter of touch: "[T]he very fingers of her glove, resting on the seat of the sofa, had thrilled at the touch of an old velvet brocade, a wondrous texture she could recognise, would have recognised among a thousand, without dropping her eyes on it" (10:71). As these quotations suggest, the novel has a great interest in the point of contact between the human hand and the objects that lie imme-diately adjacent to it; it zooms in on some of the hand's most ordinary movements, raising them to a surprisingly high level of significance, or at least of narratability. *The Spoils* is full of characters stalling for time by fid-dling with their hats or busying themselves with the tea things; testing the quality of china by giving it a few "raps" with their knuckles; leaning on objects and, often, each other, for support in times of stress; grabbing each others' hands and wrists to demonstrate loyalty or affirm affection; even smearing varnish, as, Fleda imagines, the tasteless Brigstocks do with "their own hands" as a pastime on rainy days (10:35, 7).

In *The Spoils*, then, James is committed to making visible a moment in which vision is largely subordinated. The novel takes upon itself the proj-ect of seeing how finely detailed an account it can render of the tactile rela-tionships between persons and things; it is as if James wants to see how intimate his portrayal of what *The Portrait of a Lady*'s Madame Merle calls the "flow" between the self and the objects that lie outside it can become (3:287). My general purpose here is to offer an analysis that keeps faith with James's own particularity: I want to stay inside acts of acquiring and using objects, and so to avoid the distancing effects that must result when we consider nineteenth-century culture in terms of display and the abstracting effects that must result when we consider it in terms of "com-modity culture." Employed as shorthand for a vast world of objects, the latter term operates in critical discourse in much the same way that Marx argued exchange-value does in political economy: it deprives objects of their "coarsely sensuous" properties, casting them not as "objects of utili-ty" but instead as "bearers of value." I seek in this chapter, then, to con-serve the "coarsely sensuous" properties of the spoils, and to identify the larger political and social structures of thought that are embedded within and sustained by those objects' very grains and textures.[2]

The particular social structure delineated here will be class, along with some of its cognates, like taste and refinement and property. In a recent essay, Mary Poovey focuses the seemingly endless and slightly stale debate over the concept of class by observing that this debate centers on whether class describes "an objective set of material conditions" or constitutes instead a mode of self-understanding, a way of "articulating one's place in a social hierarchy."[3] Poovey seeks not to take a position within this debate but instead to show how it reflects a certain foundational incoherence within what she calls "classificatory thinking": a tension between description and theory that makes class both a perpetually unstable concept and a deeply powerful one. In other words, while class will always be open to question because there will always be an "interpretive element" to what it presents as "pure description," it can never be thoroughly dismantled or summarily dismissed because its empirical contents give it the shading of a stubborn reality.[4] While Poovey seeks to show how this epistemology established itself in seventeenth- and eighteenth-century English state politics and economic theory, my own contribution comes almost at the end of the process she describes, for I seek to show how this tension between theory and description plays out in the lived experience of class the Jamesian novel represents. In this chapter, I will argue that out of the smallest touches and gestures emerges a double conception of class: at once a set of standards that can be articulated and rationalized, promoted, even shared, and a bodily truth that is indisputably real but absolutely unsharable. Further, I will argue that through this double account, the language of class becomes inseparable from the language of identity. And I will close by showing how both the touch of class and the concern for the specifics of the material world it implies persist in the final, seemingly renunciatory gesture with which the Jamesian plot typically draws to a close. As the moments I have already glanced at suggest, I begin with the sensing hand.

One reason the hand figures so prominently in *The Spoils* is that the objects at its center reflect the hand; they anticipate and invite its touch. They are things with handles, like teacups and cabinets, or with contours that reflect the shape of the whole body, like sofas and chairs, or things that, like vases and figurines, are scaled to be arranged by hand, fondled, toyed with. Significantly, there are "not many pictures" at Poynton; the valuables are mostly decorative arts like brasses and china, enamels and cabinets (10:22). These objects are a material record of the details of the body; they anticipate and objectify bodily needs and characteristics. In an extraordinary essay, Philip Fisher argues that "every instance of imagination or making installs the conditions of the body into material separable from the body and detachable from the self."[5] The human body's attributes are thus embedded within objects. A coffee cup, Fisher suggests, has a handle that reflects the shape and movements of the thumb and fingers, and a rim that fits against the mouth. Its size, dimensions, and materials reflect facts about the human appetite, its tastes, even body temperature. Thus,

Fisher concludes, "the features of the cup can only be understood by preserving a hovering human image nearby"; "the cup is adjacent to the body
even when seen alone."[6]

Fisher's view of objects as things that imply the close presence of the
human body matches exactly the interests of *The Spoils* and the ways in
which this novel typically arranges its materials. While Poynton is sometimes referred to as a museum—and so a place where objects are seen
rather than used—it is really the use of objects and the narrowness of the
distance between person and thing that the novel repeatedly emphasizes
(10:147, 214). Indeed, to take the objects wholly as objects of vision is to
take them in the wrong way. While from the start Fleda values the experience of "living with them, touching them, using them," Mona's initial
response to the spoils is strictly visual; she spends her first visit to Poynton
"sitting there like a bored tourist in fine scenery" (10:156, 25). And while
the novel draws numerous contrasts between Waterbath—the tacky home
of the Brigstocks—and the splendors of Poynton, in both cases it stresses
the nearness of people and objects; thus to be at Waterbath is to be subjected to an "intimate ugliness," while to be at Poynton is to be in "warm
closeness with the beautiful" (10:6, 12). Similarly, when Mrs. Gereth
invites Fleda to Ricks, she writes that she "shall have warmed the place a
little by simply being [there] for a week" (10:61). Underlying the emphasis on the differences in the decor of the three houses is James's fascination
with the close proximity of—the narrowness of the space between—persons and their environments.

But touch is also emphasized in *The Spoils* because the spoils have the
sense of touch built into them, instilled in them at the moment of their
creation. They are all works of the hand: "wrought substances," like "old
golds and brasses"; carved objects, like ivories and cabinets; hand-decorat-
ed, like china; or woven, like tapestries (10:58). The objects are "figured,"
"chastened" and refined to a high degree of intricacy; Poynton is thus said
to be "written in great syllables of colour and form" by "the hands of rare
artists"—as if it possesses not only the individuality of literary style but
also the idiosyncrasies of handwriting (10:78, 22). And it is precisely
because the objects possess both the refinement and the idiosyncrasies of
the handmade that Fleda can "kn[ow] them each by every inch of their
surface and every charm of their character" (10:73). Only the worked surface that reflects an individual touch contains the swirls and nubs and
nuances, the improvisations and irregularities, that allow for intimate
acquaintance; the "maddening relics" of Waterbath, largely purchased at
department stores and bazaars, are too uniform, too mass produced, to
possess a "character" that one can really "know" (10:19).

Thus, the handmade object simultaneously embodies the physical actions of its maker and the physical characteristics of its user; it reaches backward and forward, forming a physical link between the hand of the artisan and the hand of the connoisseur.[7] In understanding objects in this way, and in adopting the handmade as a crucial test of worth, *The Spoils* follows the emphases typical of the commentary on craftsmanship that proliferates at the century's end. In *The Decoration of Houses*, published the same year *The Spoils* first appeared in book form, Edith Wharton and Ogden Codman conclude their survey of the principles of interior design with a chapter on bric-à-brac that matches this strand of James's novel both in its disparagement of the mass-produced ("that worst curse of modern civilization—cheap copies of costly horrors," as Wharton and Codman put it) and in its tendency to evaluate objects in terms of touch.[8] Fine objects reveal "the master-artist's hand"; they have "the distinction," "the personal quality," that comes only from what Wharton and Codman repeatedly call the "touch" of the "virtuoso" (195, 191, 185). What's wrong with machine-made reproductions is that they lack the artist's "individual stamp," the "skilful handling" and improvisation that is the work of the all-important "finger-tips" (192–94).

Like James's novel, *The Decoration of Houses* reflects a moment of inten-sified interest and a distinct shift in the aesthetics of interior design. Emphasizing the careful discrimination of household artifacts and the need for shaping the interior according to the rules of architectural propor-tion, Wharton and Codman's manual seeks to sweep away mid-Victorian clutter by stressing unified designs based on a new appreciation for the architectural lines of a room and for surfaces unbroken by the "piling up of heterogeneous ornament" into a "multiplication of incongruous effects" (xx). *The Decoration of Houses* thus styles itself as something of a con-sumer's guide for the Gilded Age (one that actually does at one point dis-tinguish between tasteful and vulgar uses of gilt [192–93]). Such an attempt to guide acts of acquisition and display suggests that the end of the century is not so much an era of unbridled appetites nor even a time defined by a tension between processes of commodification and their Veblenesque critique, but instead a time of growing self-consciousness over the consumption and accumulation of goods—a time when acts of acqui-sition were precisely coded, differentiated, assigned varying values. Like the body that generates and uses them, the elements of decor are itemized by a highly detailed system of thought, one that forms modern tastes and delineates modern styles of consumption. In these respects, *The Theory of the Leisure Class* does not differ significantly from *The Decoration of Houses:* both treatises seek to diagram a system of taste that governs acquisition and use; both texts mark out the aesthetic, social, and economic patterns that underlie a welter of objects.[9]

Given this tendency toward thinking of domestic space in terms of carefully delineated patterns and this newly heightened consciousness of accumulation, it is not surprising that the debut issue of one decorating magazine begins by telling readers not what they need but what they need to get rid of. The lead article in the premiere issue of *House Beautiful,* which appeared in 1896, defines the "successful house" as one "where it is evident that thought has been used everywhere," and so "the sundry bits of poor furniture or bad pictures which survive from an earlier period, or are the gifts of well-meaning but misguided friends" must be relegated to the attic. Objects that have been unthinkingly accumulated must give way to objects that together reflect a high degree of expertise so that nothing will "break the effect."[10] *The Spoils,* which James had for a time thought to call *The House Beautiful,* begins by teaching essentially the same lessons, portraying the Brigstock home as an example of a house "smothered" with "abominations" and then shifting to Poynton, the ultimate example of the house artfully arrayed (10:7, 19). Like the magazine's publishers, James had probably hoped to capture interest by invoking what had become a catch phrase for the aesthetically inclined, a phrase that Walter Pater had used in *The Renaissance,* that had given an American decorating manual its title, and that Oscar Wilde had used as the title for one of the lectures he gave in America in 1882.[11] Likewise, *The Old Things,* the title under which the novel appeared when it was serialized in the *Atlantic Monthly,* gestures toward the vogue for antiques and so connects the novel to the handbooks and magazine articles that offered advice for collectors.[12]

Perhaps there is not much distance, then, between James's novel and the "female magazine" that the clueless Mrs. Brigstock buys in the train station on her way to Poynton and enthusiastically offers to share with the extremely unenthusiastic Mrs. Gereth (10:36). Like Wharton and Codman, James took a critical view of what the former call the "fads" and "affectations" of the culture of decor; the magazine that to Mrs. Brigstock seems "so clever," with its patterns for vulgar innovations like antimacassars, has just made its debut, and so it appeals by its very novelty to an audience which, like Mrs. Brigstock, "tr[ies] to pass off a gross avidity as a sense of the beautiful," an audience on which the new lessons of restraint and proportion have been lost (10:27). Yet there are other strands of interior-decorating discourse toward which James seems far less skeptical. In fact, to one *House Beautiful* contributor he seemed a most sympathetic voice. An article on the Grueby Company, a Boston pottery workshop, begins not in Boston but in Blois, with a long quotation that exhorts the traveler to pay a visit to M. Ulysse, a potter whose work comes as a relief from what "we all know" to be "an age of prose, of machinery, of wholesale production, of coarse and hasty processes." In the ceramics of M.

Ulysse's shop, one appreciates the "family likeness and wide variations" that allow one to escape from mass-produced uniformity even as they bear testament to "a greater search for perfection."[13] This vignette, *House Beautiful*'s writer reveals, is the work of Henry James—the concluding passage of a chapter in his *A Little Tour in France* (1884). The article's author continues in the same register, praising the Boston-made pottery both for its simplicity—its avoidance of "tortured outlines" and "unnatural fantastic shapes"—and for the variation of each piece—its avoidance of "the monotony of machine-made wares." Each piece is thus an "individual effort" possessing "the wonderful charm of personality"; each bears the "stamp of individuality."[14]

That *House Beautiful*'s writer quotes James as an arbiter of taste makes the essay remarkable (it suggests, among other things, that "Henry James" had already become a proper name for a certain sort of refined discrimination), but in other respects the article could not be more ordinary; hundreds of essays like it appeared at the end of the century. In these little essays on pewter, garden ornaments, wrought leather, and Tiffany glass, a deeply formative set of associations takes shape: it is not just that good objects reflect their makers' touch, but that in touch's presence or absence the whole matter of individuality is at stake. As a *House and Garden* article on beaten metalwork puts it, fine objects reveal "the marks of the man, his skill, his idea of form and design, his originality"; "in fact one almost feels that a glimpse of his character and temperament is revealed in his work."[15] Or, as an article on garden pottery in the same magazine explains, "one always feels the life-giving personal touch" in the object made by hand, the "visible mark" of "the human eye and brain and hand."[16]

This alignment of touch and its traces with individuality pervades late-nineteenth-century writing about interior decorating and objets d'art; it links the tastes of *House Beautiful* and *House and Garden* writers, which tend toward the Arts and Crafts movement, with those of Wharton and Codman, who adopt more formal Continental models. Similarly, in his American lectures Oscar Wilde associates a "sense of individualism" with craftsmanship that reveals a "delicacy of hand."[17] Joined in their advocacy of the handmade and the values they locate within it, aestheticism, classical styles, and Arts and Crafts are further joined in seeing the handmade object as a living thing. Praising the integration of Grueby pottery's stylized floral ornament with its form, *House Beautiful*'s essayist notes, "so cunning has been the hand that the vases often seem to be emerging from their own foliage, like living things."[18] Likewise, *The Decoration of Houses* develops a whole vocabulary that links the "expressiveness" of objects with the artisan's hand; the language used to talk about home furnishings thus becomes a language of animation. Or, as Mrs. Gereth puts it, the spoils are "living things to me; they know me, they return the touch of my hand" (10:31).

It is precisely because objects are thought capable of "returning" one's "touch"—of acting upon one, in other words—that the handmade comes to seem such an urgent matter. For in an era in which machine-made goods multiply so rapidly, the worry is that their users will become mechanized as well. More exactly, it is the extreme regularity of factory-made furnishings—their uniform lines and unvaried surfaces—that troubles commentators on home decorating. "The life-giving personal touch" is lost in "the machine-made accuracy of to-day," as one writer puts it; a "purely mechanical process" cannot "transmit . . . the idiom, the enthusiasm, of the creator's hand."[19] Commenting on this difference between crafted and manufactured goods, a *House and Garden* editor clarifies the assumptions that lie behind criticisms of the machine-made: the straight line of the machine-made object "wearies" us because it "beats on the same nerves with the same monotonous and inevitable touch." "Dispiriting" and "dreary," the "monotony of an unchanging line" frustrates our "natural craving for stimulus and rest, for variety and variation."[20]

Perhaps all this explains why Mrs. Gereth speaks of her reactions to design as if they were not matters of taste but matters of what she calls her "nerve[s]" (10:3). In representing her painful "sensibility" to ugly decor, the novel moves into the realm of the somatic, construing taste not as a matter of mere preference but instead as a matter of physiological reactions (10:4). So refined is her aesthetic sense that Mrs. Gereth can't "leave her own house without peril of exposure" (as if bad design were one of those diseases you catch from the lower classes); the "depressing" effects of Waterbath cause "her face to burn," while the wallpaper in her bedroom ruins her sleep (10:12, 6, 7). These constructions could be dismissed as melodramatic overstatement were it not that they capture fairly precisely some common nineteenth-century ways of understanding the relation between houses and their inhabitants: just as figuring the loss of her objects as an "amputation" reflects the idea that decor is a bodily extension of its inhabitants, so too do Mrs. Gereth's references to her own nervous system reflect a typical way of explaining how houses become such extensions, of how the details of design shape the details of the body (10:69). Indeed, for Catharine Beecher and Harriet Beecher Stowe, understanding the one requires understanding the other, and so they include in their domestic manual *The American Woman's Home* (1869) an explanation of the nervous system, complete with a diagram of the brain and spinal cord.[21] For writers of the second half of the century, the physiological effects of the house seem so strong that sometimes the difference between body and house simply drops out, as when Poe's Roderick Usher attributes the quality of "sentience" to the house that has "moulded" him, or when a character in Stowe's 1871 novel *Pink and White Tyranny* suggests that women "have nerves all over their house[s]," or when the narrator of Charlotte Perkins Gilman's "The Yellow Wall-Paper" (who, like Mrs. Gereth, is kept awake by ugly wallpaper) imagines a body like her own behind the "sprawling flamboyant patterns committing every artistic sin" that "confuse the eye" and "irritate" the nerves with their "optic horror."[22]

Among other things, such formulations suggest the primacy of touch in thinking about design; even strictly visual impressions begin to sound like tactile ones because they cause changes in the body's reactions, the organization of its nervous system. This emphasis on the shaping power of interiors is all the more emphatic when actual touch is at work. In their chapter on children's rooms in *The Decoration of Houses,* Wharton and Codman propose that such rooms serve as scenes of the child's aesthetic initiation; they should teach "daily lessons in beauty," "communicating to the child's brain a sense of repose which diminishes mental and physical restlessness" (175, 180). Objets d'art further advance this goal of controlling the child's bodily motions: "The possession of something valuable, that may not be knocked about, but must be handled with care and restored to its place after being looked at, will . . . cultivate in the child that habit of carefulness and order which may be defined as good manners toward inanimate objects" (177). Likewise, "a well-designed bookcase with glass doors is a valuable factor in the training of children"; it teaches that books must be handled with "respect" and aids in developing the love of good bindings, which is the sort of refinement that must be instilled early on (181, 177).

In emphasizing the training of the hand, *The Decoration of Houses* falls in line with the turn toward manual training in late-nineteenth-century pedagogy; indeed, the neural paths running from the brain to the fingertips became the favored physiological locale of educators of the time. In the theories of Friedrich Froebel, the inventor of the kindergarten, simple sense perceptions are the beginning of all learning; abstract thinking develops itself out of the child's intimate contact with blocks, beads, and sticks, which Froebel thought of as objectified properties of mind. Grasping and holding are thus the child's very first lessons.[23] At the turn of the century, John Dewey and Maria Montessori each combined this emphasis on manual training (or "object-teaching," as it was sometimes called) with an emphasis on the instructional possibilities of the home; the life and objects of the house—activities like sewing, baking, decorating, and gardening—are the first lessons in arts and sciences. Montessori in particular stressed the tactile aspects of education, urging her readers to "teach the child how to *touch*" through exercises designed "to develop co-ordinated movements of the fingers"; like Wharton and Codman, she emphasized the need to discipline the hand by "educating youth in gentleness towards their surroundings—that is, in respect for objects [and] buildings."[24] As William James explained in his *Talks to Teachers on Psychology* (1899), "all those methods of concrete object teaching which are the glory of our contemporary schools" "confer precision" on the child's movements; they train the hand to adapt itself to the characteristics of a given object by fostering "acquaintance with the properties of material things" and, by absorbing the child's attention, "reduce the teacher's disciplinary functions."[25]

Objects don't just imply a body, then; rather, they imply a specific body, one that has been trained to match itself to their own specifications and attributes. When the touch of the artisan comes together with the touch of the user, the user replicates the precision and delicacy of the motions that went into the making of the object. In other words, one doesn't lift a teacup the same way one grasps a tumbler, a calibration that Mona's mother, whose "big knuckles" are a threat to the Poynton china, is incapable of making (10:35). In this respect, Mona is her mother's daughter; the "massive maiden" of Waterbath is nearly impervious to the sort of shaping pressure that interiors such as those at Poynton exert: "She was a person whom pressure at a given point infallibly caused to expand in the wrong place instead of . . . the right one" (10:199, 27). As "a product of Waterbath," Mona has been raised among objects that are durable or expendable and so has acquired not only the wrong set of habits but also the wrong physique (10:15). "Tall" and "long-limbed," her body is both too large and too athletic; when the "force of habit" takes over, it's the "reflex action of the custom of sport" that's at work, not the finely tuned, appreciative touches that characterize "little" Fleda (10:9, 36). Significantly, when Mrs. Gereth imagines what Mona will do when Poynton is hers, she assumes that the objects that must "be handled with perfect love" will be replaced by ones answering to "some vulgar modern notion of the 'handy,'" ones that obviate the need for precise movements (10:19).

That Fleda Vetch is Mona's bodily and behavioral opposite is signaled by her name alone: a vetch is a plant that takes its form from another plant, adapting its structure to something outside itself. Fleda's is the sort of figure that the interiors of Poynton figure forth; as James puts it in the New York Edition preface, a character "like Fleda Vetch had surely been latent in one's first apprehension of the theme" of the precious, intricate objects (*LC* 2:1144). When she is in the house, Fleda's smallest physical motions replicate the contours and properties of the objects around her; on her first visit, she spends her time "finger[ing] fondly the brasses" and "sit[ting] with Venetian velvets just held in a loving palm" (10:22). When she designs a piece of embroidery after the pattern of an old Spanish altar-cloth at Poynton, the details of the house pattern her behavior in the most literal of ways; her hands imitate the motions of the hand that created the original artifact (10:60–61).

As these contrasting attributes of Fleda and Mona suggest, what is at stake in the design of the house is the design of the bodies that live in it. Indeed, decorating handbooks of the time often hone in on the body as they progress; typically, they begin with public spaces like entrance halls, move to parlors and bedrooms, and end with the objects that exist closest to the body, like bric-à-brac (as does *The Decoration of Houses*) or clothing and utensils (as does Charles Eastlake's *Hints on Household Taste* [1868]). As their comments on children and design especially show, such writers assume a malleable body, one that lends itself to the shaping influence of artifacts, one that can be made to conform to the ideal type in its mannerisms and habits.

This would seem to be a fundamentally different account of the body and its objects than the one that sees decor as a matter of individual self-expression. In design manuals and decorating guides at the end of the century, an emphasis on adhering to newly demarcated standards competes with an emphasis on the individuality of one's choices. As one *House Beautiful* writer puts it, "uniformity is the last thing on earth to be sought for in different homes, either outwardly or inwardly, just as it is in persons."[26] Yet this homage to the uniqueness of the individual appears between a model floor plan and a guide to china marks—between articles construing design as a matter of expertise and the shaping of behavior to accord with an ideal type: it is thus tinged with the irony that colors any mass-market discourse of individuality. A masterfully self-deconstructing paragraph in *The Decoration of Houses* addresses this tension almost directly:

> Before beginning to decorate a room it is essential to consider for what purpose the room is to be used. It is not enough to ticket it with some such general designation as "library," "drawing-room," or "den." The individual tastes and habits of the people who are to occupy it must be taken into account; it must be not "a library," or "a drawing-room," but the library or the drawing-room best suited to the master or mistress of the house which is being decorated. Individuality in house-furnishing has seldom been more harped upon than at the present time. That cheap originality which finds expression in putting things to uses for which they were not intended is often confounded with individuality; whereas the latter consists not in an attempt to be different from other people at the cost of comfort, but in the desire to be comfortable in one's own way, even though it be the way of a monotonously large majority. It seems easier to most people to arrange a room like

> some one else's than to analyze and express their own needs. Men, in
> these matters, are less exacting than women, because their demands,
> besides being simpler, are uncomplicated by the feminine tendency to
> want things because other people have them, rather than to have
> things because they are wanted. (17)

Individuality slides here from being construed as a matter of uniqueness
to a matter of being like other people who are individuals; you give your
rooms the individual touch by giving in to the formulae followed by "a
monotonously large majority," by the class of individuals.[27] Within this
contradictory logic, women inevitably play a special part; since they're
thought more inclined to imitation, they epitomize both the hazards of
indiscriminate duplication of other people's things and the potential for
more disciplined, more carefully studied imitation to yield an "individu-
alized" decor. While women clutter rooms with bad needlepoint and "dec-
orations of the cotillon-favor type," they also, in many turn-of-the-century accounts, possess the more highly refined sensory capacities; Havelock
Ellis wrote in *Man and Woman: A Study of Human Secondary Sexual
Characters* that "there can be little doubt that as regards tactile sensibility
women are superior to men."[28] Women thus have the higher powers in
making the "exacting" discriminations that good decorating entails.

In the transformation of individuality into the class of individuals, the
properties of touch—especially women's touch—come into elaborate play.
We have seen that objects mark their users, that they confer upon the hand
their own physical characteristics. They figure forth an ideal body and
conform the hand and its motions to that body's standards. But this
emphasis on living up to a standard operates alongside—or, rather, operates indistinguishably from—an emphasis on personal uniqueness.
Wharton and Codman's almost oxymoronic phrase the "individual stamp"
captures this perfectly, forcing a link between the stereotyped and its
opposite (192). As it handles handmade objects, the hand is stamped with
their idiosyncrasies; their signs of uniqueness rub off on it until the human
body comes to seem as artfully crafted as the things that surround it. Thus
we find Mrs. Gereth described as if she were herself an object: Poynton
contains "no ornament so effective as its . . . mistress," who is always "the
great piece in the gallery" (10:47, 73).

But this is not the only way the discourse of decor accounts for the
individualizing touch. The hand that is marked by objects also marks
them; as one *House Beautiful* writer explains, achieving "individuality in
homes" means "staying in [one's house] as much as possible; living things
into shape, as it were, and making them adapt themselves to look like
one."[29] As the individually owned object is handled, its edges wear down;

the boundary between the body and its property dissolves. The loss of Mrs. Gereth's things can be figured as an "amputation" because the edges of her body and her objects have melded together (10:69). Conversely, the Brigstocks' bad habit of varnishing their house makes their things durably impervious to the effects of touch, of use, of the passage of time; as Eastlake explains in *Hints on Household Taste*, varnish is "destructive of all artistic effect" because "the surface of wood thus lacquered can never change its colour, or acquire that rich hue which is one of the chief charms of old cabinet-work."[30] Far from serving as a material register of one's personal touch, varnished wood perpetually retains the slightly alien feeling that invests any new object.

But just as making one's own "individual" choices turns out to be a matter of making the choices other individuals make, so too does giving objects one's personal stamp turn out to be an act that conforms to an established pattern. Objects of desire in *The Spoils* bear the marks of their previous owners; around the "relics" of Mrs. Gereth's aunt hovers "a presence, a perfume, a touch . . . a soul, a story, a life" (10:55, 249). To "finger fondly the brasses that Louis Quinze might have thumbed" is literally to attach oneself to a tradition by means of the sense of touch; indeed, these brasses epitomize the individualizing function of objects in *The Spoils* inasmuch as they transmit the absolute uniqueness embodied in the monarch (10:22). That the royal touch is the subject of a long tradition that endows it with healing power—and thus the power to effect change in the body of another—reinforces this suggestion, perhaps.[31] But one might also note here that objects figure significantly in late-century accounts of psychic phenomena; ghosts and poltergeists manifest themselves by clattering crockery, moving furniture, and bringing objects to the séance table (one discriminating spirit produced a pair of Sèvres salad tongs).[32] As Fleda and Mrs. Gereth find when they move to Ricks, where the "little worn bleached stuffs" and "melancholy tender tell-tale things" of the maiden-aunt figure forth a ghostly aura, ownership leaves a residue, a trace, a pattern for the hand to follow (10:248). Or, as Fleda puts it, the objects at Ricks speak to Mrs. Gereth with a "voice" that she "listen[s] to . . . unawares" as it guides her "infallible hand" (10:249).

The appeal to the supernatural here in *The Spoils*'s penultimate chapter is a curious moment; whereas earlier stretches of the novel diagram the formation of touch and hence of class with some real clarity, here the novel suggests that the touch of class is something shadowy, ghostly, even unreal. It's as if class can't quite be located in anything apprehensible to the senses, but instead operates in a mysteriously extrasensory way; you recognize good things, as Fleda does, "by direct inspiration," and if you have to ask (or to consult magazines like the ones Mrs. Brigstock reads), you'll never know (10:138). As Flaubert's Bouvard and Pécuchet discover, "What it comes to is that taste is taste," and nothing "tells you how you get it."[33] But if this late chapter in *The Spoils* repeats the mystification Flaubert identified—by suggesting that class distinctions are based on something that resists identification—then it also and simultaneously anchors class distinctions firmly within reality by means of the hand. Mrs. Gereth's decoration of Ricks has been as hurried and unconsidered as her decoration of Poynton was calculated, but this difference turns out to make no difference because, as Fleda tells her, she "make[s] things 'compose' in spite of [her]self"; Mrs. Gereth needs "only to be a day or two in a place with four sticks for something to come of it"—for her "admirable," "infallible hand" to leave its individual stamp (10:249). Her class is so much a part of her that it has little to do with conscious action but instead emerges most fully in those "unwitting" moments when her hand operates as if by rote; class thus becomes something buried deep within the body, located in the nerves and the hand they govern (10:248). Class seems real because it "borrow[s] the appearance of reality from the realm that from the very start has compelling reality to the human mind, the physical body itself," to adopt a precept of Elaine Scarry's.[34]

Something constructed and contingent like class can assume the appearance of something incontestable and inevitable if it can be redescribed as physiology, then. This strategy of redescription is given a stark rendition in the chapter on habit in William James's *Principles of Psychology*. On this account, class becomes part of the body because repeated actions wear a groove in the nervous system just as water does a river bed; a "path once traversed by a nerve-current" is "scooped out and made more permeable than before," so that the next time we face similar circumstances, the nerves follow that path until the action finally becomes a matter of reflex.[35] The principle underlying this adaptation is the "plasticity" of matter which, "in the wide sense of the word, means the possession of a structure weak enough to yield to an influence, but strong enough not to yield all at once" (110). This is a wide definition indeed; it could just as easily describe a social order as it does bodies. In fact, it turns out to be the structuring principle of both. Habits are actions that have "become embodied in the . . . nervous system" until we don't think about them anymore; you "cannot *tell*" how you perform certain actions, but your "*hand* never makes a mistake" (125, 120). But once they are set, habits are hard to modify; plasticity means a semi-rigid structure, one that is malleable but hardly fluid. Thus a social-climber can't acquire the correct vocal tone because he can't unlearn the "nasality" of his early training. He can't dress like a gentleman, even though "the merchants offer their wares as eagerly to him as to the veriest 'swell,'" because an "invisible law, as strong as gravitation, keeps him within his orbit, arrayed this year as he was the last; and how his better-bred acquaintances contrive to get the things they wear will be for him a mystery till his dying day" (126). Habit, James concludes, is "the enormous fly-wheel of society, its most precious conservative agent." It is what "saves the children of fortune from the envious uprisings of the poor"; it is what "keeps different social strata from mixing" (125).

Class structure is habit, and habit is written "down among" "the molecules" of the "nerve-cells" (131). Because it is such a thoroughly bodily matter class is incontestable. But because it is such a thoroughly bodily matter, it is also mysteriously inexplicable to others whose bodies don't already "know." In other words, the body ensures that class will be seen as indisputably real even as it also ensures its mystification. Perhaps it is because of this amorphous aspect that the *Principles* occasionally refers to more visible sorts of bodily marks like scars and brands: "Every smallest stroke . . . leaves its never so little scar"; habits "endure to the end of life, like the scar of a wound"; "what is early 'learned by heart' becomes branded-in (as it were) upon the Cerebrum" (131, 117). Passages like these conceive the formation of habits in terms of the visible marks of individual identity; such comparisons suggest that outer marks are extruded from an inner core, a suggestion that *The Spoils* also makes when Fleda considers Mrs. Brigstock in similar terms:

> Fleda had not yet been confronted with the question of the sort of person Mrs. Brigstock was. . . . She was really somehow no sort of person at all. . . . She had a face of which it was impossible to say anything but that it was pink, and a mind it would be possible to describe only had one been able to mark it in a similar fashion. As nature had made this organ neither green nor blue nor yellow there was nothing to know it by: it strayed and bleated like an unbranded sheep. (10:172)

This passage, a small mass of collapsed distinctions, puts the matter of social distinction on nearly incontestable grounds. The "individual stamp" that forms the basis for evaluating objects here becomes a psychological and physiological attribute and so a basis for describing persons; the figure of the brand, since it's usually applied to living flesh and since it marks something as property, expresses exactly this equivocation between persons and things. Further, in reshaping the language used to describe persons after the language used to describe objects, the logic of this passage ensures that persons will be more or less unimaginable apart from class—apart from the traces of material things that serve as an index of distinction; class and identity are so enmeshed (or confused) with each other that not to be a member of the class of individuals is to be "somehow no sort of person at all." In Wai Chee Dimock's words, class thinking depends on metonymy, on "a kind of cross-mapping, a cognitive traffic between" different "ontological orders"—a claim that perfectly characterizes this passage's braiding together of skin, mind, marks, objects, social class, and personal identity.[36]

One more example will help to show how touch, bodily marks, and habits work together to collapse the distinction between identity and class. In his *Finger Prints* (1892), Francis Galton famously proposes the ridges on the tips of the fingers as the infallible mark of personal identity. What is less often noticed in this text is that Galton's account links these marks both with the sense of touch and with the marks of class. The fine discriminations so crucial to the discourse of decor are made possible, in Galton's account, by the physiological fact that the tactile nerves congregate in the ridges and so are projected forward into close contact with the outer world; further, the ridges "engage themselves with the roughness" of different surfaces, and so assist us in distinguishing one material from another.[37] Because the ridges also form the fingerprints that serve as an incontestable, unchanging "criterion of identity," the notion of the individual touch comes to rest on a physiologically verifiable ground (2).

Because he conceived of them as indices of identity, Galton expected that fingerprints would correlate with such broad ways of categorizing persons as class. But here his results were richly mixed. In one sense, fingerprints bear no relation to class; no pattern, so far as Galton could discover, is more typical of a farm worker or a gentleman or an idiot. Galton considers this conclusion somewhat preliminary, and so leaves open the possibilities that more data will reveal the mark of class (19) and that the "general shape of the hand" will also prove revealing (197). Yet even while he draws this tentative conclusion of noncorrelation, he finds that fingerprints reveal class anyway. Because it is not, strictly speaking, true that the prints don't change: over the passage of time they come to reflect the work one does—or doesn't do. On the hands of laborers, the prints are "obliterated" by the calluses that form through the "constant pressure of their peculiar tools"; on the hands of tailors and seamstresses, for example, the ridges of the left forefinger are "often temporarily destroyed by the needle." But since moderate manual activity serves to heighten the ridges, the prints on the usually gloved and often idle hands of ladies are only "faintly developed" (59). Like novelistic bodies—which so often reveal their class through the shape, size, and color of their hands—Galton's bodies are whatever they are all the way down to their fingertips; Galton cannot imagine a hand that does not reflect its class, even when his evidence would seem to suggest otherwise.

Given this tendency to think of the hand as both a class indicator and as possessing an incontestably individual mark, it is no wonder that Galton envisioned a time when class could be regulated and stabilized through fingerprints. Outlining the practical applications of his work, Galton recommends that travelers and emigrants to the colonies leave

> their finger-prints behind them as a token of their identity. For in a large population like ours, whose members migrate to all quarters of the earth, the instances are numerous of men who, having left their homes in youth, find a difficulty on their return after many years, in proving claims to kinship and property. Or some alien scoundrel from foreign parts may assert himself to be the long-lost rightful claimant to an estate held in previous security by others on the supposition of his decease.[38]

The hand can provide the physical basis for class because it persists throughout the vagaries of economic, social, and physical mobility. It is the point at which one's training, the shaping of one's habits, can be referred to some inherent attribute, can be referred to a natural mark and so linked with something unchanging (even though Galton elsewhere allows that it does change). As in *The Spoils,* class becomes built into the structure, the tissue, of the body; it becomes a category that aligns habitual actions with bodily shape with material objects, discovering in each an adequate metonym for the other.

But if Galton throws into sharp relief the metonymic construction of class, then he also reflects the considerable strain class thinking undergoes at the end of the nineteenth century. For there are really two accounts of class at work in *Finger Prints.* On the one hand, class is conceived as a relation among a cluster of objects and attributes, a relation among elements that belong to different orders and so can never quite fit together, can never be bound together into a stable entity. On this account, class relies on a chain of metonymic displacements; it is something of an endless shell game, since it is never identical to any one of the elements it correlates. Class thus partakes of the substance of bodies and objects while never being reducible to any of them. While this irreducibility makes class difficult to critique, it also makes it difficult to verify: class proves largely unsusceptible to the kinds of unwavering correlations Galton seeks, as bodies and their origins, objects, and customary environments never prove to be in stable relation to each other.

Because class inevitably splinters into its constitutive elements, Galton evolves his second way of treating class, which is to reduce it to a matter of tautology: your fingerprints confirm your class because they prove you are who you are. In a world of "alien scoundrels" and contested heirs, class thinking needs to construe identity in terms that cannot be pried apart; when class thinking becomes confused and threatened, it takes refuge in the simplest of equations. Thus Galton's text moves from a rich evocation of the material world and its contingencies—touches, traces, scars, abrasions—to an unambiguous, inalienable mark.

The Spoils of Poynton follows this same movement, and for some of the same reasons; like Finger Prints, it worries that class is coming apart, and so it reduces the equivocal and the multiplicitous to the inalienable and the singular. What is most threatening in The Spoils is registered as being threatening largely because it is so numerous; as Mrs. Gereth puts it, the "world is full of cheap gimcracks in this awful age, and they're thrust in at one at every turn" (10:31). Epitomized by the department-store wares of the Brigstocks and figured as the invasion of a "foreign army," it is the very multiplicity of mass culture that threatens to undermine claims to class distinction (10:116). Similarly, at the furthermost edges of this text we see portrayed the efficient management of the economic lower classes along with the worry that they won't prove manageable enough. When Mrs. Gereth transports the spoils from Poynton to Ricks, part of her triumph lies in the way she has manipulated—"t[aken] hold of"—servants loyal to Owen, just as Owen has earlier returned to Poynton "to tackle a tenant on the property whose course with" the Gereths "had not been straight" (10:76, 50–51). These anxieties over multiplicity and the unmanageability of class snap into sharp focus in one of the novel's smallest scenes or, more precisely, in some of the smallest details of one of the novel's more compelling scenes. Uncertain whether they've lost Owen to Mona or decisively separated him from her, Fleda and Mrs. Gereth part at a London railway station and the chapter closes with Mrs. Gereth suggesting that if they have indeed lost Owen and the old things, then at least "We can always, as time goes on, talk of them together."

> "Of the spoils—?" Fleda had selected a third-class compartment: she stood a moment looking into it and at a fat woman with a basket who had already taken possession. "Always?" she said, turning again to her friend. "Never!" she exclaimed. She got into the carriage and two men with bags and boxes immediately followed, blocking up door and window so long that when she was able to look out again Mrs. Gereth had gone. (10:233)

The aesthetic and social "horrors" that Mrs. Gereth continually invokes become real here for a moment, as the novel's deep background pushes its way into the foreground. If this passage lightly presages the outcome of the contest over the spoils—Fleda's place is occupied by a large woman with common objects—then it also registers much more emphatically the incoherence of class, as Fleda's physical refinement and sense of aesthetic discrimination prove to be awkwardly matched (or mismatched) by her economic status, her "third-class" carriage. As Anthony Giddens has argued, class is a mode of "structuration," a process by which economic relationships are translated into ostensibly noneconomic social forms. Hence, class always fits together elements that never fit together exactly, as class markers like refinement float away from their economic referents.[39]

This small scene at the railway station suggests both some of the larger strategies that shape *The Spoils* and some of the anxieties that lie behind the novel's obsessive references to social distinctions—anxieties that its larger strategies are meant to manage. The novel keeps pointing toward realms of culture that escape its management, that lie just beyond the reach of its ability to render them coherent: unruly tenants, crowded railway stations, "smelly cottages" and "smellier shops" (10:180). With these moments, the novel represents class as bounded into an entity and simultaneously reveals class as an entity that keeps falling apart. In other words, these moments in which the novel wanders outside the drawing room give class an edge, so to speak: they allow class to be conceived as spatial, as something with recognizable borders. Indeed, these moments might be said to sketch class along the lines of some of this novel's characteristic objects: vessels like cabinets or teacups that materialize the social properties of control and containment.[40] But *The Spoils* also makes it clear that edges fray, meld, wear down, unravel—and when this material property finds its narrative analogue, class becomes hard to maintain as a bounded entity. When Fleda moves beyond Mrs. Gereth's drawing room she gets mixed up in—and so insufficiently distinguished from—a world that is materially confusing, as at the Oxford Street bazaar or at the train station, and in need of regulation, as at her sister's house, where her brother-in-law the curate diagrams "with a fork on too soiled a tablecloth" the "scandalous drains" of the local convalescent home (10:180).

Conceiving class as an entity with certain boundaries leads to acknowledging how porous those boundaries are; if certain moments in *The Spoils* succeed in giving class edges and a shape, of sorts, then those moments also reveal that such margins are points of traffic, susceptible to blurring. Perhaps this is why the novel chooses, as a sort of compensatory move, to devote most of its energies to making discriminations *within* a class, staying inside the boundaries that are never drawn very finally. In other words, having uncovered classes that escape its expertise, the novel takes refuge in the activity of making discriminations within a single class, developing its elaborate distinctions between Fleda and Mona and between Mrs. Gereth and Mrs. Brigstock as compensation for the confusions it encounters else-where. But this sustaining principle of the novel is also a conceptually con-fusing one: it is hard to imagine a class that takes in both the ideal and her opposite. If the distinction between Fleda and Mona makes class legible—by dramatizing their different qualities—then it also makes class seem an inadequate description, since membership in a given class turns out not to guarantee any specific attributes at all. Here once again we see that class acquires its social force through its descriptive inadequacy, its incoherence: consisting of no particular attribute, class on James's account is always open to question and so always needs to be reasserted.

But even as *The Spoils* exposes and relies upon the incoherences of class, it ultimately renders class as something unquestionable. Like Galton's account, James's novel ends by centripetally gathering together the dis-parate stuff of class into a single inalienable bodily fact. And like Galton's account and like its own earlier accounts of class, the novel ends by appeal-ing to the indisputable reality of touch, albeit in a rather different register. Shortly before she learns that Owen and Mona have indeed married, Fleda returns to her sister's house, where she imagines from afar the "reconstitut-ed splendour of Poynton": "Thus again she lived with [the spoils]," the memory of which instills in her a kind of "equilibrium." The motions fine-tuned by manual training here become wholly internalized: "Her excitement was composed of pulses as swift and fine as the revolutions of a spinning top: she supposed she was going round, but went round so fast that she couldn't even feel herself move" (10:234–35). James's language here partakes of the vocabulary of fin-de-siècle aesthetic theory, particular-ly that of Bernard Berenson, Vernon Lee, and other theorists of empathy who held that the sensations of the perceiving body pattern themselves after the contours of a work of art. As Lee put it in an 1897 essay on "Beauty and Ugliness," a work of art makes its beholder "realise a whole organism of active and opposing movements" as her breathing, sense of balance, and muscular contractions pattern themselves after the vase or painting or cathedral she sees.[41] In his theory of what he called "tactile val-ues," Berenson argued that painting's appeal lies in its ability to intensify our grasp of the third dimension. Relying upon the theory of "ideated sen-sations" developed by Wilhelm Wundt and Hermann von Helmholtz, which held that the sense of touch is stimulated when we look at physical objects, Berenson theorized that looking at paintings involves our whole bodies: "our palms and fingers accompany our eyes"; as I gaze at painted figures, "my retinal impressions are immediately translated into images of strain and pressure in my muscles, of resistance to my weight, of touch all over my body."[42] And because art accelerates our processes of perception, it endows us with the "further pleasures of self-consciousness"; it heightens our awareness of the sensations pulsing through us as we attend to the outside world, bringing about an "exhilarating sense of increased capacity in the observer."[43]

In explaining how material objects can be transformed into a mode of consciousness, Berenson's theory replicates the contours of James's plot, which moves from intimate contact with the material world to the refined bodily state that both James and theorists of empathy call "equilibrium." Like *The Ambassadors*' Lambert Strether, who feels a change "deep down" "in his own organism" after his brush with Parisian culture, Fleda at the end of *The Spoils* possesses an enriched consciousness of her own perceptual powers, is "conscious of an advantage in being able to feel" (22:75, 79; 10:248). Hence, at the novel's end the objects of class are rendered as inalienable property: property in the sense of an attribute, instead of an object that must be subject to the hazards of everyday life like clumsy movers or unjust inheritance law or even the fire that guts Poynton in *The Spoils*'s last scene. In other words, a sense of one's own bodily processes must be the ultimate private property.[44] If, at the end of my argument, I have returned us to the deeply familiar conception of the Jamesian plot as the growth of consciousness, then I hope it is with a strengthened grasp of that plot's bodily and material interests.

CHAPTER FOUR

THE REPRODUCTION
OF PAINTING

On opening day of the Royal Academy Exhibition in the spring of 1914, a woman whom the London *Times* would the next day describe as "elderly" and "of distinctly peaceable aspect," dressed in "a loose purple overcloak" with "ample folds" was among the visitors.[1] She seems to have attracted no notice until she produced from beneath her cloak a meat chopper and used this utensil to attack John Singer Sargent's recently completed portrait of Henry James (figure 1). Striking the painting three times, she broke the glass, cutting the painting on the left side of the head, the right side of the mouth, and below the right shoulder, leaving jagged slashes that in some places stripped away the paint from the canvas. This is viewership with a vengeance.

After a "scuffle," the slasher, Mary Wood, was restrained and arrested and taken to the Marlborough Street Police Court. At some point along the way, she revealed herself as a suffragist, stating that "If they only gave women the vote, this would never have happened." In a letter to the Women's Social and Political Union, she similarly stated that "I have tried to destroy a valuable picture because I wish to show the public that they have no security for their property nor for their art treasures until women are given the political freedom." Likewise, in court, when the value of the painting was reported to be 700 pounds, Mary Wood shot back that if the picture had been painted by a woman, it would not have been worth so much.

While it may be an alluring possibility to regard this incident as the founding moment of feminist critique of Henry James's fiction—and of Sargent's paintings, which have to many readers often seemed continuous with that fiction—the historical record makes this approach hard to devel-

Figure 1
John Singer Sargent, *Henry James* (1913). Courtesy of the National Portrait
Gallery, London.

op because that record leaves Mary Wood's motives for choosing *this* portrait curiously underexplained. So far as one is able to tell, Wood never
referred to either James or Sargent in her statements; there is no evidence
either that she was a frustrated reader of James's novels, irritated by the tendency of James's heroines to capitulate and renounce, or that she found in
Sargent a confinement of women to the realm of the decorative. Indeed,
Jamesian scholarship has never quite found a *use* for this incident and so
has consigned it to the realm of the bizarre, the meaningless coincidence.[2]

I think this moment is worth dwelling on, then, not because it critiques James's poetics—although it may do so—but because it exaggerates and thus makes more clearly visible some assumptions about paintings and their viewers that have wide currency at the century's turn, and that shape James's fiction and Sargent's paintings in some important ways. My point is not merely that slashing a painting is a scenario James himself had represented in his fiction (although that's true, and I'll return to it later). Nor is my point quite that in his novel *The Tragic Muse*, James had, like Mary Wood, understood painterly and political representations in terms of each other (although that's also true, and I'll return to it later, as well). Rather, my argument is that both James and Wood work from a conviction that a painting *makes* its viewers, that viewing a painting is a physically intimate, almost immediate process that shapes and forms and frames the body of the viewing subject. The work of painting, then—shaping bodies on a canvas—is understood as continuing in front of the finished canvas in the body of the person viewing it. To consume a painting is to be produced by it.

Understood in this light, Mary Wood's motives become far more comprehensible: she attacks James's portrait because she sees in it a set of social and economic circumstances that have defined her life as a woman. Her statement that the painting would not have been worth so much money if it had been the product of a woman's labor implies that the painting's exchange value in turn calculates the value of her own labor: this painting makes her what she is and holds her in the role it has created for her. In proclaiming that she wished "to show the public that they have no security for their property nor for their art treasures until women are given the political freedom," Wood draws an implicit connection between the pictorial frame and the political framework: for her, violating the one and redrawing the other go hand in hand. As David Freedberg has shown in his study of iconoclasm, to deface an image is to attest to that image's power.[3] To put this in another way, to slash a painting is to argue that painting has material consequences for its viewers.

Considered as such, Mary Wood's knife-work constitutes a critical argument about painting, one that corrects some persistent scholarly misunderstandings of how paintings function in the Jamesian text and its culture. It corrects, first of all, the assumption that painting is construed in James as an overwhelmingly ocular and dematerializing practice, one in which the Jamesian text abstracts itself from history into the relatively atemporal realm that painting offers. I wish to argue quite the opposite by saying that when the Jamesian text imagines painting, it imagines it either under production, as a matter of paint and brushwork, as an act of labor in a studio, or as in turn producing something else, as remaking its viewer or as exemplifying and so upholding a social order. More particularly, I want to argue that when the materiality of painting comes forward—when painting is described in terms of what it is rather than what it represents— it's the social force of painting that's being revealed. The very matter of painting—brushwork, paint, canvas, and frame—gives James purchase on the social and the political. To put this point in terms of Mary Wood's vandalism, we can say that reducing Sargent's portrait to jagged canvas and chips of paint and protesting the political shaping of women in England are one and the same action. While I don't quite mean to restore to James a mastery that Mary Wood left in tatters, I do want to claim that the conception of painting Wood holds is one that James had developed in his own acts of figuration.[4]

Before going on to develop these claims and to support my reading of Mary Wood, I want to state clearly that my argument is about how painting is understood in a particular time and a fairly specific locale: set mostly in London, it concerns moments from the early 1880s to the 1910s. There is no claim here, then, toward a general aesthetic, no attempt to offer a transhistorical theory of what painting is. The work of the present chapter is opposed to arguments like that made by Norman Bryson at the end of his *Vision and Painting: The Logic of the Gaze*. There, Bryson argues that Western paintings "negate" the "space of the studio, of the body of labor"; what is invisible in painting, except as a trace, is the body that produced the artifact.[5] In a very general sense, that claim must be literally true, yet adopting it as a precept makes one a most imprecise historian; in the period under discussion here, the labor of painting is understood as reappearing in the body of the viewer. Painting is understood as a shaping of the body on canvas that in turn shapes the bodies that stand before it. To make that claim specific, I want to consider in some detail first radical suffragism and its strategy of violently attacking the objects of high culture and then the veneration of high art by aestheticism, which would seem in this regard to be suffragism's opposite.

Mary Wood was not the first suffragist to slash a painting; indeed, attacks on works of art became almost stereotypically associated with such activists at the time. Hence Mary Wood's attack on the Sargent had a successor: nine days later a woman described in the *Times* as "a well-known militant" eluded the Royal Academy's heightened security, produced an ax from her muff, and dealt three blows to Sir Hubert von Herkomer's portrait of the Duke of Wellington.[6] Wood also had a highly notorious precursor: two months before, a suffragist named Mary Richardson attacked with a meat chopper the *Rokeby Venus* of Velázquez (also known as *The Toilet of Venus*) in the National Gallery (figure 2). Like the acts of making that they reverse, destructions of works of art come in series; as the use of the meat chopper suggests, this destruction of a model of femininity—of a Venus, no less—must itself have served as a model for Mary Wood's subsequent attack. Mary Richardson's vandalism of the *Rokeby Venus* establishes the conventions of the genre of suffragist picture slashing, as we shall see.

In an interview forty years later, Richardson explained her attack on the *Rokeby Venus* this way: "I didn't like the way men visitors gaped at it all day long."[7] Significantly after the fact, Richardson thus accounts for her motives along the lines of what late-twentieth-century critics think of as the politics of the gaze: the equation of looking, especially by men, with the sexual violation and objectification of what is looked at, especially women. But Richardson's earlier explanations of her actions and the way the event itself unfolded in 1914 were considerably more nuanced than the later comment about "gap[ing]" suggests. According to the London *Times*'s report the day after the vandalism, "Slasher Mary" (as she immediately became known) said as she was led away from the Gallery, "Yes, I am a suffragette. You can get another picture, but you cannot get a life, as they are killing Mrs. [Emmeline] Pankhurst," the woman widely regarded as the mother of the Suffragist movement, who was then imprisoned and on a hunger strike. In a prepared statement, also published in the *Times*, Richardson wrote, "I have tried to destroy the picture of the most beautiful woman in mythological history as a protest against the Government for destroying Mrs. Pankhurst, who is the most beautiful character in modern history. Justice is an element of beauty as much as colour and outline on canvas."[8]

As Richardson's comments suggest, the theme of representation is at issue at every level of both the *Rokeby Venus* and the act that violates that painting; mirrored reflection runs as a connecting motif from the painting's provenance to the politics of suffragism to the little mirror in the painting's center by which Velázquez's woman looks at herself—or her viewer. There is, to begin, the fact that the painting had been purchased for the Gallery by a much-publicized subscription of donors eight years prior to this attack: this painting may have seemed to Richardson a fitting target because it became national property through the accumulation of individual acts of expression, almost like the voting process from which women were excluded.[9] Moving inward, from the painting's economic frame to the structure of the painting itself, we can see how Richardson's attack on this painting is a faithful reversal of the painting's principle of composition: the act of slashing this painting, in other words, critiques the female role the painting produces, even as that act also mimetically follows the painting's own logic. In slashing this portrait and so violating the boundaries of its frame, Richardson does not so much contradict or negate

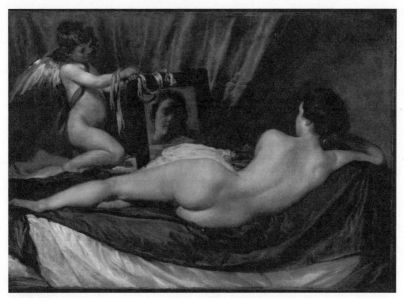

Figure 2
Diego Velázquez, *The Toilet of Venus (The Rokeby Venus)* (1647–51). © National Gallery Picture Library, London.

the painting as she reverses and rereads its dramatization of the themes of representation and framing; her work with the meat-chopper uncovers the political nonrepresentation of women that results when women are reduced to embodying an aesthetic ideal. At the same time, Richardson implicitly relies on the painting's highly elaborated metaphor of the frame to make manifest the tightly constricted space women occupy within the social framework: the female personality, epitomized by the face, requires a frame within a frame, a boundary within a boundary, in Velázquez's painting. Similarly, Richardson adopts the painting's theme of doubling, of mirroring, in order to connect the fate of this physically beautiful, painted body with the fate of the morally beautiful, real body of Emmeline Pankhurst; indeed, the meat-chopper, because it's meant to cut flesh, serves as a metonym that links the two, so Richardson's choice of implement is imagistically consistent with her conception of the politics of painterly realism. In slashing the painting, Richardson turns it into an image that mirrors the violation of Pankhurst, a violation that this painting has itself, in some sense, produced. As an unnamed woman at a meeting of the Women's Social and Political Union in Bayswater put it a few days later, Mary Richardson's attack on the Velázquez was a "stroke of genius," so deft is its touch in handling a cultural poetics of extraordinary density.[10]

In describing the slashing of the Velázquez in such self-reflexive terms, I am implicitly suggesting a link between this incident and its cultural poetics and the poetics of that most self-reflexive artistic movement, aestheticism. This sense of endless mirroring and this practice of categorizing experience and artifacts into "life" and "art" only so that those categories may swap attributes are what aestheticism depends on. This implicit link between suffragist and aestheticist conceptions of portrayal becomes especially evident if we turn to the most famous portrait stabbing in British literature, which occurs in the final moments of Oscar Wilde's *The Picture of Dorian Gray* (1891). Having come to believe that the hideously decrepit portrait is what keeps his tormented conscience alive, Dorian seizes a knife and "stab[s] the picture with it."[11] But in the few paragraphs that come between that sentence and the novel's close, Wilde blurs this scenario so that portrayed and portrayal, agent and object, become wholly confused with each other in a condensed series of symmetries so excessively reversible they seem impossible to sort out or stabilize. Actually, the confusion between real and painted bodies begins even before the stabbing takes place as Dorian uses the same knife to stab the picture he earlier used to stab Basil Hallward, the picture's painter, concluding that "as it had killed the painter," whose incinerated corpse has left "no trace," "so it would kill the painter's work, and all that that meant" (223, 222). Further, since the first knife one sees in *Dorian* is not this dagger but a palette-knife instead—a palette-knife with which Basil, the painter, threatens to stab his own creation—the acts of destroying a painting and making one are imagistically referred to each other (27). At the novel's end, the confusion between the painting and its subject becomes one of agency: the painting, which had physically recorded Dorian's moral decay and which the novel says he stabs, returns to its pristine, ravishingly beautiful state, while before it lies Dorian's now "withered" and "loathsome" corpse with the "knife in his heart" (224). The novel leaves the action of its closing scene suggestively murky (cloaked in gray, as it were), but the suggestion is that the painting somehow stabs Dorian even as the painting returns to him the physical signs of degeneration that it had assumed in his stead.

This not-quite-rational understanding of the novel's ending makes a good deal of sense given how emphatically the text has imagined that the painting makes Dorian's identity, sustains his beauty by mysteriously assuming the symptoms of aging and endowing him with the permanence, the atemporality, traditionally associated with portraiture. By stabbing the painting, Dorian attempts to destroy the artifact that has produced him, then; conversely, the implication at the close that the painting stabs Dorian reinforces the argument about painting the novel has been making all along. Here it will be useful to think about how Wilde echoes and redirects the imagery of the foundational myth of Western pictorial realism. In Pliny's story of the competition between the painters Zeuxis and Parrhasius, Zeuxis produces a painting of grapes so lifelike that the birds fly down and peck at it with their beaks. Assured of winning the palm, Zeuxis asks Parrhasius to pull back the curtain concealing his own picture, only to discover that it is actually a painting *of* a curtain and that while he has tricked the birds, his rival has fooled another artist.[12] The story hinges on the kind of multiple reversals of the represented and the real which we have come to think of as characteristic of aestheticism in general and of Wilde in particular. Understood in this light, Parrhasius's painting becomes a triumph of realism because it so successfully maintains the illusion that it covers up the real; realism turns out to be a matter of surfaces, of ornament, an inversion central to Wilde's decentering poetics.[13] Perhaps Wilde means us to hear, then, and to hear as distinctively and transumptively Wildean, Pliny's story, first behind the episode in which Dorian unveils his own portrait for Basil, and then again at the end, where painting's force is dramatized by the violation of a canvas. In the former of these moments, Basil, who has "put too much of [him]self" in the painting, and Dorian, who sees "his own soul" mirrored in the canvas, stand in front of the picture, which is covered by "a large purple satin coverlet heavily embroidered with gold, a splendid piece of late seventeenth-century Venetian work" (115, 119, 118). The scene is like a hall of mirrors, a *mise en abîme* of representation and desire: in Wilde's version of Pliny's story, the curtain, a work of art in its own right, really does cover a painting, but this painting is one that has taken over a basic attribute of the human body, leaving its subject a figure more artificial than itself. Everything and everyone in this scene are changing places, being exchanged, projecting themselves into other substances, other artifacts, other persons; the relation of artist, model, objet d'art, and painting is one of endless circulation. If we pull this moment into relation with the other half of Wilde's revision of the Plinean myth—the last scene, in which the attempt to violate the canvas turns into a demonstration of painting's agency—then we can say both that painting makes its viewers and that the way that it does so characterizes within *Dorian* a far more general economy.

For even as the novel places tremendous emphasis on Dorian's efforts to hide the painting from others' eyes, the work of the painting proves throughout the novel to be uncontainable; what the novel construes as painting's endlessly circulatory nature is reproduced in the smallest corners of the text and what the novel construes as painting's work of producing its viewers is generalized into an economic model. Wilde dramatizes this circulatory and reproductive nature of painting through Dorian's attempt to keep the painting secret and contained. When he realizes that the painting is recording and displaying his moral degeneration, Dorian places a screen in front of it and then, deciding that keeping it downstairs is too risky, moves it, in its ornate frame and covered by the tapestry, to his attic, which is kept locked. To move the painting upstairs, Dorian sends for some men from the frame-maker's shop and is surprised when Mr. Hubbard, "the celebrated frame-maker of South Audley Street," appears in person (120). The passage is one of those in *Dorian* in which Wilde seems deflected from the real business of his novel; there is too much detail about the frame-maker, about moving the painting, about the labor involved in going up the stairs, about the need to use the front stairs since the picture is too bulky for the narrower ones in back. Wilde seems to overinvest in the peripheral here, except that the whole episode is devoted to keeping representation centered *and* to showing how impossible it is to do so, hence showing the distinction between center and periphery to be an unstable one. The frame-maker appears at this moment because he is in the business of containing representation; his profession is one of preventing paintings from leaking out into the world. In an essay on the picture frame, Georg Simmel writes that the frame's purpose is to keep the viewer's gaze "flow[ing] back into itself"; the frame "must never offer a gap or a bridge through which . . . the world could get in or from which the picture could get out."[14] Moving the painting upstairs is a hugely laborious and messy task because it strains against the tendency paintings have to get out—to seep into other representational spaces—when they appear in narrative.[15]

This seepage becomes apparent when we consider for a moment the characteristic objects and activities of its social world that *Dorian Gray* accentuates. In no particular order (indeed, they are unorderable because they are how Wilde disrupts a hierarchy of significance), these include cosmetics, costumes, dyed hair, love affairs, orders to the florist, and the pursuit of the "exquisite," a category that keeps on changing its contents (164). All of these activities and appurtenances have an element of self-maintenance; they all perform the work of maintaining the self's newness and its youth (which in Wilde is to say its artistry, so thoroughly does his novel equate freshness with the artifactual). More specifically, the maintenance of the self and of its materializations in *Dorian* tends to be a matter of conservation, of keeping things (like hair, or love) from fading, or otherwise disintegrating or decaying. When Dorian occupies himself with obsessive collecting, many of the objects on which he focuses, like antique musical instruments and old tapestries, are ones that present curatorial challenges, which challenge the conservator's art to deflect "the ruin that Time brought on beautiful and wonderful things" (137). When he first sees his painting in its degenerated state, Basil suspects that the painting has been improperly cared for, that "mildew has got into the canvas," a momentary suggestion that reinforces the way in which the materials and principles of painting come to be associated with the maintenance of the self (156).

Looking at Dorian's portrait in light of this economy that generalizes on the painting's work, we can say that the portrait epitomizes the novel's characteristic economy because it takes over for Dorian the work of daily life; it assumes the labor of living by maintaining Dorian as he is, as an agelessly beautiful young man. As in the episodes from the history of suffragism with which I began, portraiture is understood here as a genre that makes its viewers, that holds them in place, holds them perpetually within a compositional and social frame.

There is a more specific set of cultural assumptions at work in these narratives of slashed portraits, a code or style to which Henry James is highly attuned, and one which he submits to its most searching analysis in his own tale of a stabbed painting, "The Liar" (1888). James's story is set in motion when a painter, named Oliver Lyon, encounters among the visitors at a great country house a woman he once loved and tried to marry. Her husband, Colonel Capadose, is a vivid personality, "handsome and clever and entertaining," an "odd" "mixture of the correct and the extravagant: as if he were an adventurer imitating a gentleman with rare perfection, or a gentleman who had taken a fancy to go about with hidden arms. He might have been a dethroned prince or the war-correspondent of a newspaper: he represented both enterprise and tradition, good manners and bad taste" (12:331, 317–318). He is also a tremendous liar, who will invent marvelous stories about adventure in India—or lie about the time of day or the name of his hatter. As one of the other characters explains, "It's quite disinterested," not at all malicious, a kind of "natural peculiarity" (12:344). It's almost, Oliver Lyon the painter concludes, like a "love for beauty," "art for art" (12:350).

When Lyon comes to paint the portrait of the liar (the pun is one James obviously means us to hear), he determines to convey this duplicity in the painting itself. "How he did it he couldn't have told you," but he insinuates falsehood in his representation of "every line of the face and every fact of the attitude, in the indentation of the chin, in the way the hair was planted, the mustache was twisted, the smile came and went" (12:361). The painting is so successful in this regard that when Colonel Capadose and his wife are alone with the portrait, she breaks down completely and he impulsively reaches for a dagger and "plunge[s] it into the canvas . . . dash[ing] it again several times into the face of the likeness, exactly as if he were stabbing a human victim" (12:375–76).[16]

I want to argue that the texts and episodes I examined earlier unpack the significance of this story and its climactic moment, and this will become clearer if we look at two passages, two ekphrastic companion-pieces, each of which describes a husband and wife, each of which simultaneously portrays the couple and assesses their potential to serve as the subjects of striking portraits. The first is a description of the Ashmores, the couple who host the country-house party at the story's opening:

> Arthur Ashmore was a fresh-coloured thick-necked English gentle-man, but he was just not a subject; he might have been a farmer and he might have been a banker; you could scarcely paint him in character. His wife didn't make up the amount; she was a large bright negative woman who had the same air as her husband of being somehow tremendously new; an appearance as of fresh varnish—Lyon could scarcely tell whether it came from her complexion or from her clothes—so that one felt she ought to sit in a gilt frame and be dealt with by reference to a catalogue or a price-list. It was as if she were already rather a bad though expensive portrait, knocked off by an eminent hand, and Lyon had no wish to copy that work. (12:316)

The passage comes very close to saying that Arthur Ashmore is not a subject because he's a subject: the passage describes him in pictorial terms that, it then goes on to insist, make him unfit to serve as the subject of a picture. This description relies on its reader's ability to recognize this type of English masculinity and then transforms that type's characteristics into a lack of distinguishing attributes. The gap between the passage's techniques of portraiture and its claims about portraiture widens when the paragraph moves to Mrs. Ashmore, who is somehow both "bright" and "negative," vivid and bland. To paint her would be like copying the work of another painter because Mrs. Ashmore has styled herself along the dictates of the genre of portraiture; her air of newness conveys a sense of the high degree of recognizability, of immediacy, upon which portraiture so often depends, just as that newness stems from either her complexion or her clothes and so replicates the shifting and ambiguous relation between figure and ground that is characteristic of painting. Similarly, her varnished look suggests that the finishing touch of the painting process that accentuates the polish of a portrait has now looped back and is being applied to the real thing. When the ancient family patriarch, Sir David Ashmore, sits for his portrait, Lyon finds him "a beautiful subject" because the hand of time has done the work of "crystallisation"; his face shows "the sum of his experience" without any "leakage," by which the passage presumably means the kind of blurring into accessories by which portraiture so often identifies its subjects (12:342). The metaphor of "crystallisation" makes only the bare minimum of sense in the text because it conjures up the properties of shininess, of "bright[ness]," which, the description of the Ashmore son and daughter-in-law indicates, make persons poor subjects, not good ones like Sir David.

"The Liar," then, becomes a logically confusing text when it tries to represent and to sort out its characters according to their potential for portraiture; underneath the distinctions it draws lies a strong sense of common ground as the sense of characters as somehow already painted turns out to blur such discriminations. The later description of the Capadoses opposes this one of the Ashmores because it values this couple quite oppositely, but in spite of this different valuation, it, too, describes the couple as looking like portraits even before they are painted:

> He [Colonel Capadose] appeared ten minutes later in the smoking-room, brilliantly equipped in a suit of crimson foulard covered with little white spots. He gratified Lyon's eye, made him feel that the modern age has its splendour too and its opportunities for costume. If his wife was an antique he was a fine specimen of the period of colour: he might have passed for a Venetian of the sixteenth century. They were a remarkable couple, Lyon thought . . . as he looked at the Colonel standing in bright erectness before the chimney-piece and emitting great smoke-puffs. . . . (12:335)

The Colonel is already a portrait because he wears a "costume," because he is a "specimen" of a period of art history, because he conveys the "splendor" of a portrait, because with his "great smoke-puffs" he creates an atmospheric effect for himself, because his "bright erectness" mimics the immobility of the painted figure, and because he places himself "before the chimney-piece" and so in the space always furnished with a picture. When he stabs the painting of himself later in the story, the Colonel stabs the genre that has produced him. For as his colorful self-presentation and his penchant for colorful lies both make clear, the Colonel has been produced by a culture of portraiture, a culture structured around the ideal, which it finds epitomized in painting, of an engagingly distinctive yet adequately conventionalized portrayal of one's self. This presentation of one's self is portraiture's "social product," to use a term from *The Tragic Muse,* the novel James published two years after "The Liar," the novel in which James interweaves the modes of painterly and political representation (7:191). A particularly clear example of this kind of product comes in a famous passage in *The Portrait of a Lady* in which Ned Rosier catches his first sight of Isabel in the role of Mrs. Osmond at one of the couple's weekly receptions in Rome: "framed in the gilded doorway, she struck our young man as the picture of a gracious lady," a picture designed to appeal to a culture with an "eye for decorative character" (4:105). In this understanding of culture, every person carries with him or her the air of appearing in a *tableau vivant,* the air of reproducing in dress and posture the codifications of a genre of painting. What becomes accentuated in persons is that which is visible when figures are seen in a relatively formal situation, against a ground of material things, from a distance of four to eight feet away.[17]

The implication of this argument is that "the real thing" is always artificial, which is exactly what James argues in the tale of 1892 that bears that catch-phrase as its title. Major and Mrs. Monarch are the products of drawing-room and club culture; "twenty years of country-house visiting" have "given them pleasant intonations" along with an impervious "blankness," an imperturbably "deep intellectual repose" (18:316). Their bodies have been refashioned into the stereotypes of perfect gentlepeople right down to the "orthodox crook" of Mrs. Major's elbow; they carry portraiture in their very postures (18:313). Because they are suited for nothing but making appearances, when they become financially strapped they apply for work as artist's models—work they are completely unsuited for because their statuesque rigidity defies the ability of the painter's brush to make them look natural (in her youth, Mrs. Monarch was "known as the Beautiful Statue" [18:314]). By comparison, the artist's usual model, Miss Churm, is "only a freckled cockney," but she can "represent everything, from a fine lady to a shepherdess"; since her physical self is not "already made," like Mrs. Major's, she can lend herself to any artistic genre (18:321, 322). Because they really are upper-class, the Majors are too artificial to serve as models for a realist aesthetic, while the lower-class woman lacks all aesthetic polish and so can mold herself into a convincing semblance of the real thing.

This chiastic patterning of the tale's plot carries with it a view of portraiture as endless reflection and reproduction. Almost every element of "The Real Thing," and of "The Liar" as well, is self-reflexive in one way or another; every element has its matched opposite. The tale's title itself matches opposed elements because while "real" suggests the absence of artifice or ornament, "things" in Jamesian idiom carries the implication of objets d'art (*The Spoils of Poynton* was serialized under the title *The Old Things; The Portrait*'s Madame Merle has "a great respect for *things*"; Balzac, James writes, had a "mighty passion for *things*").[18] Persons and portraits in these tales trade attributes just as narrative and portraiture do (the artist's current project in "The Real Thing" is making woodcuts for the collected works of Philip Vincent, a once-neglected novelist who has been reappraised with the dawn of aestheticism). Husbands and wives are matched pairs like vases or figurines on a mantel-piece; when the Monarchs first appear in his studio, the narrator wonders at their silence (they are embarrassed at their impoverished circumstances), and muses that "the gentleman might have said 'I should like a portrait of my wife,' and the lady might have said 'I should like a portrait of my husband,'" a grammatical reversal that captures in small the pattern governing these stories (18:308). When the liar slashes his portrait, he "literally" "hack[s] himself to death": the work of the knife undoes the work of the brush even as it attests to the brush's success, a compelling mimesis that the reflexive pronoun underlines (12:376). The playful-seeming doubles of James's stories of portraiture together form his account of how such artifacts reproduce themselves in the living bodies of their viewers.

But just as a chiasmus is always both a reproduction and a reversal, so too are the productions of portraiture both mimetic and antithetical: faithful reproductions and endlessly reproductive illustrations of an ideal, yet modeled on and so generated by that ideal's opposite. This is so first of all because James's artist in "The Real Thing" does not actually make enough money painting portraits to support himself; he needs to supplement that income by making "'illustrations'" "for magazines, for storybooks, for sketches of contemporary life" (18:310, 309). These works, which he sees as "pot-boilers" and which call for the service of a model as endlessly adaptable as Miss Churm, are what underwrite his career as a portrait-painter (18:310). Further, since Miss Churm also models for the plates of the *édition de luxe* of the works of Philip Vincent, the labor of the lower-class woman produces an object that epitomizes refined aesthetic sensibility, that attests to the discrimination of those who have come to treasure this "rarest of the novelists," newly reissued by "a publisher of taste" (18:318).

In "The Liar," this sense that portraiture does not stand free of the classes that support the leisured person so depicted is more pronounced, even lurid. During one of the Colonel's sittings in Lyon's studio, a "soiled and tarnished" woman wanders in, a woman with "something about her" that "savour[s] of a precarious profession, perhaps even of a blighted career" (12:365). Vaguely described as a prostitute, the woman is also described as a particularly bad portrait, with "a face that was rosy, yet that failed to suggest freshness," and dressed in an overabundance of cheap versions of the accessories indispensable to portraits of the upper class, "a hat with many feathers, a dress with many bugles, [and] long black gloves encircled with silver bracelets." She is also an artists' model, come to Lyon's studio looking for work. When Lyon turns her away, saying that he is "so busy with portraits," Geraldine, the would-be model, responds, "Yes; I see you are. I wish I was in the gentleman's place. . . . I do hate them portraits . . . It's so much bread out of our mouths" (12:366). Geraldine conceptualizes the situation of portraiture here as one in which the upper-class man's occupation of the position in front of the canvas economically deprives lower-class women and keeps them "in place." Even so, the leisured class's position depends on the labors of women like Geraldine, as she herself implies: "many" painters, she insists, "couldn't do anything without me" (12:366). Further, with her artificially rosy complexion and her superabundance of appurtenances, Geraldine is the antithetical mirror image of the upper-class woman, a negative model by which that woman and her class know themselves. Finally, she contributes to the maintenance of London's social order in another way because she is potentially a painted woman in both senses; when Lyon tells her he doesn't need her, she turns to Colonel Capadose and says, "If *you* should require me, sir—" (12:366). Colonel Capadose would need her for sex, not modeling, of course, and the verb "require" suggests that fulfilling such a need would be a matter of maintenance; modeling and prostitution are interchangeable for Geraldine because both endow the social order with the stasis of a fine portrait.

At the end of "The Liar," when Colonel Capadose and Lyon meet once more, it becomes necessary for the Colonel to account for the damage the painting sustained in the painter's absence so as to cast suspicion away from himself. Almost needless to say, he pins the vandalism on Geraldine, spinning a lie supported by a chain of circumstances (a woman lurking in the road as he and his wife visited the studio, a door left unbolted, the unemployed model's resentment). Actually, the Colonel invents two lies about Geraldine. The first, concocted after her first appearance in the studio, is a long and lugubrious tale, a completely fictitious story about saving a family friend, "a young jackanapes," from Geraldine's clutches before she "plucked" him of his fortune (12:368). The second lie about the slashed portrait compresses this narrative—a story about the preservation of class structure—into the much tighter space defined by the painting's frame. The elaborate tale about keeping her in her place by separating her from the vulnerable upper-class young man is recast into the second lie, which is centered on the painting in which, Geraldine has said, the Colonel takes her "place." This painting, then, definitively frames the model it does not portray even as the Colonel's lie frames Geraldine for the painting's destruction.[19]

This moment in "The Liar" may seem uncannily prescient, even prophetic. James imagines in 1888 a scenario in which a woman blames her economic deprivation on the production of portraiture, which leads one of the tale's characters to allege that she slashes a painting; in 1914, a woman slashes a painting of James in order to dramatize the political disenfranchisement of women. This odd similarity between the two incidents seems to me significant not because either mimetically produces the other—suffragists would not begin to slash paintings until 25 years after James wrote his story, and there is no evidence that when they did begin damaging works of art they were inspired to do so by reading James—but because taken together, the two moments focus some of the ways in which painting is understood at the turn of the century. Specifically, painting is regarded as an image that is itself part of a larger economy; its material making and subsequent exhibition shape the socioeconomics of the world beyond its frame. Further, painting's images exert a social force because they have the capacity to make themselves real, the capacity to do something to their viewers, to bridge the distance that observation entails. Consequently, the motifs that dominate and structure thinking about painting in this time are those of loops and matter. With the term "matter," I mean to emphasize the way in which paint, bodily matter, and clothing and ornament mix with each other, forming the *fin de siècle*'s political economy of portraiture. With the term "loop," I mean to emphasize the way in which making a painting, posing for one, and viewing one are understood as circuitous and reflexive, as routes of endless exchange. To make these figures more particular, I want first to dwell on a series of small moments in the careers of James and Sargent, including those moments in their careers where they represent each other (and find their own representations in each other), before turning to Bernard Berenson (the aesthetician who gives these motifs their most minutely-rendered delineation) and then to *The Tragic Muse* (the novel in which James most emphatically interweaves the painterly shaping of bodily matter with the matter of political representation).

When James sat for his portrait by Sargent in 1912, he was sitting for an artist he had had a hand in making: James's 1887 essay on Sargent not only helped to establish Sargent's reputation but also established some of the terms in which Sargent's paintings would be understood, the language that would come to seem an effective and compelling reflection of these nonlinguistic surfaces. In other words, James forms a vocabulary that facilitates the linguistic circulation of Sargent's art, an idiom that allows the paintings to come down off the walls and be passed around, replicated in journals and magazines and salon gossip. The idiom James forms for writing and talking about Sargent's paintings itself represents a flowing economy because that terminology centers on Sargent's precocious fluency and his free and fluid handling of the figure, especially the female figure. For James, Sargent's talent lies in his "facility," the speed with which he perceives and conveys the human figure.[20] Sargent works so quickly and assuredly that "perception with him is already by itself a kind of execution"; "it is as if painting were pure tact of vision" (217). This rapid grasp is how Sargent's paintings "arous[e] even in the profane spectator something of the painter's sense, the joy of engaging also, by sympathy, in the solution of the artistic problem" (219). What James limns in, then, is a series of exchanges by which the painter apprehends his subject in an act of the eye so readily translated to the painting's surface that this visual act seems itself tactile, and then a reproduction of this experience in the experience of the painting's viewer. This sense of exchange is further substantiated in James's essay by an emphasis on the shimmering, "glow[ing]" quality of Sargent's paint and by the way in which objects, clothes, and bodies "shine together" and so mix their properties, as in the complex reflections between the children and their aprons, the mirror, and the porcelain jars in *The Daughters of Edward D. Boit* (219, 222). Implicitly, then, James's essay draws a parallel between the relation of painting and viewer and that of the painting's figure and the objects that surround her.

Roughly half of James's account of Sargent is wrong, but his error is a revealing one. James confuses the process of making paintings with the experience of looking at them, assuming that what a painting's viewer can grasp instantaneously must have been for the painter a matter of rapid apprehension as well. As even a glance at the pencil studies for a painting like *Madame X* indicates, Sargent's portraits are produced by a series of tentative experiments, not by a glance so rapid that it works like a grasping hand.[21] What is revealing about the error is that it highlights James's strong tendency to understand the production of painting as repeating itself in the viewer's experience, his assumption that the labor of the studio replicates itself in the space of the gallery.

When he is painted by Sargent in 1912, James realizes that he has been misperceiving Sargent's working methods all along, but he maintains his understanding of the reshaping power of artifacts by moving that assumption to another locale. Writing to Edith Wharton, who had led the project to commemorate James's 70th birthday with a portrait by Sargent, James reports,

> I have already sat *twice* to the great man, & am as soon as possible to sit again—to sit in fact till the thing rightly shapes. It proved, the 1st time, not to be a matter of the famous "one" impressionistic sitting at all—& he finds me difficult, perverse, obscure—quite as if I were a mere facial Awkward Age or Sacred Fount. The end of the 2nd séance left us rather off & away—& if the next one doesn't bring us back & more into line again I think he will make a new start—on a clean slate.[22]

The scene of portraiture here is one of almost dizzying circulation; what makes the passage hard to keep still or lock in place is that its different loops of exchange are themselves crossed and exchanged with each other. The productions of James's art rub off on—bestow their qualities upon—

his body so that the verbal medium of the novel reshapes the visual appearance of the texts' author; the characteristics of the notoriously "obscure" prose of *The Awkward Age* and *The Sacred Fount* become a matter of embodiment. James's novels almost function like appurtenances here, not because they are adornments but because they recast his bodily shape. The comparison of the situation of portraiture to that of a séance reflects without resolving the confusing quality of this embodiment, because it implies both a sense of contact between or even a melding of consciousnesses but also a sense of disembodiment; it is very nearly the wrong metaphor in this case, because you need to have a body in order to be painted, but you need to be disembodied in order to be the subject of a séance. In this sense, the séance metaphor does not so much disembody the scene as it reflects the way in which physical identity becomes problematic in the passage because that physicality shifts around so much, doesn't stay grounded in a stable ontology. In *The Portrait of a Lady*, when Isabel encounters Madame Merle for the last time, the effect of seeing this woman at a moment when she is "so present" to Isabel's mental "vision" is "like suddenly, and rather awfully, seeing a painted picture move" (4:375), but here in this very late text, the construct of portraiture is so much in flux that it doesn't even resolve itself into a definite image, cannot be brought "into line," as James's letter puts it.

Here it will be useful to abstract this analysis of James's letter into a simpler set of points. What portraiture portrays at the century's turn is a body in process; portraiture's interplay between figure and ground, subject and setting, body and object, becomes a way of representing the production of persons, of getting a handle on the political economy of the human body at its minutest level. Further, this interchange depicted on canvas between figure and ground becomes a model for understanding the interchange between paintings and their viewers; the material wavering represented in paintings is understood as repeating itself in the vicissitudes of the viewer's own body.

To make these points more specific, we can turn to a painting in which Sargent submits them to sustained analysis, a portrait of his sister from about 1883, *The Breakfast Table* (figure 3). The painting is also known as *Violet Sargent*, and this wavering between the two titles, one of which names an interior environment and the other of which names that environment's inhabitant, reflects the way the painting's own focus oscillates between figure and ground. This oscillation happens within the painting itself in several different ways. It happens, first of all, in the way the viewer's eye travels between figure and ground as it pulls together the pink of the hair ribbon with the pink of the roses on the table, the glint of the knife in Violet's hand with the glint of the table-settings and the mantelpiece silver, the black dress with the black recess behind the figure. The viewer's eye works in loops of production and consumption as it discovers pathways between figure and objects, pathways that replicate the acts of reading, eating, and carving, because like those acts, they stitch together figure and objects. Part of the reason these oscillations stay in motion has to do with the small size of the figure as contrasted with the expansive and finely delineated setting: the figure is a little too small to hold the eye's focus for long, while the surfaces that frame her become of central interest. The figure's material frame here almost *is* the painting's central commitment. In keeping with this skewed scale of values is the way in which the interior of this flat both foregrounds the woman and threatens to swallow her, both delineates and attenuates her physical identity. Half of the figure dressed in black appears against a white wall and is thus highlighted by the contrast; the other half blurs into the black recess of the hallway behind her. This turning configuration itself forms the backdrop, the context, for the oscillation the painting puts at its visual center, the play between hand and eye, between reading a book and carving an apple.

For the carving knife is central to the viewer's involvement with this painting, and while this is a rather different sort of knife than those of the suffragists or Dorian or Colonel Capadose, and while it is used for a rather different task, it is like those knives because it is at the center of an account of painting and of production. The act of looking in this painting is referred to and counterpoised with the act of cutting both because the cutting hand is the first thing the painting's viewer lights on and because reading and cutting are the two things the figure in this painting is doing. In other words, *The Breakfast Table* equates the tactile and the visual, and involves the viewer in this equation by implying that when we see (or read), something tactile is happening to our bodies.

This oscillation between eye and hand is at the center of the dominant theories of aesthetic response in turn-of-the-century intellectual circles in England and America, theories that often lie adjacent to James's novels in the pages of the *Atlantic Monthly* and that were developed by two members of James's social circle, Vernon Lee and Bernard Berenson. In the developing practice of connoisseurship and in the merging of sensation psychology and aesthetics into the theory of empathy, painting comes to be understood as an object that forms its viewers, that bestows its attributes upon those who look at it, that exerts a material force upon its audience.

We can begin here by considering one famous attempt to educate the sense of vision. In Giovanni Morelli's method of connoisseurship, looking at paintings becomes a matter of detecting the individual touch of a Renaissance master—of determining which paintings are the work of a master's assistants or early copies or forgeries and which reflect the work

Figure 3

John Singer Sargent (Florence, Italy, 1856–1925, London, England), *The Breakfast Table* (1883–84). Courtesy of the Fogg Art Museum, Harvard University Art Museums, Bequest of Grenville L. Winthrop, 1943.150. Photo by Rick Stafford.

of the master's own hand. Morelli theorized that while such large and conventionalized aspects of paintings as faces and overall composition are often indistinguishable from one artist to another, in a painting's tiny details the pressure of convention relaxes and the painter's individual habits take over. Like Francis Galton's *Finger Prints* (1892) and like James's *The Spoils of Poynton* (1897), Morelli's work assimilates the habits of the hand with marks of identity.[23] Hence in such small regions of a painting as a subject's ears and especially hands (which Morelli regards as "one of the most expressive and characteristic parts of the human body") appear the master's own characteristic gestures, which escape the notice of a copyist or an assistant. We can identify a genuine Raphael if we have learned to recognize bodily details like "the broad metacarpus and somewhat stiff fingers" with "the nails extending to the tips" that characterize the hands of his noblemen and Madonnas.[24]

What one sees in the painted hand, then, is the hand that painted it. This is true not only because Morelli follows Leonardo's suggestion that painters reproduce their own physical attributes in the bodies of their subjects; it is also true because in the morphology of the painted body we glimpse "the habitual modes of expression," the gestures and "flourishes" that distinguish one Renaissance master from another.[25] As Richard Wollheim suggests, drawing is conceived by Morellian connoisseurship as "the residue or traces" of movement; it is a trail the hand leaves behind as it glides across canvas or panel.[26] For Morelli, these traces of movements governed by habit are the marks of identity; they are the painter's true signatures since, unlike actual signatures, they cannot be forged.

These motions are ones that, in studying paintings, we learn to follow and to reproduce. As Berenson, Morelli's most famous Anglo-American disciple puts it, becoming a connoisseur means "living one's self sympathetically into the situation" of the artist; to be an expert on paintings requires the "careful training of [one's] eye" so as to recognize a painter's "habits of visualization and execution."[27] Following his Harvard teacher William James's account, Berenson characterizes habits as impulses that "tend by the inevitable necessity of mechanical laws to dig deeper and easier channels for themselves," and so they are the only reliable signs of "identity."[28] Berenson's conception of the connoisseur's project holds, then, that the painter's identity shapes and customizes the viewer's own; the habits that form paintings also form those paintings' viewers.

When Berenson comes to formulate his general theory of aesthetic experience, he makes this argument in an extraordinarily literal way, developing much further the psychological and physiological bonds between the art object and its viewer. Attempting to identify the source of pleasure in the act of viewing paintings, Berenson proposes that paintings quicken and heighten our perception of the material world by giving us an intensified and immediate grasp of the third dimension. Berenson bases this account on the interrelation between vision and touch developed by nineteenth-century sensation psychology, which hypothesized that our recognition of form, space, and motion not only depends on linking our visual perceptions with our memories of tactile sensations (we must feel with our fingers that a ball is round before we can recognize its roundness through sight alone) but also somehow activates the tactile nerves. In looking at or even just thinking of a manual object like a pencil, we experience "a weak feeling of innervation of the hand as if touching the pencil's surface."[29] This is why Berenson believes that looking at paintings involves our whole bodies as its figures set

in motion the sense of touch; painting makes us "realise the material significance of things," makes us make real in our bodily sensations the depicted
objects we see before us.[30] The material exchanges between body and canvas
that James, Wilde, and the suffragists in different ways dramatized here form
the basis of a theory of aesthetic response.

Underlying Berenson's argument is the idea, developed by German theorists of empathy, that with our bodies we imitate the forms we see. As
Robert Vischer put it, when I observe an object, I "place myself within its
inner structure. . . . I can think my way into it, mediate its size with my
own, stretch and expand, bend and confine myself to it."[31] Just as I follow
a melody by tracing it in the air with my finger, so too I reproduce the contours of a visual form by tracing it with my eyes. But I also alter my breathing, shift my weight, and contract my muscles to accord with the form's
shape and size. In their 1897 essay advancing a psychophysiological definition of beauty, Vernon Lee and her companion, Clementine Anstruther-
Thomson, outline the bodily changes apart from "chemical or muscular
change in the eye" that occur when we study a form.[32] When we look at a
jar, we feel in our feet the weight at the object's base, and then we feel lift-
ed up as our eyes travel toward the jar's top. The jar's symmetrical sides
"bring both lungs into equal play"; "we seem to be breathing according to
the proportion of" the object.[33] On this model, vision is not solely visual;
it affects and shapes the whole body, and the whole body aids us in realizing the objects we see. As Berenson phrases it, "we more than half become
the things we admire" as our bodies emulate the objects we look at.[34]

In *The Tragic Muse,* James uncovers the ways in which this aesthetic theory grounded in the body is also a political technique. By interweaving
plots about painting and the theatre, James structures this novel as an
economy of vision and gesture; by setting this economy within a plot
involving parliamentary politics, James draws lines between the minute
material things and tiny physical motions of daily life—the world of still
life, of Sargent's *Breakfast Table*—and the maintenance of a macropolitical
order. For while James's hero, Nick Dormer, must choose between a career
in politics and a career in painting, this choice is one the novel keeps
encouraging its readers to deconstruct as its puns create a resemblance
between these different sorts of "representation," playing on the painterly
resonance of terms such as "canvass" and finding a grammatical similarity
between "standing" for Parliament and "sitting" for a portrait (7:80, 300).
Inasmuch as the world of state politics in *The Tragic Muse* is one of almost
total stasis while the world of painting is one of motion and exchange, of
"ocular commerce," politics in this novel somehow seem more painterly
than painting does, even as painting's productive capacity becomes a way
for James to represent the political (7:26).

To begin diagramming these reciprocities, we might examine the chiastic relations between vision and gesture as they appear in a small and revealing moment in which Peter Sherringham, the novel's diplomat, visits the Louvre with *The Tragic Muse*'s heroine, the aspiring actress Miriam Rooth. Here in the museum, Miriam finds a new source of what the novel elsewhere will call her "mimetic capital" (7:337):

> . . . in the long summer days, when he had leisure, [Peter] took her
> to the Louvre to admire the great works of painting and sculpture.
> Here, as on all occasions, he was struck with the queer jumble of her
> taste, her mixture of intelligence and puerility. He saw she never read
> what he gave her, though she sometimes would shamelessly have
> liked him to suppose so; but in the presence of famous pictures and
> statues she had remarkable flashes of perception. She felt these
> things, she liked them, though it was always because she had an idea
> she could use them. The belief was often presumptuous, but it
> showed what an eye she had to her business. "I could look just like
> that if I tried." "That's the dress I mean to wear when I do Portia."
> Such were the observations apt to drop from her under the sugges-
> tion of antique marbles or when she stood before a Titian or a
> Bronzino. (7: 225–26)

Here painting gives rise to gesture, costume, and performance as Miriam consciously plans to model her stage appearances after the examples of old masters. Behind the passage's statement that Miriam "felt these things" lies the aesthetics of empathy, with its assumption that the viewing body realizes the figures it sees as it maps their contours onto its own self, a making-real that, Berenson theorized, yields a "quickened sense of" physical "capacity," a heightened awareness of one's own body and consequently of that body's malleability.[35] In *The Wings of the Dove*, James would similarly associate Bronzino with the mutual pliability of painted figure and viewing body as Millie's tears return the painting to its liquid state; here, in *The Tragic Muse*, the artistic shaping of the painted body merges with and remodels the "elastic substance" of Miriam's own (7:190).

Miriam is "constructed to revolve like the terraqueous globe"; like all of James's worldly, self-dramatizing women, she is a perpetually turning figure (8:195). This "flexibility" is a textual and economic motor in *The Tragic Muse* as the actress's molding of her body and the shaping of bodies on canvas recreate and reproduce each other, keep each other in a state of fluid suspension (7:190). Acting and painting form an economy in the text: painting reproduces the gestures and shapes of bodies that then give rise to bodily performances that are themselves recaptured within painting; Miriam models her acting on painting and then becomes a painter's model when Nick portrays her later in the novel. Once Miriam becomes famous, the process requires the speed and mass-replicability of photography in order to meet demand: "she made almost an income out of the photographers—their appreciation of her as a subject knew no bounds" (8:385). As the novel progresses, the scale of its economy of images keeps expanding; the images the novel traffics in become more and more a matter of advertisement, of newspapers, of representations that appeal to "the eye of the public" (8:386). But even after Miriam becomes a celebrity, she is "still accommodating enough . . . from time to time, to find an hour to come and sit to Nick Dormer," who paints two portraits that Miriam's impresario, Basil Dashwood, means to hang facing each other in the theatre's vestibule, supplemented by photographs arranged around them. This relatively massive economy of endless reproduction is founded in the moment in which a woman looks at portraits, founded in moments like the one in the Louvre, where Miriam borrows from Titian and Bronzino the bodily styles that she will expertly manipulate in climbing the "steps in the ladder of fame" (8:385–36). As the suffragist slashers would later, James locates the conceptual core and basic unit of political economy in the scenario of a woman gazing at a painting. As the arrangement of the photographs around Miriam's portraits makes especially graphic, portraiture is understood as endlessly generative, endlessly productive.

Given this extraordinary generativity, it makes a kind of intuitive sense that *all* economic activity in *The Tragic Muse* is represented in terms of painting and that not to be portrayed is, in the world of this novel, somehow not to exist, not to be real. Early in the novel, Nick meets up with the arch-aesthete Gabriel Nash at a Parisian cafe, a setting that Nash finds repugnant as he sits down with Nick, and then

> at the end of five minutes uttered a protest against the crush and confusion, the publicity and vulgarity of the place, the shuffling procession of the crowd, the jostle of fellow customers, the perpetual brush of waiters. "Come away; I want to talk to you and I can't talk here. I don't care where we go. It will be pleasant to walk; we'll stroll away to the *quartiers sérieux*. Each time I come to Paris I at the end of three days take the Boulevard, with its conventional grimace, into greater aversion. I hate even to cross it—I go half a mile round to avoid it."
> (7:165)

The terms that leap out here as parts of an instantly recognizable idiom are "vulgarity," "conventional" and "aversion"; together they signal the presence of the aesthete's pose of exaggeratedly shrinking from a world of commerce

into a wholly artistic realm. But another set of terms in the passage under-
cuts that flight into the more picturesque streets of Paris: "crush" and
"brush" together cast in artistic terms the economy Nash opposes to the
realm of art.[36] This rhymed pair of words implicitly compares the work of
self-maintenance to the work of making a portrait; "brush" and "crush" suggest a process of embellishment and disfiguration, of the disfiguring of the
body as its outlines are lost in a crowd, and of the compensating remaking
of the body as its needs and desires are fulfilled by the waiters. To appear in
public is to "shade off into other people"—there is a great deal of "jostling
and shuffling and shoving" in this novel—and to appear against a ground
necessary for making one's own figure stand out (7:81, 8:244).

Because he attempts to remove himself from this economy of portraiture, Nash eventually disappears from the novel. All along, other characters have remarked on Nash's seeming lack of reality in precisely the terms
of graphic representation of the person; Nick says that Nash is "too simple to give an account of. Most people have a lot of attributes and
appendages that dress them up and superscribe them, and what I like
Gabriel for is that he hasn't any at all." Nash is "as neat as an outline cut
out of paper with scissors" (7:80, 81). Without appurtenances or circumstances, there's nothing for the realist novel to know him by, and so by
the end of *The Tragic Muse* he has vaporized, "melted back into the elements" (8:419). Having removed himself from any scenario that would
compromise the neatness of his cut-out figure, Nash also removes himself
from any scenario that would identify it: like the "crush" of the social,
"appendages" and appurtenances highlight the identities they also threat-
en to compromise. Hence when Nash offers a definition of portraiture,
he defines it wrongly, at least on the novel's own terms. When Miriam
matures her acting style and tones down the histrionic displays of her
apprenticeship, Nash congratulates her by commenting that she is now
"just the visible image, the picture on the wall" (8:54). Nash understands
acting as portraiture here and portraiture as static, a set of misunderstandings that go against the grain of every other layer of *The Tragic Muse*
and against the ways in which portraiture was conceived at the end of the
century.

For even maintaining persons within an undeviating order requires a
great deal of economic activity, requires the sustaining work of painting,
as all the texts represented in this chapter suggest. The strand of *The Tragic
Muse* devoted to Parliamentary politics never actually depicts the House of
Commons at all; the work of status-quo politics is instead conducted in
and by great houses, private homes that are picture-perfect representations
of the idealized English town and countryside, houses "where an
immutable order appear[s] to slant through the polished windows"

(8:153). Julia Dallow, the politically ambitious young widow engaged to Nick, appears as "a composed picture" in the grounds of her estate; her house, with its "tiresome insistence on harmony," holds its occupants within a social frame, narrows their frame of reference, ceaselessly iterates a political order (7:264, 238). In the *Philosophical Investigations,* Wittgenstein writes of the intellectual trap of thinking that one has traced a phenomenon's true outlines, when really all one has done is to reproduce a conventionalized view: "A *picture* held us captive. And we could not get outside it, for it lay in our language and language seemed to repeat it to us inexorably."[37] The objects and paintings of Julia's house keep a political order continuously present to its subjects, make them the "incarnation of politics," make them figures both in "perpetual motion" and figures who are "perpetual sitter[s]," a contradiction that makes sense because such subjects in *The Tragic Muse* constantly labor to portray the order they embody (8:75, 11, 15).

This equation between motion and stasis helps us to see why for James portraiture is sometimes equivalent with a lie. For the static appearance of a portrait bestows a sense of permanence, of unchangingness, on the culture that its endless reproductive quality must nevertheless keep generating. Political stability turns out to have a wholly fictive basis, turns out to be based on the endless cultivation of convention, the perpetual shaping power that late-century aesthetics finds exemplified in the act of viewing a painting. For ultimately the aesthetics of empathy in *The Tragic Muse* are James's way of explaining and representing the way that paintings and objets d'art produce a political order. In one of the novel's most complex moments, Mrs. Gresham, who functions in the novel as a sort of campaign manager, remarks to Nick that she's "almost part of the house, you know— I'm one of the chairs or tables" (7:257). And then she remarks, rather puzzlingly, "It's a wonderful constitution." Nick thinks for a moment she means the British constitution, "the great unwritten instrument by which they were all governed," before Mrs. Gresham's elaboration makes it clear she means Julia: "The surface so delicate, the action so easy, yet the frame of steel" (7:257). Constitutional law becomes bodily constitution here, and the delicate surfaces of portraiture, along with the frame that rigidly keeps those surfaces in place, are adopted by the citizens that law portrays. Like the suffragists, with whom he otherwise differs so markedly, James finds in the language of painting an account of how a political order realizes itself in the minds and bodies of its subjects.

CHAPTER FIVE

BODIES, PAPERS, AND PERSONS

At certain points in the *Principles of Psychology*, the self seems to exist in the marks it makes, in the writing of its own hand. An "extensive work in manuscript," for example, is so "intimately" part of one's self that "few men . . . would not feel personally annihilated" if it were "suddenly swept away" (281). But at other points, persons feel themselves somehow present not just in papers they have written, but also in papers they have read or owned or even just touched. Characterizing secretiveness, which he classifies as an instinct, James notes that

> some persons will never leave anything with their name written on it,
> where others may pick it up—even in the woods, an old envelope
> must not be thrown on the ground. Many cut all the leaves of a book
> of which they may be reading a single chapter, so that no one shall
> know which one they have singled out, and all this with no *definite*
> notion of harm.

Even when such "habit[s] of concealment" seem the product of conscious calculation, James suggests, their "motive is far less often definite prudence than a vague aversion to have one's sanctity invaded and one's personal concerns fingered and turned over by other people" (1049–50). And in these cases, at least, to have one's personal books and papers "fingered" by others is to suffer a physical intrusion of sorts: the physical motions involved in the acts of reading a person's papers and of intruding upon a person's body cannot quite be kept discrete here. Indeed, so tightly does the passage bind together persons with their papers that it isn't even imme-diately clear if the reason the envelope must not be discarded in the woods is that it is somehow a part of one's self, as if writing's ability to betray bodily presence somehow makes writing part of the body. Perhaps the point where the hand grasps the page, then, is a point at which the edges of the body shade into other objects, raveling out into what is adjacent to them. Acts of reading and writing tend to happen close to the body; perhaps that is why it seems possible to imagine here that bodies and papers can lend each other their qualities or attributes, compromising each other's physical integrity as they do so. Are our bodies "simply ours, or are they *us?*" James asked earlier in the *Principles;* here this equivocal status of the body seems to transfer itself to the objects lying alongside that body, which passes along its ambiguities to anything it touches (279).

Inasmuch as it can be linked with other passages in the *Principles* that treat of reading and writing—which attempt to diagram the relations between the psyche that composes, the body that writes, and the language that materializes itself in writing—this meditation on secretiveness is fairly typical of James's concerns. Yet what makes the passage worthy of note is not so much the role it plays in any of the *Principles'* major arguments, but the extent to which it reflects a preoccupation characteristic of late-nineteenth-century English and American culture. Indeed, the possibility I want to explore is that in the last two decades of the century, strands of that culture are committed to the metonyms, the displacements, the curiously fluid logic—the curiously fluid *materiality*—with which this passage treats the relationships between bodies and papers, persons and texts, selves and writing: committed, that is, both to the difficult work of stabilizing these displacements and to ordering large segments of experience by means of them.

These commitments become clearer when we move from the psychological analysis of secretiveness to the concurrent legal analysis of privacy. Published in the *Harvard Law Review* in 1890—the same year the *Principles* appeared—Samuel Warren and Louis Brandeis's "The Right to Privacy" argues that embedded within the common law is the right "to be let alone," a phrase Warren and Brandeis take from a standard text on tort law and subsequently reinterpret as "the immunity of the person."[1] This right to one's own person is fundamental, but how the law defines the person to be protected changes over time. Protections afforded by law once stopped with the body, "serv[ing] only to protect the subject from battery." Then "came a recognition of man's spiritual nature, of his feelings and his intellect," and with it the development of those areas of law designed to protect a person's reputation—the law of slander and libel—and a person's feelings—laws governing threats, nuisances, and interferences with the family. Thus, Warren and Brandeis conclude, "regard for human emotions soon extended the scope of personal immunity beyond the body of the individual" (193–94).

In articulating the legal right to privacy, Warren and Brandeis would push this extension further, past the body and past the emotions, to one's papers. Reviewing cases in which private papers have been protected, Warren and Brandeis argue that even when these decisions appeal to copyright law or other laws governing ownership of intellectual property or breach of contract, they are really based on the common-law principle that upholds the inviolability of the person. One's papers are private not because they're owned by one's self but because they are legally part of one's self. Indeed, the rhetoric of "The Right to Privacy" implies that one's papers are as much a part of one's self as one's body is, or at least the thoughts rendered material upon them are: "the protection afforded to thoughts, sentiments, and emotions, expressed through the medium of writing . . . is merely an instance of the enforcement of the more general right of the individual to be let alone. It is like the right not to be assaulted or beaten" (205). To be traced in the history of the law, then, is a path that leads from the law of battery—and the right to one's own body—to the law of privacy—and the right to one's own writing. The growth of the legal definition of the person thus ends by folding together body, mental life, and papers.

These formulations are partially dictated by the logic of the law: legal traditions and precedents account for some of the emphasis on writing here, and for some of the effort to merge papers and persons. Yet as the *Principles of Psychology* suggests, such formulations are not confined to the realm of law. And as Warren and Brandeis indicate, problems of the boundaries of the person and of the sanctity of those boundaries had, by 1890, been constituted as a topic of public discussion. Seeking "to protect the privacy of private life" against a press that is "overstepping in every direction the obvious bounds of propriety and of decency" so that it may satisfy the "prurient taste" of its readers, Warren and Brandeis take it nearly for granted not only that protection of the person must be extended, but also that invasiveness will be recognized as something deeply characteristic of their own time; they assume, in other words, that the matter that crystallizes in and is epitomized by the relation of person to paper has already achieved legibility as a matter of wide concern (215, 196).[2]

In characterizing its time as "the age of newspapers and telegrams and photographs and interviewers," Henry James's *The Aspern Papers* (1888) invokes and contributes to this legibility (12:8).[3] James's fascination with the problems of privacy and publicity is well known and fairly explicit; he himself recognizes it as crucial to his project, writing in his notebook in 1887 that "one sketches one's age but imperfectly if one doesn't touch on . . . the invasion, the impudence and shamelessness, of the newspaper and the interviewer, the devouring *publicity* of life, the extinction of all sense between public and private."[4] But what makes *The Aspern Papers* a most pertinent text to consider here is the extent to which its concern for privacy entails a concern for papers, and further (and more hyperbolically), the ways in which it edges toward equating the act of reading with the act of physical intrusion. Such equations are most obviously rendered in the story's broad outlines: the papers of the tale's title are part of the trail left behind by an affair between the late poet, Jeffrey Aspern, and the now-aged Juliana Bordereau, who keeps herself shut up with her niece in a crumbling Venetian palace. For the Aspern-obsessed man of letters who narrates the tale, reading these "personal, delicate, intimate" papers necessitates a "horribly intrusive" act of virtual home-invasion, of infiltrating the house, creeping into the sitting room, and rifling through the cupboards (12:11, 17). A story of reading, then, is synonymous with a story of privacy's violation.

This much occurs on the level of plot. But on a less schematic, far more microscopic level, a whole grammar and vocabulary operate to associate papers with the body and to define privacy in terms of that association. Thus committing to paper the details of another's life is treated as an act of "pry[ing]" (12:65). Thus to subject someone to close scrutiny is to have "turned [him] over"—as if he were pages (12:69). Thus it's not just bodies that have the capacity to "transmit" the touch, to relay knowledge of other bodies (though this is odd in itself: it's as if by touching my body you also touch the bodies I've touched); "esoteric knowledge" of others' sexuality also "rub[s] off on" one in the process of handling papers like the love letters of Jeffrey Aspern and Juliana Bordereau (12:8, 44). As in the passage from William James's *Principles,* the tale's concern with violated privacy, with "fingering another's personal concerns," leads it to literalize the metaphor embedded in that phrase: the act of the invading eye materializes in the act of turning pages. And as in the *Principles*—and, more notably, as in Warren and Brandeis—in *The Aspern Papers* privacy is construed as a problem of the relation, the ontology, even, of bodies and their papers.

This tendency to associate bodies and papers and to understand in terms of each other the protections afforded to each is not exactly new at the end of the nineteenth century; the fourth amendment to the U.S. Constitution (to think of just one area of the realm of law) guarantees "the right of the people to be secure in their persons, houses, papers, and effects, against unreasonable searches and seizures." But the fact that, with the 1886 Supreme Court case *Boyd v. United States,* fourth-amendment jurisprudence very nearly shares its point of origin with the other narratives of search and seizure I am considering here indicates that a newly intensified pressure is being brought to bear upon these associations of bodies and papers: in large part the issues that converge in *Boyd* hinge on whether compelling a person to produce his papers should be considered just as much an intrusion as rifling through his drawers; on whether "the eye" can "be guilty of a trespass"; on whether doctrines protecting "the sanctity" of the home and "the privacies of life" extend protection to one's papers.[5] Staking out a right to privacy thus entails scrutinizing impulses like the ones present in the *Principles of Psychology*, holding steadily visible the elusive—and formative—relation between the materiality of writing and the physicality of the body.

Insofar as texts like "The Right to Privacy" and *The Aspern Papers* do render visible this relation, they offer a somewhat unusual opportunity to examine quite closely a matter of much interest to contemporary criticism. The body has emerged as the favored subject of literary thematics as contemporary criticism tends to prioritize them; the body is now one of those things we pay attention to when we read. Likewise, for recent accounts of the social shaping of the body, the act of writing has become chief metaphor and model; we tend to think of bodies and their sexualities, subjectivities, desires, classes, and diseases as both malleable within the field of writing and as decisively formed—subjected to restriction—within that same field. The body has thus become a cultural and historical index crucial to the way we read now; in the process of writing, "language [is] inscribed by history on the bodies of living beings," as Stephen Greenblatt influentially puts it in *Renaissance Self-Fashioning*.[6]

Writing writes bodies just as much as bodies produce writing, then, but these relationships are not stable and unchanging ones; rather, they shift and slip and develop over time, sometimes coming to the foreground and sometimes receding from view. The end of the nineteenth century is one point at which they come to the fore in fairly decisive ways: in social, legal, and literary commentary, the "materials of the writer"—and of the reader—"come also to be ways of inhabiting and conceptualizing the body," to use Jonathan Goldberg's formulation.[7] Further, texts like "The Right to Privacy" rather consciously invest a good deal of their energies in arranging this relation, in forming and shaping the range of implications bodies and writing have for each other. As the interests of contemporary criticism suggest, these implications are still at work, still forming our conceptions of the texts we read and the bodies with which we read them. Indeed, one reason for retracing this episode in the history of the point where the hand grasps the page is to see something of how that point came to be so formative and generative and interesting in the first place. In an essay on the use of words within paintings, Meyer Schapiro suggests that by collecting representations of print, one can uncover and "reconstitute" a culture's "beliefs about the senses and language."[8] That is what I aim to do here: to uncover a set of associations and assumptions that govern James's conception of writing, associations and assumptions that at least in part govern our own habits of mind.

One fascination *The Aspern Papers* shares with the texts that surround it in James's career is its fascination with writing itself—a fascination not only with the role of the writer, nor only with the effects of reading, but also an absolutely concrete interest in writing as a material thing. An extraordinary passage in *The Princess Casamassima* (1886) suggests how intense this concentration can be in James and gives at least a glimpse of its associations and consequences. At the start of his holiday at Medley Hall, Hyacinth Robinson experiences a moment of overwhelming desire while exploring the great house's library:

> It was an old brown room, of great extent—even the ceiling was brown, though there were figures in it dimly gilt—where row upon row of finely-lettered backs returned his discriminating professional gaze . . . there were alcoves with deep window-seats, and arm-chairs such as he had never seen, luxurious, leather-covered, with an adjustment for holding one's volume; and a vast writing-table . . . furnished with a perfect magazine of paper and pens, inkstands and blotters, seals, stamps, candlesticks, reels of twine, paper-weights, book-knives. Hyacinth had never imagined so many aids to correspondence, and before he turned away he had written a note . . . in a hand even more beautiful than usual—his penmanship was very minute, but at the same time wonderfully free and fair—largely for the pleasure of seeing "Medley Hall" stamped in crimson, heraldic-looking characters at the top of his paper. In the course of an hour he had ravaged the collection, taken down almost every book, wishing he could keep it a week, and put it back quickly, as his eye caught the next, which appeared even more desirable. . . . Altogether, his vision of true happiness, at that moment, was that, for a month or two, he should be locked into the library at Medley.[9]

There may not be another passage in all of James that focuses more intently on the materials of reading and writing, nor one in which the attraction toward paper things is more sensual, nor one that more thoroughly extends the processes of reading and writing to everything it details; here even the ceiling is brown like a calf binding and inscribed like the gilt lettering on a book's spine. The language of handcraftedness and its way of folding together body and object (the subject of chapter 3 above) are here focused on the matter of reading and writing. Furthermore, there may not be another passage in James that points more clearly to the ways in which two crucial Jamesian preoccupations intertwine. On the one hand, Hyacinth exemplifies James's interest in what he would come to call "my usual narrator-observer."[10] As a spectator, Hyacinth is "condemned to see . . . things only from outside" (as James puts it in the New York Edition preface) and so develops a voyeuristic, even prurient, relation to a world that excludes him (*LC* 2:1087). Thus, the longing he feels toward the paper world of Medley Hall reflects his exclusion from the class that uses monogrammed stationery as a matter of course; and his marginal relationship to the objects in the library follows the same logic as his voyeuristic relation to the world of lived sexuality in which he spies on scenes of seduction between Paul Muniment and the Princess and between Captain Sholto and Millicent.

All this has been a focusing concern for much recent discussion of James and consequently is fairly well known. What is less often recognized is what the quoted passage makes nearly inescapable: for James, a concern for the observer entails a concern for the materials of reading and writing. This seems obliquely reflected at the start of the passage when "the finely-lettered backs" of books seem to "return" Hyacinth's "discriminating professional gaze." Because this line casts the act of reading in the language of observation, it has the effect of suggesting that the two are equivalent. And since the books seem to Hyacinth to meet his gaze, they apparently operate as if they were human faces, their lettering miming a facial reaction to the observer's attention.

Then, too, the "professional" quality of Hyacinth's "discriminating" gaze, along with his expert appreciation for the library's amazing array of writing paraphernalia, implies a close tie between his role as observer and his occupation as bookbinder, between looking and the materials of writing. This connection seems all the more important to make when we realize that James's fictions routinely make it. Not only are there figures like reporters (in "The Papers" or *The Reverberator,* for example) and novelists ("The Lesson of the Master," "The Middle Years") whose professions require that they write what they observe; there are also those observers with other sorts of "knowledge occupations," to use a term from economic theory.[11] Lambert Strether of *The Ambassadors,* who edits the Woollett Review, and the literary reviewers of "John Delavoy" and "The Figure in the Carpet" are obvious examples here, but less obviously the category includes the docent of Shakespeare's early home in "The Birthplace" (who at the tale's beginning is a librarian) and the clerk of "In the Cage," an "intense observer" whose relation to paper is as intimate and immediate as Hyacinth's, a woman who sells stamps and converts handwritten messages into telegrams, who weighs envelopes and counts words (11:426).

In emphasizing the Jamesian observer's involvement with papers, I am suggesting that a fascination with bodies and a fascination with writing coincide, that writing fascinates because it somehow reveals bodies. Yet regarded from a certain point of view, these are interests which we might expect to resist becoming intertwined, which might just as easily be kept separate from each other. Inasmuch as the body is what is absent in— indeed what absents itself from—writing, it might appear more logical to argue for an opposition between the two rather than for the sort of simultaneity outlined above. In *On Longing,* her essay on narrative's relation to the body and its objects, Susan Stewart clarifies this absence, arguing that "what disappears in writing is the body and what the body knows—the visual, tactile, and aural knowledge of lived experience."[12]

The body disappears in writing: this principle would lead us to expect that papers are not revealing enough to serve the purposes of the voyeuristic gaze, the gaze which seeks to know others' bodies. But as Jamesian observers seem intuitively to grasp, this principle is open to resistance of several different kinds. Most obviously, they seek to observe the body before it has detached itself from writing, as "In the Cage" exemplifies, or as the observers of "The Private Life" also demonstrate when, acting on their "insane desire to see the author," they steal into a playwright's darkened study to find him hunched over his writing table (17:251). Then, too, Jamesian observers are drawn to situations in which the authorial body makes a sudden, thrilling reappearance, as in the several stories in which novelists are among the guests at parties in great country houses, and to texts that seem less than thoroughly mediated, that seem to offer some sort of bodily trace, like the galleys an author has worked over or letters that offer a glimpse of the author's own hand.

These examples suggest that bodies can be read back into papers, and that such acts of reading complete the meanings of texts. When the voyeuristic gaze trains itself on papers, it seeks to discover a secreted body, seeks to reattach bodies to the papers they've all but detached themselves from, as *The Aspern Papers* makes clear. Thus, for the editor, close reading inevitably leads to collating bodies and texts; to see most deeply into Aspern's poems necessitates "opening lights into his life," reconstructing his life as a body (12:6). In this respect, it makes a certain amount of sense that the act of reading Aspern's poetry widens into a fascination with Aspern's portrait, with his papers, with the living body of his lover. For by the logic of *The Aspern Papers,* the meanings of texts remain incomplete until the bodies they stem from and refer to can be reattached to them.

This is why Miss Bordereau represents such a rare opportunity for the editor; whereas his previous sources have been disembodied "phantoms and dust, the mere echoes of echoes," she offers the chance not only "to look into a . . . pair of eyes into which [Aspern's have] looked," but also "to feel a transmitted contact" in a hand Aspern's has touched (12:8). Meeting her for the first time, the editor marvels at finding himself "face to face with the Juliana of some of Aspern's most exquisite and most renowned lyrics," an experience that not only gives Aspern's poems a body but also a voice, an "individual note" that "had been in Jeffrey Aspern's ear." All this comes early on in the tale; much of what follows is taken up with the editor's further efforts to see Juliana, who usually keeps herself shut up in her rooms, and more particularly, his efforts to touch her hand, which she will not give him, and to see her eyes, which she keeps veiled. Much of what follows, in other words, details the editor's efforts to know the secrets of Miss Bordereau's body, a body which seems "somehow to contain and express" Aspern's own, and which seems to bring the editor "nearer" to the poet than he has ever been before (12:23–25).

For the editor, the pleasures of reading are the pleasures of knowing the body, of reading the body back into writing, of restoring the visual, tactile, and aural qualities the body seems to lose when committed to paper. Indeed, so thoroughly does the tale associate the body with the pleasures reading offers that when it imagines the act of reading, it imagines it as a physical—almost a physiological—process. Of course, reading always *is* a physical process—a coordination of manual and ocular actions, say— though we don't usually dwell on that fact, just as we don't dwell on the fact that reading generally necessitates bringing our bodies into contact with objects that are outside them. *The Aspern Papers,* on the other hand, seems as obsessed by this physicality of reading as it is by the reproduction in writing of the physical body. Thus the editor imagines Miss Bordereau going through the nightly "solemnities" of "pressing" Aspern's letters "to her withered lips," a ritual which he would give "a good deal" to see (12:35). Thus, too, he considers Miss Tina a potential source of knowledge not because she might be able to summarize the contents of the papers, but because she has "seen and handled all mementoes" and so "some esoteric knowledge" has "rubbed off on her." As we have already seen, the editor imagines Miss Bordereau's body has the ability to "transmit" Aspern's touch; these further examples suggest that this is an ability it shares with the papers which (if he could ever get his hands on them) would make the editor's life "continuous, in a fashion, with the illustrious life they had touched at the other end" (12:43–44). (It is here that the meaning of "Bordereau"—"memorandum, note"—becomes relevant.) The act of reading papers is thus construed along the lines of touching bodies—so much so, in fact, that the acts of touching (or reading) bodies and reading (or touching) papers come to substitute for each other, come to be confused with each other much as they do in the *Principles of Psychology*'s meditation on secretiveness. In this respect, *The Aspern Papers* might be seen as literalizing, and thus exaggerating, the sentiment that the act of reading makes our lives continuous with those of others; here the continuity is construed as a material one.

This extraordinary emphasis on the tactility of reading and this insistence that in the process of reading the body is doubly involved (reading is not only something bodies do, but also something they have done to them) go more than a little way toward suggesting that reading can be an act of intrusion. The various analogues the text supplies for reading further advance this suggestion. As already noted, these analogues align the editor with the forces of publicity in this "age of newspapers and telegrams and photographs and interviewers" (12:8). Similarly, when the editor's search for information leads him to exploit the ingenuous Miss Tina, he feels "almost as base as the reporter of a newspaper who forces his way into a house of mourning" (12:82). Further, when Juliana discovers him testing the lock on her bureau in the middle of the night, her rebuke—"Ah you publishing scoundrel!"—aligns an act of physical intrusion with the sort of violation we associate with the revelation of secrets, of personal information (12:118).

Now a bureau is a container: kept in a sort of boudoir, it contains the secrets of the body, serving as a "model of intimacy," a "veritable org[an] of the secret psychological life," as Gaston Bachelard puts it.[13] In this respect, it resembles a house, which really does contain bodies, and the editor's attempt to unlock the bureau's secrets resembles his attempts to gain access to Miss Bordereau's house and then her rooms. When he passes through the hall that links his own rooms with Juliana's, the editor customarily lingers there, watching the door that leads to the "treasure." "A person observing me might have supposed I was trying to cast a spell on it or attempting some odd experiment in hypnotism," he remarks—a passing comment that itself might seem odd, except that hypnotism in the nineteenth century epitomizes the threat of visual intrusion, and that, since hypnotism or mesmerism is sometimes thought to endow with physical consequences the act of the intruding eye, it repeats *The Aspern Papers'* account of reading (12:43). These factors aside, I highlight the remark as one more alignment of reading with an act of intrusion into a receptacle that contains the body. This equation begins to reach its fullest and most literal expression in an edgy conversation between the editor and Juliana. Questioning the ethics of those who write about the lives of great writers who "are dead and gone and can't, poor darlings, speak for themselves," as the editor puts it, Juliana asks, "Do you think it's right to rake up the past?" To which the editor responds, "How can we get at it unless we dig a little?" (12:89–90). The implication of these remarks clarifies itself in an exchange between the editor and Tina after Juliana's death. Having given up on the papers, he suggests to Tina that what Miss Bordereau really intended was for Aspern's "literary remains" (12:12) to be buried with her own corporeal ones:

> Miss Tina appeared to weigh this suggestion; after which she answered with striking decision, "Oh no, she wouldn't have thought that safe!"
> "It seems to me nothing could be safer."
> "She had an idea that when people want to publish they're capable—!" And she paused, very red.
> "Of violating a tomb? Mercy on us, what must she have thought of me!" (12:133–34)

The last container of the body that reading threatens, then, is the grave, and if the image seems less than fully developed in *The Aspern Papers,* we have only to remember that, like hypnotism, and like the intrusion within a house, the violation of a tomb is in the nineteenth century a fascinating, repellent, and notorious topos for the invasion of the body's privacy.[14]

With these images of the bureau, the house, and the tomb, reading aligns itself with the act of intruding within the body's containers and wrenching it forth. Not only are these acts of invasion propelled by the experience of reading Aspern's poetry, but reading itself seems so body-directed, seems so much to take the body as its object, that it comes to seem an invasion in its own right, and bodies appear to be contained within papers as surely as they are contained within houses or tombs. Thus, for at least a moment in *The Aspern Papers,* the whole point of reading Aspern's lyrics is to discover Miss Bordereau's body within them, to find their revelation of what she and Aspern once did with each other's bodies. Along these lines, Aspern's poems might well be viewed as containers of secret knowledge of the body; the body would then be "as concrete there as a bird in a cage," "stuck into every volume as your foot is stuck into your shoe," to borrow Hugh Vereker's description of the pattern that unites his work in "The Figure in the Carpet" (15:233). But if this remark suggests the body's presence in writing, it also begins to suggest the difficulty of knowing that body; the figure in the carpet never swims up clear, just as the outlines of Juliana's career never become specific. The editor notes that while "most readers of certain of Aspern's poems" have "taken it for granted that Juliana had not always adhered to the steep footway of renunciation," one would be hard-pressed "to put one's finger on the passage in which her fair fame suffered injury" (12:48). The implication is that the poems contain a body from which one is excluded; they objectify knowledge of a world that one cannot infiltrate.

This construction of reading does not quite tally with ways of thinking about reading I have identified earlier; more particularly, the implication that bodies have disappeared from writing—and so one must read bodies back into it—conflicts with the implication that bodies are inside writing—and so readers have "to dig a little," as the editor puts it. But resolving this logical incoherence may not be as important here as recognizing how these conceptions together overdetermine the body's place in reading, constructing it as a problem and insisting on that problem's relation to privacy. Indeed, if we momentarily regard *The Aspern Papers* as a sort of gloss to Warren and Brandeis, then it begins to look like the "prurient" readers they found so plentiful—and so worrisome—in late-nineteenth-century America are those who, like the editor, read in order to know the secrets of the body. And though Warren and Brandeis imply that this sort of "prurient taste" is confined to scandal sheets, *The Aspern Papers* begins to suggest that writing is also framed as a bodily problem in the highly literary contexts that might otherwise seem to be yellow journalism's opposite.

This question of the body's place in writing is pursued within literary commentary, then, and is pursued within the wider context of a question of the ethics of seeking the sort of knowledge the editor seeks. One thing that has always made *The Aspern Papers* seem a resonant text in James's career is its tight focus on the figure of the author and, more particularly, on the relation between an author's lived experience and his or her writing. In James, this relation is always figured as a sort of double question, one in which the boundaries between epistemology and ethics begin to blur. On the one hand there is the question: how do the writing life and the rest of a writer's life intersect with each other? At the same time James asks: is it right to try to find out? As early as 1872, in a review of a selection of passages from Hawthorne's notebooks, James's anxieties on this score show themselves:

> These liberal excisions from the privacy of so reserved and shade-seeking a genius suggest forcibly the general question of the proper limits of curiosity as to that passive personality of an artist of which the elements are scattered in portfolios and table-drawers. It is becoming very plain, however, that whatever the proper limits may be, the actual limits will be fixed only by a total exhaustion of matter. (*LC* 1:307)

The image of ransacking the writing table that these lines suggest is one *The Aspern Papers* would develop in full, while the suggestion that the writer's "personality" is present in his papers and therefore threatened by the curious reader seems, at least in this context, to forecast the ways in which William James and Warren and Brandeis would write about persons and papers eighteen years later. As James's notes and preface reveal, *The Aspern Papers* is based, first of all, on the attempts of Edward Silsbee, an extraordinarily devoted Shelley-obsessive, to get at the papers of Claire Clairmont, the last surviving member of the Byron-Shelley circle. But as these early comments on Hawthorne suggest, the tale also has points of contact with other authors who have, by 1888, come to epitomize for James questions of privacy and the life of writing.[15] Not only is the tale characteristic of the ways in which James thinks about Hawthorne, but, as Laurence Holland has argued, it is also formed by James's fascination with George Sand and her affair with Alfred de Musset.[16] Aspern might, then, most accurately be seen as a sort of composite figure that epitomizes James's characteristic ways of conceiving of authorship.

Although they lurk behind the tale, neither Byron nor Shelley nor Hawthorne nor Sand is mentioned within it. Indeed, the only explicit mention of a real author comes as the editor explains to Mrs. Prest, his confidante in the tale's beginning, why he finds it so revealing that Juliana refers to her old lover as "Mr. Aspern":

> It proves familiarity, and familiarity implies the possession of mementoes, of tangible objects. I can't tell you how that "Mr." affects me—how it bridges over the gulf of time and brings our hero near to me—nor what an edge it gives to my desire to see Juliana. You don't say "Mr." Shakespeare. (12:12–13)

And later, as the editor ponders what Aspern's poems reveal about Juliana's past, comes the only explicit mention of an actual literary text:

> It was incontestable that, whether for right or for wrong, most readers of certain of Aspern's poems (poems not as ambiguous as the sonnets—scarcely more divine, I think—of Shakespeare) had taken for granted that Juliana had not always adhered to the steep footway of renunciation. (12:48)

These references to Shakespeare seem the most passing of allusions, and ought not to make much of a difference in the way we read *The Aspern Papers* and its obsession with the relation between writing and the body. Yet when we look for analogues to the metaphors with which *The Aspern Papers* characterizes reading, we find them with an odd frequency and sharpness in the texts that swirl around what came in the late nineteenth century to be thought of as the Shakespeare "mystery."

This is not surprising inasmuch as Shakespeare might be said to be the period's exemplary private character, at least in literary contexts, its most alluringly mysterious, most secret subject, the writer who manages to efface his own personality from his writing most thoroughly, disappearing behind his characters. Thus Walter Bagehot takes the occasion of meditating on "Shakespeare—The Individual" (1853) as the occasion for characterizing privacy itself:

> Behind every man's external life, which he leads in company, there is another which he leads alone, and which he carries with him apart. We see but one aspect of our neighbour, as we see but one side of the moon; in either case there is also a dark half, which is unknown to us. We all come down to dinner, but each has a room to himself.[17]

If one accepts this characterization, as many nineteenth-century commentators did, then it seems almost inevitable that reading will take the shape of a desire to penetrate the author's secret, to peer into the room Shakespeare kept to himself. Which may well be what Virginia Woolf's Richard Dalloway is getting at when "seriously and solemnly" he says that "no decent man ought to read Shakespeare's sonnets because it was like listening at keyholes."[18]

In banning the sonnets, Richard recycles what must have seemed by the time Woolf wrote *Mrs. Dalloway* a cliché of Victorian literary commentary: that in the sonnets Shakespeare gives voice to his own experience and emotions, for once allowing what Bagehot calls his "dark half" to speak. Not all critics believed that, as Edward Dowden argued in his 1881 edition of the sonnets, these poems represent "real feelings and real experiences."[19] But for personalists and anti-personalists alike, the issue in large part shaped the nature of debate over Shakespeare, determining its characteristic concerns and metaphors. As the quotations from Woolf and Bagehot suggest, these metaphors draw on the language and imagery of privacy, especially imagery that conceives of privacy in terms of domestic space. Indeed, the dominant metaphor of nineteenth-century Shakespeare studies in general, and of studies of the sonnets in particular, may be the one Woolf plays on: Wordsworth's characterization of the sonnet-form as the "key" with which "Shakespeare unlocked his heart," an image consistent with and amplified by the comparison of the sonnet to a "narrow room" in "Nuns Fret Not."

Woolf was not the first to recognize that one possible implication of this image is that reading the sonnets can be a form of voyeurism. In the poem "House" (1876), Robert Browning developed this suggestion in terms peculiarly relevant to *The Aspern Papers*. One more statement of Browning's credo of the objective poet, "House" begins by mockingly toying with the possibility of writing a self-revealing poem:

> Shall I sonnet-sing you about myself?
> Do I live in a house you would like to see?
> Is it scant of gear, has it store of pelf?
> "Unlock my heart with a sonnet-key?"[20]

Having invoked the standard Wordsworthian image, the poem turns to literalizing it, sketching a tableau in which an earthquake has left the interior of a house open to view. A crowd gathers before it, "feast[ing]" its eyes on the late occupant's domestic arrangements and idiosyncrasies—noticing, for example, that he smoked ("no wonder he lost his health!" the crowd concludes); that he seems not to have bathed before he dressed; that, as "the neighbours guessed," "His wife and himself had separate rooms" (31, 22–28). "House" thus turns a mode of reading into an act of ocular invasion, an invasion in which the secrets of the body are not only revealed but are turned into spectacle. Further, the poem turns a poetic form into a physical space that contains evidence of the body's activities; the physical dimensions of the sonnet make it participate in what Bachelard calls the "homology between the geometry of the small box and the psychology of secrecy."[21]

This homology is relevant to the status of Shakespeare's sonnets because two questions that dominate—and sometimes titillate and sometimes unnerve—readings of the sonnets toward the end of the century are whether the poems represent actual bodies and whether the actions the poems represent are the actual experiences of the bodies represented. Not only does criticism of the time increasingly pursue the identities of the Dark Lady, the Fair Young Man, and the Rival Poet, but it comes to think of the poems as somehow *containing* Shakespeare himself; it's as if reading writing so tied up in experiences and representations of the physical body is equivalent to knowing the body that wrote what one is reading. When the narrator of Oscar Wilde's *The Portrait of Mr. W. H.* (1889) claims that in reading the sonnets with the Willie Hughes theory in mind he has his "hand upon Shakespeare's heart, and [is] counting each separate throb and pulse of passion," he expresses feelings that appear in the wholly un-ironic criticism of his real-life predecessors and contemporaries.[22] Likewise, when Samuel Butler, in *Shakespeare's Sonnets Reconsidered* (1899), insists that in the sonnets "we look upon" the poet "face to face" even as we also look "over [his] shoulder" to read the poems that are actually "a very private letter," he speaks for assumptions present in mainstream criticism even if his bizarre thesis that Mr. W. H. worked as a cook at sea is anything but.[23]

The intensity of this emphasis on the authorial body may seem extraordinary in later nineteenth-century writing on Shakespeare's sonnets, but the habits of reading it reflects are not so unusual. Inasmuch as deducing biographical, lived experience from texts is a main critical project of the time, Shakespearean studies epitomize the assumptions that govern nineteenth-century literary commentary in general. As Marjorie Garber demonstrates, conceptions of authorship in the nineteenth century are routinely referred to Shakespeare; the question of what an author is is defined through Shakespeare even as it gives definition to Shakespeare himself.[24] This is true not only of the controversy over who wrote Shakespeare, which begins to attract attention in the middle of the century. It is also true of questions about the body's presence in Shakespeare's writing, particularly the sonnets, as the remarks of Wilde and Butler suggest. That the sonnets themselves conceive of persons living on through writing—and thus, in a sense, living within it—may have seemed to underwrite this emphasis on the body in writing. But we should also consider this emphasis as part of what Foucault identifies as an "intensification" of the body in the nineteenth century: a growing tendency to determine meanings and to specify individuals through recourse to corporeality.[25]

This discourse surrounding and reconstituting the sonnets is not, of course, one that merely constructs and worries over a general corporeality, a universal state of embodiment (indeed, it is one of those episodes that reveals the emptiness of "the body" considered as an uninflected abstraction). As Eve Sedgwick observes in *Between Men*, Shakespeare's sonnets "have been a kind of floating decimal in male homosexual discourse," a point where gay male critics have sometimes and prominently found the English literary canon reflecting same-sex desire and a point where critics with a deep and insistent *lack* of interest in sexuality have been forced to confront the issues of embodiment and sexual desire they have worked to exclude from their projects.[26] In Wilde's *Portrait of Mr. W. H.*, male same-sex desire is mediated through debate on the sonnets, mediated through lyric scholarship; in the narrator's characterization of reading as equivalent to placing his "hand upon Shakespeare's heart, and counting each separate throb and pulse of passion," contact with the textual artifact substitutes for direct physical expression with the sonnets' other readers, Cyril Graham and Erskine. As William Cohen notes, Wilde "embeds" his theory of the sonnets "in a nested series of narratives, where it is exchanged through successive pairs of desiring men."[27] As in *The Aspern Papers*, where reading is conceived both in terms of a hauntingly spiritual connection and in terms of a tactile physicality, in Wilde and the discourse around the sonnets more generally reading is pulled in opposite directions, simultaneously construed as something that looks a lot like a sexual act and something purely cognitive.

Given both these tensions and this insistently corporeal impulse in the debates circling around Shakespeare, it is not surprising that the desire to see Shakespeare "face to face," as Samuel Butler put it, received in the mid-1880s a most literal construction. In 1883, five years before *The Aspern Papers'* publication, a pamphlet by C. M. Ingleby, a life trustee of Shakespeare's birthplace at Stratford, ignited a small controversy by renewing earlier calls for a new approach to Shakespeare studies, one best summarized by Ingleby's long title: *Shakespeare's Bones. The Proposal to Disinter Them, Considered in Relation to Their Possible Bearing on His Portraiture: Illustrated by Instances of Visits of the Living to the Dead.* As his title suggests, Ingleby calls for exhumation as a means of determining, through an examination of Shakespeare's skull, which of the portraits of the poet most resemble him. Other disinterment advocates hoped as well that an examination of the skeleton might reveal whether Shakespeare was lame, an implication many readers saw and took quite literally in Sonnets 37 and 89. As it does in *The Aspern Papers,* reading here becomes a matter of seeing the body and of (very respectfully, Ingleby's tract emphasizes) touching it. And as the examples of the portraits and of Shakespeare's lameness further imply, one conviction that motivates would-be resurrection men like Ingleby is that it is the body that resolves not only the ambiguities of graphic representation, but also those of language itself. Or, rather, the body resolves such ambiguities because it is itself a superior language: a bone contains a "message," "an intelligible language"; a skull requires no interpreter but rather "sp[eaks] for itself."[28]

What eventually quashed Ingleby's proposal—which did have its supporters, and which was considered in an 1884 meeting of the Shakespeare Trust—was an international outcry against disturbing the sanctity of the poet's grave. Ingleby had anticipated such objections, arguing that since a respectfully conducted scientific investigation was hardly the same thing as grave-robbing inspired by "morbid curiosity," the malediction engraved upon the tomb ("Blessed be the man that spares these stones, / And cursed be he that moves my bones") hardly applied. But the examples—the "instances of visits of the living to the dead"—Ingleby gathers together to establish a precedent for exhumation under such circumstances do little to gain support for his proposal. Ingleby follows the odd rhetorical strategy of arguing for the exhumation of Shakespeare by devoting a quarter of his short book to examples of how the job ought not to be done, detailing oddly harrowing stories of the posthumous careers of the famous: Swedenborg becomes the target of souvenir-hunters, one of whom carries away the cartilage of an ear; a skeleton purported to be Milton's is displayed for a small fee; Cromwell's embalmed head makes such a quixotic journey that it isn't quite possible for Ingleby to say where it has finally come to rest.[29]

Henry James was hardly unaware of the controversies swirling around

Shakespeare; indeed, it seems unlikely that any literary person of the time could escape them. And like Emerson before him and like his contemporary Mark Twain, James was not always immune to the efforts of others to question Shakespeare's authorship of Shakespeare. When, in 1877, he made his second visit to Stratford, James wrote of the "torment" of Shakespeare's "unguessed riddle," as well as of the charms of being on the spot where "the greatest genius who has represented and ornamented life" had walked.[30] Much later he would happen upon a new book proving that Bacon wrote Shakespeare; shortly after that he would confess that he was

> haunted by the conviction that the divine William is the biggest and most successful fraud ever practiced on a patient world. . . . I can only express my general sense by saying that I find it *almost* as impossible to conceive that Bacon wrote the plays as to conceive that the man from Stratford, as we know the man from Stratford, did.[31]

But if James was not quite immune to the ideas of "maniacs who embrace some bedlamitical theory of the cryptic character of Shakespeare," as "The Figure of the Carpet" calls them, this did not quite keep him from coming to define himself and his own privacy in Shakespearean terms (15:244). Especially when he considers that the searching lights and prying fingers that were taking Shakespeare as their object might eventually be turned on himself, James takes Shakespeare's impersonality as exemplary. When, in 1914, he gives instructions to the nephew who would become his literary executor, James not only adopts Shakespeare as his model, but further, he replays the whole association of writing and the body that *The Aspern Papers* and the Shakespeare controversy both establish:

> My sole wish is to frustrate as utterly as possible the post mortem exploiter . . . and I have long thought of launching, by a provision in my will, a curse no less explicit than Shakespeare's own on any such as try to move my bones. Your question determines me definitely to advert to the matter in my will—that is to declare my utter and absolute abhorrence of any attempted biography or the giving to the world . . . of any part or parts of my private correspondence.[32]

The injunction to keep papers private is here conveyed by relating those papers to the body, by speaking of them as if they were body—whether hidden in the grave or dismembered and scattered as "parts." In constructing papers as such by way of reference to Shakespeare, James not only relies on the general image of Shakespeare that emerged in the nineteenth century; he also relies, more particularly, on a relationship that he had worked out eleven years before in his study of prurience at Stratford-on-Avon, "The Birthplace," a story which revisits *The Aspern Papers*' linkage of intrusion into a house with investigation of the life of the author. The tale centers on a young couple, Morris and Isabel Gedge, who become the new caretakers of the national "shrine," "the early home of the supreme poet, the Mecca of the English-speaking race." The poet, obviously Shakespeare but never named, is simply referred to as "Him"—as if his name were too venerable to pronounce. The new docents, blessed with a modicum of taste and discernment, believe that as holders of "the key" of "this trans-figured world," their role is to correct and circumvent the assumptions of "vulgar" tourists (17:134–36). But the vulgar, it turns out, want to hear not just what Morris regards as the very few known "facts" about the author; they want, instead, "everything . . . they want to see where He hung up His hat and where He kept His boots and where His mother boiled her pot" (17:138, 177). They want, in other words, an embroidered account of what is most "personal" rather than skeptically revisionist his-tory. Gedge's style of presentation does not exactly meet these desires, con-vinced as he is that Shakespeare "covered His tracks as no other human being has ever done" (17:165). Indeed, he finds the tourists' intrusions upon the Birthplace as akin to "kill[ing]" Shakespeare not just because such intrusion pries into his life, but also because it substitutes his life for his works (17:180). As in Browning's "House," then, reading Shakespeare's body back into his writing is equated not only with intrud-ing within a house, but also with subjecting its occupant to violence.

When faced with the prospect of being fired by the Birthplace's govern-ing committee, however, Gedge manages to "strangle" his own "critical sense," and evolves an extraordinarily showy routine that makes him so celebrated that the committee doubles his stipend (17:189, 188). Whereas before his conversion he holds that one should "let the author alone," his new style of presentation promises that in the Birthplace, "the whole tenor of existence" is "laid . . . bare"; here one experiences absolute "intimacy" with "Him" (17:180, 194–95). Whereas before his conversion Gedge insists that "the play's the thing," now the Shakespearean writing that mat-ters most, that means most fully, is not anything so mediated as the col-lected works but instead is the mark made directly by the body. As Gedge informs the breathless tourists: "It is in this old chimney-corner, the quaint inglenook of our ancestors—just there in the far angle, where His little stool was placed, and where, I dare say, if we could look close enough, we should find the hearthstone scraped with His little feet" (17:180, 195–96).

As this climactic tableau in "The Birthplace" suggests, reading and see-ing, writing and bodily identity, all give off on each other, becoming fluid and protean. The turning matter I have described in previous chapters comes to be a way of imagining what a text is and how readers interact with it. These ontological blendings characterize the thinking of both James's Shakespearean tourists and of social conservatives, like Warren and Brandeis, who regard with anxiety the prying masses James's tourists exemplify. For in seeing writing as a bodily function or extension or trace, James's Shakespearean tourists assume a relationship that Warren and Brandeis delineate at length. Relying on the analogue of intellectual and artistic property, Warren and Brandeis argue that common-law doctrines of intellectual ownership are themselves but "instances and applications of a general right to privacy" (198). What allows Warren and Brandeis to put the matter in this odd way is the assumption that my ownership of, say, this book is not a matter of my owning the pages on which it is printed; rather, my ownership is of its intellectual and rhetorical content. My common-law publication right, then, is a right to decide which of my thoughts and expressions will become public and which will not. And there's no significant difference, according to Warren and Brandeis, between expressing my thoughts "in writing" and expressing them through the body "in conduct, in conversation, in attitudes, or in facial expression"; from the point of view of privacy law, these all amount to the same thing (206). In rendering immaterial the material through which ideas and emotions are conveyed, then, the right to privacy subsumes the difference between bodies and papers, understanding in identical terms the protections afforded to each. To construe writing as body is at once to claim for it a high degree of protection and to suggest that the boundaries of the body are fluid, unstable, capable of shading into the objects that exist around and alongside the body.

This instability is central both to the way Warren and Brandeis try to protect privacy and to the way they imagine privacy's invasion. Part of what makes late-century social conservatives uneasy about the dissolving boundary between public and private is their conviction that such dissolutions have come to characterize large segments of American society. Running alongside the strong fear of invasion that shows itself in documents like "The Right to Privacy" and "The Birthplace" is a fear that many Americans *want* to be invaded, that they want to give up their privacy— and their selves—to the forces of publicity that Warren and Brandeis critique at the beginning of their article. James's friend E. L. Godkin, in an 1890 *Scribner's Magazine* essay on reputation that partially anticipates Warren and Brandeis, notes that while it causes some people "exquisite pain to have their private life laid bare to the world, others rather like it"; "the passion for notoriety . . . has been fostered to such an extent" by the "wide diffusion of printed gossip that there is a large number of people who . . . put themselves in the way of having their private life explored in the press."[33]

These people who "rather like it" are ones who are "*all* self-advertisement," as James puts it in the long 1903 tale "The Papers."[34] They are people who so thoroughly define themselves on the basis of being "paragraphed . . . and . . . published" that, at least in James's view, they might be all print, wholly publicity effect (378). This applies most obviously to figures like the star celebrity of "The Papers," Sir A. B. C. Beadel-Muffet K.C.B., M.P. (whose very name underlines his definition as an effect of the alphabet, of writing), who are "universal and ubiquitous, commemorated . . . on every page of every public print every day in every year" (317). Here an intertextual connection will indicate more fully the extent to which James imagines the publicly disseminated self in emphatically embodied terms. In "The Papers," Maud Blandy, James's journalist-heroine, imagines that were the celebrity Beadel-Muffet to attempt a retirement from public life, he would be haunted by the public persona she has, with Beadel-Muffet's own cooperation, crafted for him: he would be pursued "by the lurid glare that he has himself so started and kept up, and at last literally devoured (like Frankenstein, of course!) by the monster he has created" (324). This image of the outstanding citizen as a dismembered body with a name full of decorative flourishes (including the initials A. B. C.) echoes Poe's "The Man That Was Used Up," the tale of Brevet Brigadier General John A. B. C. Smith, a veteran of the Indian wars whose famously handsome body proves to be nothing but discriminatingly chosen appurtenances.[35] This continuity between bodily and scriptive identity also characterizes figures like the publicity-craving Selah Tarrant of *The Bostonians,* who noses his way into newspaper offices,

> always trying to find out what was "going in"[to the papers]; he would have liked to go in himself, bodily, and, failing in this, he hoped to get advertisements inserted gratis. The wish of his soul was that he might be interviewed; that made him hover at the editorial elbow.[36]

What James saw as the collapse in America of privacy as a value is registered in examples like these as a crisis in the relationship between bodies and writing; when persons "go into" print to the extent that they seem to be physically constituted of writing, privacy ceases to function. This "scriptively remade body" (the phrase is Jonathan Goldberg's) typifies not only celebrated subjects of writing like Beadel-Muffet or would-be celebrities like Selah Tarrant; it also comes to characterize the writer, or at least those who engage in certain kinds of writing.[37] Thus it is not only the consciousnesses of Maud and of Howard Bight, the journalists of "The Papers," which are wholly "furni[shed]" by "the Papers"; this is also true of their bodies. Maud is "really herself . . . an edition, an 'extra special'"; Howard is "papery all through" (313, 314, 340). Likewise *The Portrait of a Lady*'s journalist, Henrietta Stackpole, is "as crisp and new and comprehensive as a first issue before the folding. From top to toe she had probably no misprint" (3:117).

Privacy, as we have seen, depends for its definition on a relation between writing and body. But the metaphor loses its efficacy when it is tugged too far in either direction: body and writing must become neither too detached from each other nor too indistinguishable. James's clearest exemplum of this uneasy logic comes, of course, in "The Private Life" (1892), a story in which the private self almost literally dissolves before its subsequent recuperation, one that is realized through the body of the writer. Lord Mellifont is "so essentially, so conspicuously and uniformly the public character" that he is "all public" and has "no corresponding private life" (17:246). Celebrated simply for the "tone" he imparts to any event, he is all "style" and no substance—so much so that, in the tale's extraordinary literalization of the proverb, he disappears when he has no audience (17:227).

In contrast to Lord Mellifont, who "isn't even [one] whole" person, Clare Vawdrey, a celebrated playwright, has not one self but two (17:245). One is a "bourgeois"-about-town who has all the usual unremarkable foibles; he has "his hours and his habits, his tailor and his hatter, his hygiene and his particular wine" (17:244, 220). The other self, from whom the bourgeois is wholly cut off, is "the genius" who "stays at home" (17:244). So separated are these two lives that they go on simultaneously; at the same time "the bourgeois" socializes in the parlor, "the genius" hunches over a writing table in his darkened room. This conceit carries to a fantastic extreme the division of the self into one half that comes down to dinner and another half that has a room to itself—the division which Bagehot and other nineteenth-century commentators saw as so eminently Shakespearean. It also follows the conception of the artistic personality that Browning outlined in "House," among other poems—a connection all the more compelling in that James's remarks about the tale in the New York Edition reveal that Vawdrey is modeled on Browning himself (*LC* 2:1255).[38]

The self—or the part of Vawdrey's self—that writes is an ambivalent figure. At one point it is suggested that the man who can only be seen in the darkened room is someone Vawdrey gets to do his writing for him; he is thus doubly a ghost writer. Inasmuch as a ghost is neither wholly substantial nor so wholly disembodied that it cannot be recognized as the trace or outline of a body—inasmuch as it is body and not body—it figures exactly the equivocal, highly generative relation between body and writing that has been my subject.[39]

This chapter has argued that in the twin discourses by which writing and privacy are figured together, a material model of textuality emerges: a cluster of prevailing metaphors, ones that carry into the act of reading a set of concrete analogues. Governed by the logic of the private dwelling and shaded by the nineteenth-century sexualization of things hidden—and, even more generally, by the intense somatic bias of nineteenth-century thought—the concept of the text becomes that of an intimate space, one with definite borders that are also permeable, susceptible to violation. As is especially evident in the commentary on the sonnet form, the physical dimensions of the text are thought through architecture and architecture's social functions; writing's materiality is confused both with the architectural spaces that bespeak intimacy and with the bodies those spaces protect. If this argument holds, then we can say that few concepts, at least in literary criticism, have effaced their own origins more successfully than that of reading, than that of the text.

As a coda, and as a way of developing still more explicitly the significance of the preceding analyses, I offer the following: In 1964, W. H. Auden wrote the introduction for a Signet Classics edition of Shakespeare's sonnets. Auden opened up his subject with a polemic against biographical readings of imaginative literature; he did so in terms of privacy and, even more specifically, in terms of private papers located within an enclosed architectural space: "A great deal of what today passes for scholarly research is an activity no different from that of reading somebody's private correspondence when he is out of the room, and it doesn't really make it morally any better if he is out of the room because he is in his grave."[40] Following in the tradition established by Browning and many other Victorian readers (or nonreaders) of Shakespeare, Auden decrees that Shakespeare's "room" and "grave" must remain sealed against "the desire for truth," a desire hard to distinguish, Auden says, from "idle curiosity" (89). But if the room, the grave, and "Shakespeare the man" must remain impervious to "desire," this desire works its way back into the solely textual kind of reading Auden advocates, as he imagines the "shade" of Shakespeare feeling "grateful" for the "loving care" bestowed on his texts by William Empson in an explication of one of the sonnets (91, 90). Nor is that all, for in speculating about the dating of Shakespeare's sonnets—are they the product of youth or maturity?—Auden hesitantly adopts the former, "because the experiences the sonnets describe seem to me to be more likely to befall a younger man than an older" (91). It is hard in such moments to tell whose experiences Auden is talking about, or whose privacy he would protect—his own or

Shakespeare's. It is hard, in other words, not to associate the kind of reading Auden both forbids and practices with his own sexual history, his slowly emergent sense of himself as a gay man. What *is* clear is that figuring the text as an enclosed and private space—a room or a grave—cannot be disentangled from homosexual reading here, and that Shakespeare's sonnets are still, in 1964, giving that model of textuality its distinctive shape. I would suggest, then, that the material models of reading I have traced in this chapter rework the textual condition, bestowing upon it the shape of the closet. Similarly, the constellation of texts assembled here affirms one of the crucial arguments Eve Kosofsky Sedgwick makes about the closet, which is that the private/public distinction is one of those "contestation[s] of meaning" which is "indelibly marked with the historical specificity of homosocial/homosexual definition, notably but not exclusively male, from around the turn of the century."[41]

CHAPTER SIX

ADULTEROUS MATTER

I would like to begin with two working principles of James's late fiction that together prove enormously generative even as they seem, from a strictly logical viewpoint, only barely reconcilable. The first is that these narratives are centered, with enough obsessiveness to make one suppose that James had fully recognized and embraced his master-metaphor, on the act of adultery; the second is that these narratives so complicate their claims to reference—their own allegations that their grip on a reliably solid world outside themselves is firm—that to ask about the reality of, say, *The Turn of the Screw*'s fornicating ghosts, is, fundamentally, to mistake the nature of the text being read. To put this dual claim more succinctly, the late fiction centers on and effaces the adulterous body, posits that body as both a central and an absent truth. One way this tension appears within the late fiction is as an impulse to "trace" bodies, to locate them within a set of spatial coordinates: "People are always traceable . . . when tracings are required," Colonel Bob Assingham remarks of the presumed tryst of Charlotte and Amerigo (24:134). *The Turn of the Screw*'s governess "trace[s]" little Flora to her rendezvous with Miss Jessel by the lake and triumphantly concludes that the ghost "was there, so I was justified; she was there, so I was neither cruel nor mad" (12:270, 278). The narrator of *The Sacred Fount* considers himself "on the track of a law"—a principle of interpersonal relations that would explain how adulterous lovers transform each other—as he traces these lovers through the meanderings of a country-house weekend.[1] All of these epistemological adventures arrive at an adulterous body, an equivocal figure that will not settle into a stable ontology; they end with ghosts (*The Turn of the Screw*), perpetually transforming bodies (*The Sacred Fount*), and a woman who, defined as a turning figure, frustrates efforts to "definitely plac[e] her," to define her (*The Golden Bowl*) (23:53–54). The condition of having a body should entail the con-

110

dition of having a spatial location, but that more or less necessary truth seems one the late novels deny; they consistently characterize the body along the lines of what William Dean Howells, in his collection of stories about spiritualism, called "questionable shapes," figures that carry with them a sense of physicality that nevertheless cannot be held in physical place.[2]

If we move from the narrative patterns of the late fiction to those texts' moments of description, we find this sense of illocality borne out by the pronounced lack of a whole body, as characters are represented by a single part, a few strands of hair (like Chad Newsome's gray streaks in *The Ambassadors*) or one accessory (Miss Barrace's tortoise-shell glasses in the same novel) or a single prop (the narrator's cigarettes in *The Sacred Fount*). At an early point in *The Ambassadors,* Strether dwells at great length on the ribbon, the "broad red velvet band with an antique jewel—he was rather complacently sure it was antique—attached to it in front," which Maria Gostrey wears round her neck (21:50). At this point in the novel, this ribbon is the only part of Maria the reader can "see" clearly, save for a passing glimpse of her dress, which is "'cut down' . . . in respect to shoulders and bosom." Hence this ribbon almost floats free of the body it accessorizes, a body that is very nearly absent from the passage's representation of Maria. An appurtenance by definition appertains to some more significant entity, but here in late James, the entities to which such ornaments refer are largely missing, practically invisible as the passage stays resolutely focused on this "added" "value" and leaves only dimly adumbrated the body it adds its value to (21:50, 51). At least for this moment, then, the way the text renders reference problematic and the way it represents the accessory coincide.

This ribbon loosens referential moorings in another way as it becomes a sign of adultery. It is, after all, a red ribbon, one that inevitably points back not only to Hester Prynne's scarlet *A* but also to the "cherry-coloured ribbon" that seems so incriminating a piece of evidence in the faux-adultery plot of Dickens's *David Copperfield* and, more generally, to the taste for ornament that for Flaubert's adulterous Emma Bovary seems inseparable from a taste for extramarital liaisons.[3] The ribbon is one of what *The Ambassadors* will later call Maria's "promiscuities," a term with which the novel pulls together indiscriminate social relations with a discriminatingly chosen collection of frills and bibelots, relations and bibelots that, taken together, define the mode of women like Maria Gostrey and Madame de Vionnet. A flexible accessory that can be tied and untied, the ribbon associates itself with the body of the adulteress, which is often explicitly defined as "flexible" in James's late fiction and so reflects in physical form the looseness with which that character regards binding ties (23:47; 10:320). Further, by having an intimate dinner with a woman who is not

Mrs. Newsome, his presumed fiancée, Strether is committing something he considers akin to adultery, an effect heightened by the contrast of Maria's ribbon to the austere ruff Mrs. Newsome wears instead, by Strether's inhalation of the "vague sweetness" of Maria's perfume, and by Strether's realization that "never before—no, literally never—had a lady dined with him at a public place before going to the play" (21:50, 52).

I want to bring to a close these readings of Jamesian matter by arguing that in James's late fiction, a suppressed account of adultery reappears as an account of the material world. At its simplest, this argument will be that the late Jamesian object takes on the characteristics of bodies that have come unstuck from their social moorings and floated into illicit unions: the objects of the last novels are both "slippery" and "sticky," like Lionel Croy's repulsive sofa at the opening of *The Wings of the Dove;* they are full of "duplicity," overly capable of flexible redoubling, like the proper things that serve as cover for the adulterous Selina in *A London Life;* they are "promiscuous properties," like the ornaments and relics that furnish Madame de Vionnet's apartment in *The Ambassadors* (19:3; 10:292; 21:244). With these promiscuously ambulant, amorphous, sticky yet slippery objects, James endows the slippage of reference with material properties; the missing accounts of sexual liaisons work their way into the novel's representations of the concrete world as the material things of these novels paradoxically objectify the condition of groundlessness.[4]

More generally and more complexly, this chapter will argue that the instability of the late Jamesian text equals and is accomplished through an instability of the body. What is radical about the late fictions is that they evolve a materialism without reference, a concrete materiality that will not fix itself to its bodily referent; persons come to be defined through material processes that won't sit still, figures that turn perpetually. As in the representation of Maria's ribbon, the superficial ornament does not necessarily refer to any substantial integrity; the ribbon functions as the focal point of a passage that only barely gestures toward a body held within its knot. In this sense, James's late style functions at the point where synecdochic logic begins to break down as it elaborates a part at the expense of a whole that is ostentatiously absent.

James's term for this nonreferential matter is "promiscuous properties," a phrase that first of all reflects the typical understanding of adultery as a threat to the orderly inheritance of the estate, a concern that finds its way into and shapes the plots of all the late novels as the Verver fortune, the Newsome family factory, and Millie's "thumping bank account" seem in danger of becoming floating inheritances or of being falsely assigned. Further, the phrase "promiscuous properties" carries this sense of adulterous, wayward matter into the domain of perception and, ultimately, ontology; it suggests that the qualities of material things become detached from the things they're proper to. They thus have the capacity to mix with and meld together consciousnesses as textures, sheens, glazes, lights, and smells seem to exist in the late Jamesian text without the need to stay situated within an object. In his book on Baudelaire, Sartre observes that the smell of bodies was for Baudelaire a way of possessing the body of another—"the smell of a body is the body itself"—but it is also the possession of a body "with the flesh removed, a vaporized body which has remained completely itself but which has become a volatile spirit." Such scents, Sartre concludes, are "at once bodies and, as it were, the negation of the body."[5] In *The Ambassadors,* James conveys a very similar conception of decorporealized embodiment through the sense of smell, as in the "soft fragrance" Maria exudes in Strether's pretheatre dinner with her, or in the "charming scent" that, Strether explains to Waymarsh, made him linger in Chad's flat: "I don't know what to call it . . . It's a detail, but it's as if there were something—something very good—*to* sniff" (21:50, 105). Both are presumably scenes of adultery (as the contrast between Maria and Mrs. Newsome underscores in the first, and as Waymarsh's question about whether Chad "live[s] there with a woman" underscores in the second); in both, the adulterous relation that is not quite visible but only presumed is reenacted at the level of the senses, reenacted as a tiny sensory plot that operates in a zone between the emphatically physical body and its vaporization into what Sartre calls "volatile spirit."

James is at his most materialist, then, at the point where matter can't be held to or contained within the objects and bodies to which it rightfully belongs. In saying that James is at his most materialist at this point, I mean to underscore the way in which the extreme focus on consciousness in the late novels is conceived according to a bodily model: the small sensory plots that compose so much of the late Jamesian text account for and count as consciousness, even as they mold themselves after a larger, largely absent plot about adulterous bodies, a plot that is wholly inferential, never spoken, only assumed and disowned. *The Sacred Fount,* the novel that prefaces the major phase, is James's full-length study of this displacement and dispersal of the adulterous body into the realm of the intellect, for in hypothesizing that one lover siphons off the wit and intelligence of another, the novel places at its center a metaphor that displaces bodily matter even as that metaphor is impossible to understand without imagining it in bodily terms: it is hard to think of exchange without thinking of substance, and hard to think of persons exchanging something without thinking of either objects or, in this case, the bodily fluids swapped in sexual union.

The connections drawn in late James among adultery, matter and property, and consciousness are ones at least latently present from the origins of modern British philosophy; an exploration of the relations and metaphoric resemblances among some key concepts in Locke's thought will clarify how adultery, mixed matter, and thinking verge on each other's domains and employ each other as examples. In *The Second Treatise of Government*, Locke famously defines property as whatever man has "remove[d] out of the State" of nature, "mixed his *Labour* with, and joyned to it something that is his own."[6] Locke's theory of property relies on the concept of mixing, a concept that in turn is based on the inalienability of what the body has incorporated, physiologically made part of itself. Developing his definition through the example of harvesting acorns, Locke argues that the acorns become one's own as soon as one picks them up. But the whole example is prefaced by an assertion of the fact that whoever "is nourished by the Acorns he pickt up under an Oak . . . has certainly appropriated them to himself. No Body can deny but the nourishment is his." Similarly, Locke earlier in the same chapter observes that "The Fruit, or Venison, which nourishes the wild *Indian* . . . must be his," must become "a part of him," before it can fulfill its function.[7] This theory of property, which finds its inarguable base in bodily fact, cannot be wholly disentangled from Locke's theory of cognition; indeed, owning and knowing will remain entangled in Anglo-American philosophy for hundreds of years (they remain emphatically so for William James, for instance).[8] Hence the mind in Lockean epistemology is imagined in similar terms, as a "Storehouse" "furnished" with objects of knowledge, a "stock" of "materials," "plain *Idea[s]*" it can grasp. Possessive individualism becomes a model for cognition not only because the Lockean mind knows by acquiring, but also because it forms a "Collection" out of the material it acquires, a collection it keeps in a "Store-house"; both the contents of the mind and its nature as a container are thus shaped after things that epitomize ownership.[9] The very idiom with which Locke characterizes thinking—"mixed," "flow," "properties," and "figures"—reflects a model of bodily appropriation; thinking in Locke is the mixing of cognitive labor with the world, and that account implicitly carries with it and derives much of its intuitive appeal from the mixing of bodies and substances.

Perhaps this commitment is why, in explaining the nature of "mixed Modes" or abstract ideas, Locke gives as one example the "*Idea* of *Adultery*," for adultery inheres in an improper mixture of bodies that reflects the type of thinking Locke is trying to explain at the same time that it only exists between bodies and so is irreducible to substance. As a complex (as opposed to simple) idea, adultery is for Locke empirically wayward, almost licentious, resistant to referential precision; in forming such ideas, "the Mind takes a liberty not to follow the Existence of Things exactly." Such ideas are formed without comparison to "the real Existence of Things," are not verified and perhaps not even verifiable through an examination of "Nature" (429). Hence adultery emerges in the *Essay* as both wholly embodied and wholly abstract: wholly embodied because it obliquely reflects the Lockean devotion to mixed matter and because it is a name for something bodies do, and wholly abstract because it names no one substance and is left unsubjected to ocular proof.

This chain of overlapping metaphors in Locke's philosophy usefully highlights the structure imagined for consciousness in late James. It brings forward, first of all, the image of the mind as a storeroom, a cabinet, closet, or gallery, in which James's protagonists lodge their perceptions, their "accumulations," as *The Golden Bowl* puts it, of the hints and dark glimmers of an adultery plot unraveling around them (24:14). In *What Maisie Knew*, this "collection of images and echoes to which meanings were attachable" is housed in a "dim closet" with "high drawers," a "receptacle" in which stray remarks of Maisie's promiscuous parents are "tumbled" together (11:12). In *The Golden Bowl*, this space is figured as "a roomful of confused objects, never as yet 'sorted,'" a "confusion" or "heap" of things Maggie knows she doesn't know, a closet that is her own version of Amerigo's "cabinet" containing all the things he knows intimately well (24:14; 23:46). In *The Sacred Fount*, this space is a "little gallery," "a small collection," a "museum" of adulterous couplings (29). A long and voluminous tradition of commentary centered on consciousness in late James has often obscured the principle that these passages make striking: consciousness in these fictions becomes thinkable, representable, susceptible to being given a structure through adultery. Adultery makes consciousness graphic, and the material properties of adulterous bodies, which I have argued always give off on the world of things, are what make the process of thinking in late James seem substantial, concrete, replete with tangible acquisitions. Consciousness only acquires the minimum degree of opacity necessary for representation when it is adulterated.

But if James falls in line with Locke's account of the mind as a storehouse, he also perceives the instability of the matter he places there: in the passages quoted above, material instabilities convey epistemological ones as James's prose hovers between construing matter as significance and matter as concrete substance that slides away from its signifiers. As in Locke's *Essay*, adultery in late James is a coupling of bodies that fails to inhere in any substance and so uncouples words from their referents. Hence the figure of the storehouse is in these fictions emphatically materialist and referentially troubled at the same time. In *The Golden Bowl*, the "confused objects" Maggie accumulates make up a "mass of vain things, congruous, incongruous," a "heap" (24:14–15). Evidence of promiscuity is itself promiscuously intermingled, "never as yet 'sorted.'" Like a mass of secondhand goods, cognitive property is here so jumbled that things appear to slide away from their names even as they take on momentary "affinit[ies]" with each other; they are hence "congruous" and "incongruous," slipping away from referents while sometimes sticking to each other in new and alarming combinations (24:14, 15). In *Maisie,* such objects of knowledge are a "tumbled" "assortment" of things "to which meanings were attachable," a phrase that casts the relation between signifier and signified into a materialist idiom even as that relation is undone by the very copiousness of this jumble of matter (11:12). In *The Sacred Fount,* the narrator thinks of his own mind as a "museum" that contains embodied questions: he thinks of his collection of transformed adulterers as "the museum of those who put to me with such intensity the question of what had happened to them" (29). They are materialized aporias, then, turning figures that are simultaneously understood as solid bodies and ungraspable flow.

The image of the cogito as storehouse oscillates in another important way as James's names for it shift between characterizing it as a private "closet" and a public "museum" and so shift between thinking of it as a place where goods are consumed in solitude and a place where goods are publicly displayed but never used up. These images are nearly interchangeable for James, as they are for much of the prehistory of the museum, in which private cabinets serve as quasi-public signs of status and in which civic museums originate in the collection of an individual.[10] The Ververs' career as collectors is a study in this shifting boundary between private goods and public treasures as they travel with their "smaller pieces" that they "arrange" in their hotel rooms (to make these transiently private commercial spaces "less ugly," Maggie says), store their larger pieces in "warehouses, vaults, banks, safes, wonderful secret places" on the Continent, and plan a municipal museum for American City (23:13). Maggie's mental "closet" carries with it, then, a sense of ambivalent movement between the deeply subjective and the openly shared: consciousness in late James is construed in terms of a figure that very nearly forms a continuous surface between highly private spaces and places of public access. Indeed, the sense in the late novels that consciousness can be externalized depends in large part *for* its sense, its comprehensibility, on the material practices I have been highlighting, the practices of collection and display.[11]

These indeterminacies in the storehouse metaphor—between public and private, between the materially sticky and the referentially slippery, between embodiment as something graspable and as ontologically fluid— replicate the scene of adultery. For in the late fiction, the art gallery becomes for James the locus of the adulterous couple, and the processes by which bodies give off on each other and objets d'art give off on bodies become fused. The museum, the headquarters of high culture, becomes a space of promiscuous properties; James's last fictional account of what I will call the matter of culture lies in this recurrent association of illicit or barely licit sex with the highly valorized, nearly officially sanctioned practice of museum-going. By the word "culture," I mean both the narrower sense of personal cultivation through exposure to works of art *and* the broader sense of all a society's forms, objects, and attitudes; my argument is that in his gallery scenes, James is concerned with the material blurring or blending of these senses and that gallery-going, with its combination of static of works of art and directionless, even random movement of spectators, epitomizes his sense of daily life as the endless equivocation between persons and things. As I have already briefly sketched, the figure of the gallery is furthermore the image that blurs the difference between the Jamesian investment in consciousness and the Jamesian investment in embodiment which, I have argued throughout this book, underwrites and is itself overwritten by James's epistemological and psychological interests. In the homology between the mind figured as storehouse and the gallery figured as the scene of promiscuity, the distinction between the cognitive flexibility of which James's protagonists are so capable and the bodily flexibility of which his adulteresses are so capable dissolves.

In a bracing footnote in *Capital,* Marx defines "the only materialist" historiography as one that uncovers how abstractions and apotheoses arise from "the earthly kernel," "the actual, given relations of life." The history of technology is what produces "every particular organization of society," even when that social form seems most abstracted from the machines, the concrete arrangements of tools and laborers, that have made it.[12] While my goal is more modest than those of Marx's philosophy of history, I am going to begin my reading of James's adulterous matter in the same spirit by claiming that the abstractions of the late fiction originate in a highly particular moment and a specific turning body in a novel of the late 1880s, *A London Life.*

Squarely centered on—and ultimately decentered by—adultery, *A London Life* announces itself early on as a novel about the "duplicity" of objects, of houses and decor, of the interior architecture of upper-class England (10:292). James's American heroine, Laura Wing, sees the settings characteristic of English country life as producing the gentry and holding in place the persons it has made. "English things" have the "bright durable sociable air" of "being meant for daily life, for long periods, for uses of high decorum"; they tell a "story" of stasis, "of a comfortable, liberal, deeply domestic effect, addressed to eternities of possession" (10:271, 291). The estate that Laura's sister Selina has married seems like "immutabl[e] 'property'" (the quotation marks in the text suggest not just the iteration of the idiom as a constantly invoked description, but also the term's potential

undoing) (10:270). Lady Davenant, the aged friend of the family dowager, personifies this sense of "symbolic security" conveyed by the knick-
knacks characteristic of the upper-class drawing room; seeing her seated
amidst "chintz and water-colour," Laura has a momentary glimpse of how
comforting it would be to "jump all the middle dangers of life," pass
through the awkward hazards of courtship and desire, and arrive "at the
end safely, sensibly, with a cap and gloves and formulas and phrases"
(10:283). The image of security in this novel, its very picture—Lady
Davenant is both "full of life" and more like a "fine portrait than . . . a living person"—is that of a woman nestled among her things, her habitual
accessories that are so thoroughly established that it's not clear whether
they're her own innovations or ones inherited from her forbears (10:272).

   As this nearly impossible image of the living but static portrait suggests, what stabilizes the social order in *A London Life* is a most precarious ontology. While the early pages of the novel manage to bring a diagrammatic neatness to their vision of upper-class culture, every one of the
figures they advance hovers on the edge of logical impossibility, carries
with it the germ of its own disintegration. The static "story" told by the
accoutrements of country life is barely a story. The watercolors and
chintz, which image security, seem too amorphous or flimsy to serve as
things that could anchor a social structure, even symbolically. Property is
by definition not "immutable," but alienable. More precisely, the relation
between persons and the objects that should hold those persons in place
is a hazardous one, prone to detachment and to new and promiscuous
combinations: bodies in *A London Life* tend to come unglued from the
concrete things that might stabilize them and to mix indiscriminately
with alien matter. The text explicitly names these slippages as a problem
of reference: thinking of the "stable-stamped composition" of her randy
brother-in-law Lionel and of the "fine things," like "the sweet old wain-
scoted parlour," that surrounded his upbringing, Laura wonders, "what
visible reference was there" in the former to the latter? (10:291). Such settings, Laura concludes, convey a "sense of . . . curious duplicity (in the
literal meaning of the word)"; they project a tone of "peace and decorum," while the real "spirit" that "prevail[s]" is "contentious and impure"
(10:292). By the "literal meaning" of "duplicity," Laura appears to mean
the figurative one: while the more usual sense is "deceitfulness," the literal sense is merely "the state or quality of being numerically or physically
double" (*OED*). Duplicity is itself doubled between the sense of a cun-
ningly false front and the sense of physical doubling; the loss of referential hold yields a text where the literal and the figurative keep turning,
keep exchanging places. For perhaps Laura does mean the literal here in
the sense of the doubled bodies of the adulterous couple, the beast with

two backs, the "monstrous" creations generated when the hold objects have on persons gives way (10:321).

Uncontainable within any single figure, this duplicity is nonetheless exemplified by the body of the adulterous woman, in this case Laura's sister, Selina, for whom trips to Parisian dressmakers serve as minimal cover for trysts with her lover, Captain Crispin. From the beginning, the text cannot decide whether Selina is a "foreign element" that has poisoned the estate, introducing desires that cannot be held in place, or whether somehow the estate has corrupted her American innocence. While Selina and her "doings" seem to Laura wholly "discordant" with the values materialized by Mellows, the country house, there is still a suspicion—one clearly enunciated but left unrationalized—that at Mellows Selina "had found her occasion, all the influences that had so transformed her" (10:271–2). The adulterous woman cannot quite be relegated to some social margin here because she exemplifies and exaggerates both the text's model of culture and the weak point of that model: Selina's "flexib[ility]" and acquisitiveness, her ability to accept so readily "the mark of her *couturière*," are both ideal and deviant (10:320). In other words, the same material processes that produce a person designated as "wife" or "mother" are the ones that threaten to undo that designation. *A London Life* tends to understand persons as generated and perfected by the objects from which they must somehow remain distinguishable. To use the text's own characteristic figure for this difficult position, persons must be portraits framed by their material circumstances, but only framed by them, not mixed with or adulterated by them. Even so, objects are the "frame" that has "made" persons into ideal "picture[s]," into "the perfection of human culture" (10:292). And as the texts and episodes discussed in chapter 4 indicated, frames can be points of traffic instead of rigid boundaries.

It is not surprising, then, that the frame of reference will be definitively broken in a museum scene, a scene that merges the disorienting confusion of person and thing with the adulterous disruption of marriage. Museums are almost by definition places for objects that have floated free of their contexts, come unstuck from their referents, and merged into new combinations; perhaps that is why James habitually associates them with sexual desire and thinks of them as likely settings for relatively chaste courting (Strether, having married young, had "missed the time natural in Boston for taking girls to the Museum" in *The Ambassadors*), or for more random and less licensed encounters (Kate and Densher meet at a gallery opening in *The Wings of the Dove*) (21:52). In *A London Life,* this association of the museum with the collapse of context is at its strongest, for the museum in question is the weird assemblage of architectural models, classical busts and fragments, funerary urns, mirrors, landscapes, portraits, a human skeleton, a model of Stonehenge, and an Egyptian sarcophagus, crafted by the architect Sir John Soane (1753–1857) in the building adjoining his house in Lincoln's Inn Fields in London.

Recent studies of the cultural poetics of museums place strong emphasis on the rationalized narratives museums make out of their objects, and on the ways that objects wrenched out of original context are systematically classified into an artificial and hegemonic unity. In his disciplinary critique *Rethinking Art History,* Donald Preziosi writes that "everything takes place in the museum in some eternal contemporaneity; all diachrony, all difference, all multivocality is enframed in synchronicity." The museum "orchestrates . . . contradiction into a single visible field" and "situates all objects within . . . spaces that evoke and elicit a proper viewing stance and distance."[13] This description is largely what the Soane Museum is not, nor is it the way nineteenth-century museum-goers experienced what they saw. Indeed, James almost directly answers this understanding of the museum as hegemonic in his description of the Soane collection as one of "heterogeneous objects," a "queer" collation of "thing[s] you couldn't find anywhere else" (10:356–57). Further, Soane was far more a connoisseur of spatial disorientation than a classificatory thinker, and his principles of composition owed at least as much to the sensibility governing the Gothic novel as it did to a Palladian ideal of order. An early admirer of Piranesi's etchings, Soane recreated their visual disorientations—their confusion of surface and depth—in his chambers, particularly in the basement area known as the Crypt, where the climax of James's novel takes place.[14]

Everything about Laura's journey down into the Crypt defies rationalization: she is going there with Mr. Wendover, a man she has picked up at one of her sister's receptions and so a man who, for all his seeming innocuousness, is also associated with Selina's adulterous household; the city appears a great "labyrinth" through which one must "thread" one's way; the Museum itself, although a public institution, is also "one of the most curious things in London and one of the least known" and seemingly empty of other visitors (10:355, 356). Along the way downstairs, Laura and Wendover inspect "the sarcophagi, the mummies, the idols," and then admire Soane's collection of Hogarths (Soane owned *The Rake's Progress*), paintings redolent of the adulterous atmosphere Laura has come to the Museum to escape. The effect of the strange antiquities similarly intensifies the anxious-making "duplicity" of things in the earlier scenes at the country house: "there were uncanny unexpected objects Laura edged away from and would have preferred not to be in the room with," phrasing that itself edges away from its objects and, in doing so, associates those objects with the kind of impure woman one ought not to visit or even name except by such syntactic indirection (10:357). As a thunderstorm gathers its force (this scene pulls out every Gothic stop), the labyrinthine quality of the "dim irregular vaults" and "little narrow avenues" intensifies, as does the "ambiguous sinister look" of the fragments and figures, until the journey downward and inward ends where all journeys through a labyrinth do—with a discovery of the monstrous, perpetually turning figure:

> "It's very fearful—it looks like a cave of idols!" [Laura] said to her companion; and then she added, "Just look there: is that a person or a thing?" As she spoke they drew nearer the object of her reference— a figure half blocking a small vista of curiosities, a figure that answered her question by uttering a short shriek as they approached. The immediate cause of this cry was apparently a vivid flash of light- ning, which penetrated into the room and cleared up both Laura's face and that of the equivocal person. The girl recognised her sister, as Mrs. Lionel had unguardedly recognised hers. "Why, Selina!" broke from her lips before she had time to check the sound. At the same moment the figure turned quickly away, and then Laura saw it accompanied by another, a tall gentleman with a tawny beard that shone in the dusk. These wanderers retreated together—melted away as it were, disappearing in the gloom or in the labyrinth of wonders. (10:357–58)

At the center of the labyrinth in Ovid lurks the Minotaur, half-bull, half-human, a monstrosity born of the adulterous affair of Minos's wife and hidden away in Daedalus's spatially disorienting maze, a maze Daedalus constructed by "confusing the usual marks of direction, and leading the eye of the beholder astray by devious paths winding in different directions."[15] Spatial and sexual confusion are traditionally linked in this way, a tradition James follows as he locates his Hogarthian plot in a Piranesian setting, exploiting the varied properties of the Soane Museum by finding the thread between them. The turning figure, "the equivocal person," here is momentarily indistinguishable from a thing and so is a hybrid creature, half one substance and half another, like the Minotaur. Already duplicitous, this figure is redoubled by the presence of her lover, a figure presumably intertwined with hers. Hence as an "object of reference," the figure escapes Laura's perceptual grasp and escapes the firm mooring of the marriage contract even as this groundlessness itself becomes an account of the material world. The equivocations of adultery and the equivocal relation between persons and things become indistinguishable in this passage set in Soane's Crypt, a place which spatializes the loss of reference points, points by which the eye may orient itself. Consequently, the passage actually spatializes the Jamesian lie (Selina has lied about what she is doing on this afternoon, saying that she will be visiting a friend who is ill) because it maps onto an architectural space the endlessly protean, ceaselessly malleable quality that James's liars bestow upon the world around them.[16]

In this scene, then, James materializes the adulterous loss of reference that will be a hallmark of the late fiction; the last major novels are tales from this Crypt, narratives that unfold and disperse the disorientations of this episode in *A London Life*. In this scene set in a collection, James gathers together the tropes of the late fiction, focuses within a narrow space the uncanny ontology that will characterize the novels of adultery. On their way down to the museum's basement, Laura and Wendover take time to inspect the "medals" and "pagodas," images that will figure Amerigo and his adulterous liaison with Charlotte in *The Golden Bowl*. The pagoda in the later novel would appear to be a fundamentally different sort of object than it is in *A London Life* because it is a purely mental image, a metaphor with which Maggie pictures to herself her life's strangely mixed filial and marital attachments. But what is striking is how many of its material properties the pagoda retains as it is transformed into an object of cognition, a thing that exists only in the space of metaphor. For example, Maggie imagines the pagoda as creating an area around itself for her to "circulate[e]" in, "a space that sometimes seemed ample and sometimes narrow," a space that recreates on a purely metaphorical level the wavering dimensions of the museum in *A London Life* (24:3–4). The pagoda of *The Golden Bowl* is "impenetrable and inscrutable," hence an object that excludes Maggie even as it appears as an object enclosed within her consciousness. An unrationalizable object, the pagoda is a structure shut up within Maggie that shuts her out. A material thing with a hard objectivity—it is described as "plated with hard bright porcelain"—the pagoda has an emphatically durable character, which makes it an odd choice for something that is so ontologically amorphous as a mental image. Finally, while readers practically always take this pagoda as an image for adultery, doing so means taking it as referring to nothing so much as a textual gap, a hole in the novel's account of relationships. For what is conceptually most difficult about images like this one in late James is that they have a lavish material specificity—the pagoda is "coloured and figured and adorned at the overhanging eaves with silver bells"—without the firm referential moorings that should accompany such a finely specified image. Even if we tacitly agree to fill in the epistemological gaps of the late fiction and take a figure like this one as an image for adulterous relations, we are still left with the image as a materially objective sign for the coming-loose of the marital frame of reference adultery represents.

As the trajectory of this pagoda from *A London Life* to *The Golden Bowl* implies, the materialism without reference generated in the Soane Museum is generalized in the late fiction; the slippages and adherences of the adulterous body can no longer be contained within a highly eccentric space like the Crypt. Rather, the unmoored matter and the uncanny dimensions of that episode in *A London Life* recreate themselves everywhere—in individual consciousnesses, in landscapes, in domestic interiors and public spaces—until the logic of inside and outside (and even just the logic of *in*) loosens and unravels. Spaces and contexts in the late James take on the properties of the ribbon, an appurtenance that intimates the presence of a body, is associated with adultery, and has no inside or outside. Or, to shift to a metaphor even more central to these decentering texts, all spaces in the late fiction become like the museum, a space that takes materialism as its very basis, yet that can only barely contain its material properties within any kind of context, a space constructed around the paradox of preserving objects while also making their qualities ambulatory.

These claims would probably hold loosely true of museums throughout history, but there are particular reasons for making them of museums as conceptualized in the years around 1900, reasons that lend historical depth to an understanding of James's nonreferential materialism. Indeed, the matters of context and adulteration, the poetics of metamorphosis, and the functions of the "storehouse" are explicitly at issue in the first history of the museum, the Scottish historian David Murray's three-volume *Museums, Their History and Their Use,* published in 1904.[17] Murray's work is part of a much larger effort to rationalize the curatorial profession and so to bring structure to the kind of cornucopian jumbles that collections like the Soane Museum represent; the Museums Association in Great Britain began holding an annual conference and publishing a monthly journal in the same years as Murray was writing his history.[18] For Murray, the contemporary state of the museum is epitomized by a narrative of frustration he tells several times over in his preface. He goes to a city or town museum and asks for its handbook, only to be told that the proprietors "have lost all trace of [their] catalogue" (viii). Even the British Museum is not immune to this referential crisis: it "possesses far more works on museums in general than any other library . . . but it has not a complete collection of the works relating to itself" (viii–ix). The museum is a place where things have wandered away from their names and origins, a situation repeated in the physical disarray of the collections themselves, where "odds and ends," things "presented to the museum simply because they are old," "gifts by friends in foreign lands," "birds, beasts, eggs, and fossil" are "huddled together in cabinets" (265). Murray's vision of the disordered museum is itself practically a study in the poetics of adultery as the foreign, the decadent, and the bestial promiscuously jumble together into an intimate confusion.

In Murray's history, as in the work of more recent historians of the museum, such unstable matter is central to the museum's origins. Even Enlightenment collectors, Murray notes, were "too fond of monsters and other things strange and unusual," too fond of curiosities and objects that had undergone inexplicable, marvelous transformations (195). Murray dwells at length on the seventeenth-century taste for petrified objects (especially body parts), on the fascination with water that could supposedly turn to stone, on the fixation on the story of Lot's wife, turned to a pillar of salt as she looked back at the lascivious cities of Sodom and Gomorrah (194, 196). This prototype of the perpetually turning, adulterous and adulterated body lies at the center of Murray's history not so much because of any extraordinary historical influence she might bear, but because for him she embodies the problem of the museum as a collection of objects that must be held to a referential stability but which must also give up their properties and promiscuously mix with other minds and bodies.

For while the disorderly museum is anathema to a classificatory thinker like Murray, the properly structured museum is only barely more ontologically stable than the jumble it seems to replace. In Murray's account, museums are the exemplary cultural institution because their objects escape the vicissitudes of value and the ravages of time; museums are better than libraries because their "objects are not depreciated in value by being passed through the hands of casual visitors or made vehicles of disease, as often happens with books," which are mistreated by "so-called reader[s] with foul clothes and filthy hands" (280). Yet museums must also be "open to all alike," providing "recreation and instruction for all classes"; "familiarity with [the museum's] models insensibly cultivates the taste and trains the eye" of the visitor (259, 270). Murray's conception of the museum is structured around the paradoxical goals of simultaneously containing and disseminating culture, but as the modifier "insensibly" here implicitly acknowledges, he has difficulty explaining how to do both at the same time. Unlike many other commentators discussed earlier in this study, Murray does not even move to a construction of looking as touching here as the structure of the museum cuts off the affiliations between the visual and the tactile, which much of nineteenth-century thought had woven together.[19]

But if Murray leaves a hole where his account of perception should appear, other museum theorists explained the acquisition of culture through metaphors of the porous, even the promiscuous, body. In *Museum Ideals*, Benjamin Ives Gilman, the secretary of the Museum of Fine Arts in Boston, wrote that "our enjoyment of a picture or a statue grows by contagion from that of a companion"; "any fruitful interest in fine art demands repeated contact with it."[20] Gilman's metaphors here are

those of bodily contact, of bodies giving off on each other, of persons min-
gling with art and bearing fruit, or at least "fruitful interest." His
metaphors are, in other words, the figures of *The Sacred Fount* (1901), the
novel in which James so exaggerates his metaphor of the turning, transforming body that bodies become almost too fluid to lend themselves to
convincingly realistic representation, exaggerates his metaphor of the body
that gives off so that lovers drain each other of vital fluids, and exaggerates
his metaphor of the prostheticized body so that at times all we see of a
character is a foot. All of these exaggerations yield a materialism without
reference, an instability of matter that James conveys most often in this
novel through the metaphor of the museum, which itself tends to spread
promiscuously throughout the text.

Of all James's fictions, *The Sacred Fount* may be the most difficult to
materialize, the most resistant to the kinds of reading I have pursued in this
book. It is also strangely and frankly dependent on the body it nearly fails
to make a place for. Because this novel is so heavily invested in thinking, it
would seem the body disappears; as Sharon Cameron observes, *The Sacred
Fount*'s "subject is the narrator's collusion with the thinking of *other* characters about still other characters—his attempt to make those to whom he
confides his thoughts think as he does."[21] Cameron's is the most logically
rigorous rendition of the traditional approach to this novel; it is always
taken as a comic meditation (sometimes also as a profound one) on interpretation, on the endlessness of what the hypothesizing intellect can do, or
on the dangers of adopting too radically the observer's role.[22] It is never
taken as a meditation on the body because its epistemological concerns
seem wholly to have displaced ontological ones.

And yet this novel materializes thinking in such a radical way, renders
so substantial the metaphors for cognition, that it calls for the materialist
reading it seems just as radically to efface. "The sacred fount," a figure in
the text for vitality and intellect, perpetually hovers on the brink of physiological specificity; as I suggested earlier, it only makes sense if we imagine it as a vampiric or sexual union. Hence James embodies the "Fountains
of Knowledge" with which Locke in the *Essay* characterizes the source of
our ideas (104). Similarly, the novel's fascination with intelligence as something that can flow makes literal William James's metaphor of the stream
of consciousness. It is as if in *The Sacred Fount* James set himself the goal
of rereading the epistemological tradition as if it were a materialist one.
Alternatively, it is as if he set for himself the experiment of testing his poetics of the appurtenanced body: in a novel that seems to establish a world
of pure thought, set in a place only dimly adumbrated and centered on acts
that seem totally intellectual, how might the body and its objects reintro-
duce themselves, force their way back in?

In a way, the question is slightly misleading because it almost answers itself: the epistemological tradition is already a materialist one, figuring itself in metaphors of the ownership of rarities (like Locke's storehouse) and the rushing waters of thought. This is a tradition James wholly honors in *The Sacred Fount* and in the late fiction generally; it is also a tradition he wholly decenters. He honors it in moments where *The Sacred Fount*'s narrator conceives of his theories, his hypotheses about the sexual liaisons that have so depleted one half of each couple, as his property; he "guard[s] to the last grain of gold" his "precious sense of their loss, their disintegration and their doom" (189). Here the narrator imagines himself as a miser guarding his treasure; at other points he imagines himself as a collector who arranges perceptions in his mind as if they were the bric-à-brac that adorns a house, "a perfect palace of thought," or paintings on the walls of a private gallery or "exhibition" (214, 130). The two couples who are the objects of his scrutiny become for him like "bronze groups" that accessorize either of the "two ends of a chimney-piece" (130).

With these figures, James falls in line with the tradition of construing things one knows as like precious things one owns; indeed, he very nearly literalizes that metaphor by making it one of the more finely tuned, carefully detailed elements in his text. (This is true of *The Golden Bowl*'s pagoda, as well.) But James embraces this metaphor only to decenter it: these objects the narrator collects have a material concreteness without any firm referential hold on something in the world, something known for which they serve as symbols. Indeed, for several reasons, it is hard to say what the narrator's bronze groups and horde of gold *are*. While they should be purely metaphorical, they don't stay firmly placed in the realm of the figurative because the narrator seems a Jamesian type who really does collect such things; it is hard to read his narrative without assimilating him to the category of sterile Jamesian dilettantes like Osmond in *The Portrait of a Lady* or Sanguinetti in "Rose-Agathe," who displace the emotional life onto the material one. Yet this is one of those treacherous "translations into late James" that Ruth Bernard Yeazell warns of, one of those moments in which we almost unavoidably, but also quite wrong-headedly, fill in the blank spaces of the late fictions with our knowledge of what the earlier fictions typically do in such vacancies.[23] For unlike earlier manifestations of this character-type, there is practically nothing to know the narrator by; his name, age, physical appearance, and family are all wholly absent. The "things" he "collects" have more ontological security than the narrator does—the bronze groups and the gold serve the same function as the objects that make Mrs. Gereth distinct in *The Spoils of Poynton*, for instance—but here, that security is a false one.

These objects of property convey a thick sense of materiality without stable reference in another way because the perceptions they stand for may be false; the gold may be fool's gold, in other words. *The Sacred Fount* ends with Mrs. Brissenden thoroughly routing the narrator's theories, leaving his hypotheses a "heap of disfigured fragments," or so it seems: the ending leaves the reader in a mild state of aporia over which lovers are feasting on each others' intellect and beauty and a stronger state of aporia over whether this vampiric feasting is an actual phenomenon at all (214). Hence the figures that serve to crystallize knowledge take on a stronger sense of reality than what they serve as figures for; James gives primacy to the metaphorical texture of the epistemological tradition and then cuts the strands that tie those metaphors to things outside themselves.

More precisely stated, the metaphors for knowledge in *The Sacred Fount* are both referentially unstable *and* too close in nature to the objects of that knowledge; they match the world outside them too closely and hardly match it at all. On the one hand, these emphatically material objects are in no certain relation to the world outside themselves because the knowledge they symbolize may be wholly spurious. On the other hand, these objects are so close in kind to the world of objets d'art that they symbolize knowledge of—to the bibelots, galleries, and sculpture gardens of the great country estate that is the novels' only setting—that they can hardly be symbols at all; they are so much a part of what they should symbolize that they cannot serve as abstractions, cannot make knowledge seem autonomous or distinct or self-sufficient. The bronze groups, the horde of gold, the interior gallery of paintings are all materially continuous with the world outside the narrator's mind at the same time they are referentially disconnected from that world.

James stages these continuities and disconnections most explicitly in a long scene set in the great estate's picture gallery. The narrator draws May Server into the gallery in order to watch her; he is convinced she has surrendered her intellect to some lover he cannot identify and he is bent on verifying his thesis. This particular gallery seems a very different place from the Crypt of the Soane Museum; it is ordered, light, and refined, not jumbled and dark. But it spatializes the promiscuous mixing of properties anyway, as its "high frescoed ceiling arch[es] over a floor so highly polished that it seem[s] to reflect the faded pastels set, in rococo borders, in the walls" (47). Everything here is in a state of reflection as material things exchange their properties in a setting that will, like the Crypt, serve as the scene of adulterous unions (albeit of more indeterminate couplings than in *A London Life*) and that in its own way will, also like the Crypt, make unclear whether "that is a person or a thing."

As May enters the gallery, she becomes absorbed in its frescoed ceiling, and the narrator becomes absorbed in watching her absorption:

> Mrs. Server, with her eyes raised to the painted dome, with response
> charmed almost to solemnity in her exquisite face, struck me at this
> moment, I had to concede, as more than ever a person to have a lover
> imputed. The place, save for its pictures of later date, a triumph of
> the florid decoration of two centuries ago, evidently met her special
> taste, and a kind of profane piety had dropped on her, drizzling
> down, in the cold light, in silver, in crystal, in faint, mixed delicacies
> of colour, almost as on a pilgrim at a shrine. I don't know what it was
> in her—save, that is, the positive pitch of delicacy in her beauty—
> that made her, so impressed and presented, indescribably touching.
> She was like an awestruck child; she might have been herself—all
> Greuze tints, all pale pinks and blues and pearly whites and candid
> eyes—an old dead pastel under glass. (48)

May is here a likely adulteress because, this passage opens by saying, she is
susceptible to mixing, aesthetically permeable. The "piety" she feels is a
"profane" one, and the sexual flow of the novel's title here becomes the
flow of paint which has regained its liquid quality and dropped down on
May, transforming her into a painted lady. She is both revitalized by the
painting because it touches up her "pale pinks and blues" and petrified by
it as she becomes "an old dead pastel under glass." She is, then, both a
crystallized figure, durable enough to figure as an object in a collection,
yet perpetually in a state of flowing transformation.

The novel's interests in adulterous and material exchanges become
indistinguishable here as the narrator's supposition that lovers have
"rubbed off on each other" becomes a description of the relation between
persons and things, as well (26). The gallery in this scene is a museum of
equivocal figures, just as the narrator assembles his little "gallery—the
small collection . . . the museum of those who put to me with such intensity the question of what had happened" to change them so (29). These
two museums—one presumably inside the mind and one presumably outside it—themselves mix and swap attributes even though their status as
representations of each other is wholly undecidable: it is not clear how one
would determine whether the figures the narrator mentally collects are
reliable reflections of the characters he sees in the gallery. The collection,
the storehouse, the image of achieved knowledge is literalized and redoubled in this scene; the metaphorical texture of the figure for cognitive
acquisitions is thus exaggerated, even as its material properties keep undoing the possibility that the figure does, in fact, signal the attainment of
some reliable knowledge.

The central painting in this gallery scene continues this development
of a destabilizing materialism and embodied equivocation because it por-

trays a man with a mask but renders it undecidable which is the mask and which the real face. The figure's own face is "pale, lean, livid," and "whitened"; he holds in his hand

> an object that strikes the spectator at first simply as some obscure, some ambiguous work of art, but that on a second view becomes a representation of a human face, modelled and coloured, in wax, in enamelled metal, in some substance not human. The object thus appears a complete mask, such as might have been fantastically fitted and worn. (50–51)

Of all James's turning figures surveyed in this book, this is one of the most unstable. Its instabilities, furthermore, serve as an icon for culture as *The Sacred Fount* conceives it, and as an icon for adultery. The dead face the figure wears is an image for the depleted half of each couple; the lively mask (if it is lively) serves as an image for the other half that has absorbed its lover's vitality. Yet as the narrator and the other characters stare at the painting, their visions differ radically; the painting has the quality of an optical illusion susceptible of two readings that exclude each other. Thus May Server can only see the mask as an "awful grimace," while the narrator sees it as "blooming and beautiful" (51). The narrator therefore entitles the painting The Mask of Life, while May calls it The Mask of Death. Like the wavering figures studied in the first and second chapters of this book, vitality itself is potentially lodged in an accessory, the "ambiguous work of art" that turns out to be a mask. The portrait here is itself an image of an economy between body and object, one that will not sit still. That the mask looks like May Server and the real face like Guy Brissenden, another of the depleted lovers, emphasizes the way that this portrait is practically unframeable, is both itself in motion and forges ambiguous and so mobile connections to those who view it.

This painting in *The Sacred Fount* points to the most famous ekphrastic moment in the late fiction, Strether's encounter on the river with Chad and Madame de Vionnet, a scene in which a landscape by Émile Lambinet, glimpsed by Strether in a Boston gallery in his youth, comes startlingly and beautifully to life. Here I would like to turn to *The Ambassadors,* and to that scene in particular, to indicate more fully how the unstable ontology of adultery and its materialist slipping of reference become for James a cultural model, a way of grasping the unstable physicality of aesthetic experience. All along in this book, I have been seeking to explain the place James assigns the body and its objects by studying instances of what he sometimes calls "rubbing off on," as in *The Sacred Fount*'s description of lovers as people who've "rubbed off on each other" (26). In the texts studied in these chapters, these acts of abrasion, scoring, stroking, cutting, determining distinctions and grades, taking possession, or turning pages have always carried with them problems of containment. These texts have persistently located acculturation within a fluid interchange between the body and its objects, a fluidity they have often had to work very hard to oppose to more disorderly cultural realms, as in *The Spoils of Poynton*. At other moments, James has registered the pressure of objects as a deeply and disturbingly conservative cultural force, one that carries within itself the source of its own undoing, since the relation between person and thing always carries the potential to destabilize fixed identities; that is the way James figures the relation between bodies and objects in the country-house culture of *The Tragic Muse* and *A London Life*. Because James understands culture as so thoroughly a matter of mixed matter, made up of substances of different orders and generated by processes of endless reproduction, there is always the potential in his fictions for unpredictable combinations that cannot be held in place or attached to a stable referent.

This uncontainable instability is dramatized—even uneasily celebrated, if celebration can be uneasy—in those moments in the late fiction where James dissolves the fixity of material things and lets their properties liquefy. One of these moments comes in *The Ambassadors*, in one of the early Parisian scenes, where James reworks and undoes an aestheticist cliché:

> [Strether's] greatest uneasiness seemed to peep at him out of the imminent impression that almost any acceptance of Paris might give one's authority away. It hung before him this morning, the vast bright Babylon, like some huge iridescent object, a jewel brilliant and hard, in which parts were not to be discriminated nor differences comfortably marked. It twinkled and trembled and melted together, and what seemed all surface one moment seemed all depth the next. (21:89)

The passage almost frankly reworks Pater's mandate, in *The Renaissance*, to live a life of aesthetic entrancement: "To burn always with this hard, gem-like flame, to maintain this ecstasy, is success in life."[24] James reverses the order of Pater's trope here, since he makes the jewel the more literal component of the metaphor and the melting flame the more figurative half, whereas Pater did just the opposite. Thrown in reverse, the metaphor exaggerates the protean nature of the self that was a hallmark of Pater's thought: the image in James's hands becomes almost counterintuitive, since jewels have a proverbial hardness that precludes melting. This loosening of properties from their objects happens in this passage under the sign of adultery: Babylon is a stock image of the sensual and licentious, "the whore of Babylon" a catch phrase lurking behind this passage that thus faintly associates the fluidity of the scene with the kind of flexible woman we have encountered so often in James's texts.

In the scene on the river, much later in the novel, Strether spends the day wandering around the landscape, which he experiences as if it were the Lambinet he did not buy years ago in the gallery in Tremont Street in Boston. The scene is one of "mixture" and of "liberties": the remembered landscape mixes with the actual one, and this happens as Strether gives himself up to a randomly chosen destination and to a sort of vacation from the strain of his role as go-between and confidant (22:246, 248). Like the passage that imagines Paris as a Babylonian jewel, this scene is headed toward the image of the flexible female figure, a figure who will become real when Chad and Madame de Vionnet appear as the collation of brush strokes that complete the painting. But even before that moment, the scene is a licentious one because the setting's material surfaces resist fixity. This is so first of all because of the ambiguities of landscape itself. In his aesthetic treatise *The Sense of Beauty* (1896), George Santayana writes that "the natural landscape is an indeterminate object; it almost always contains enough diversity to allow the eye a great liberty in selecting, emphasizing, and grouping its elements." The natural landscape, Santayana concludes, is "promiscuous."[25] This kind of promiscuity appears in *The Ambassadors* in Strether's sense that the relations between these elements that make up this stretch of countryside are wholly ambiguous: the river is "flowing behind or before" the village; "one couldn't say which" (22:252). While the scene seems to Strether as if contained by the "oblong gilt frame" that had contained Lambinet's painting, this frame is one that "draw[s] itself out for him," that stretches in order to match itself to wandering perceptions. Landscape is understood here as a setting that oscillates and wavers, a wavering that both Santayana and James capture in the language of adultery.

In its relation between the painting and the real thing, the episode destabilizes material surfaces in another way as well. Strether refers what he sees to the painting he did not buy, the painting he has lost sight of. Hence he sees this scene in terms dictated by a material referent that is missing. Further, the scene oscillates in Strether's vision between the view of the French countryside before him and the view of that countryside as glimpsed in the Boston gallery: "it was Tremont Street, it was France, it was Lambinet." As he circulates around this patch of countryside, Strether feels the presence of the gallery's maroon-colored walls, which had displayed Lambinet's patch of "special-green vision" (22:246–47). Strether sees the scene before him in terms of the gallery, in terms of a place that traffics in cultural objects, that exists for the purpose of exchanging aesthetic properties.

The indeterminacy of landscape and the spectral presence of the gallery should prepare us for the famous moment which unfolds next, the appearance of Chad and Madame de Vionnet, lovers who, Strether realizes before he recognizes them, are "expert, familiar, frequent," who know "how to do it" (22:256). These figures are figured as "figures," as elements that "had been wanted in the picture." Their physicality therefore hovers between a frank sense of embodiment and a sense that they are not all that real but more like the bodies in painting. These bodies are substantial ambiguities, figures both in the sense of trope and in the sense of the shape of real flesh, graphic both in the sense of representation and in the sense of an emphatic physicality that promises to obviate the need for representation's mediating work. As the presence of the gallery, the painting, and the transformative powers of the Parisian setting suggest, James conceives of culture in terms of turning bodies like these, bodies that lead Strether, and James himself, to imagine "innumerable and wonderful things" (22:266).

PART III
The Matter of Literary Criticism

CHAPTER SEVEN

LITERARY STUDIES AS SUBLIMATED PHYSICALITY

The previous chapters have offered a redefinition of Jamesian ambiguity as a matter of the body, its habitat, and its objects; in doing so, these chapters have frequently mixed their idiom and their practice, sliding between vocabularies and methods that emphasize trope and rhetoric and those that emphasize embodiment as they make claims for identifying historically specific formations. On the one hand, these chapters have tried to physicalize James's meanings and imagery, for example, replacing the materially amorphous concept of point of view with a shell of material things that defines consciousness; on the other hand, these chapters have repeatedly made use of a terminology of figure, of missed reference, and of linguistic indeterminacy. In other words, the turning body has brought with it a methodological ambiguity, a slippage between the methods associated with turns of phrase and those associated with the embodiment of meaning—methods associated with deconstruction and those associated with the history and politics of the body.

Rather than defending my own eclecticism (or the catachrestic diction of contemporary literary studies in general), in this chapter I would like to explore the relation between the two large movements in literary studies upon which I have drawn; I want especially to reveal what they share, and what the convergence of their terms means. As we will see, transformations of the body—the body's shifting shapes, the interplay between personal identity and the concrete objects that nestle against it, and the architectural spaces that supply it with a habitat and a definition—are crucial and definitive (they define discourses that might otherwise seem to compete with each other) for both deconstruction and materialism. This convergence is not accidental; rather, it suggests that there is a material model powerfully at work at the centers of both deconstruction and materialism, a model that is given its definitive shape in the late-nineteenth-century aesthetics of daily life that I have been describing. The argument here will be that we imagine and organize literary meaning and literary language by means of conceptual structures, models derived from historically specific complexes of objects in the physical world. In other words, I will be trying to identify "the material unconscious" of much criticism produced in North America in the last 30 years or so—to use the term by which Bill Brown designates "literature's repository of disparate and fragmentary, unevenly developed, even contradictory images of the material everyday."[1] In the course of critiquing the emptiness of the concept of "the materiality of the signifier," a stock phrase by which a great deal of theory laid claim to deal with the realm of physical things, John Guillory argues that the criticism that endlessly employed that term "produced no supporting analysis of the concept of materiality itself."[2] What Guillory is pointing out can be taken as the presence of an unnamed, unanalyzed concept of materiality at the heart of literary studies; some of the features of that concept are what I want to identify here. The purpose here, then, is to outline the *habitus* that much literary criticism inhabits, the "structuring structure, which organizes practices and the perception of practices," as Pierre Bourdieu has named it.[3] To give my claims focus, I will emphasize the work of Elaine Scarry and Paul de Man.

The choice of de Man is problematic, perhaps at this date unwarranted—or even "bizarre," as one reader of an early version of these pages put it. It is especially problematic because I regard de Man's work neither as a historical artifact nor as a still-viable critical resource, but uneasily as both. De Man has emerged as the bad conscience within the recesses of the discipline's psyche; he is the figure whose career, after the discovery of the anti-Semitic journalism written during World War II, presents us with the anxiety that methods of interpretation have no ethical grounding; more specifically, his example presents us with the worry that the philosophically informed, rigorous close reading so valorized in the discipline in the era before cultural studies can proceed with a perfect unawareness of its own political assumptions, implications, even its own moral grounding. For the scandal of de Man is neither that the mature work is clearly continuous with the very early fascist writings, nor that the mature work privately critiques those early writings, but instead that it is impossible to know which is the case.

As Catherine Gallagher put it, in an essay written shortly after the discovery of the wartime journalism became public knowledge, "We have not yet learned what it is we have to learn from the example of de Man."[4] But de Man functions as a bad conscience—a part of the past one does not want to examine—for another reason as well, at least for those scholars who worry, whether openly or privately, that the various abilities and approaches that characterize his work are in danger of being lost, and that the books have been prematurely closed on deconstruction and even on theory. As Avital Ronell has recently written, "his ghost took something down with it," something like "an unprecedented insistence on rigor."[5] Perhaps, then, de Man's example is still influential enough that it needs to be read while also having receded enough that we can gain some purchase on it. In any event, my goal here is to identify a conception of literary meaning in de Man that has received no attention in the voluminous commentary on his work, a conception that is also at work in a more recent and enormously influential account of language and the body. I will be emphasizing the material models by which de Man and Scarry structure their work and focus their analyses; I will be looking at the concrete things that give the conceptual its shape. As in the previous chapters, my emphasis will be on the turning body, the array of objects that surround that body, and the house that contains and blends into all of them.

In a sense, de Man and Scarry put opposite emphases on a phenomenon that they conceptualize very similarly. Both see the matter of reference as what is at stake in the twists and transformations the body can be made to undergo. For de Man, the turning body is a textual moment where language confesses its hugely figurative nature; the turning body and its accessories become the locus of "referential aberration," places where the undecidability between language as rhetorical trope and language as signification distills itself in its most dramatic form.[6] Hence in "Semiology and Rhetoric," it is the inseparability of the body and the body's motions—the dancer and the dance—that epitomizes the intertwined and mutually incompatible rhetorical and semiological sides of a text (11). In "Aesthetic Formalization in Kleist," it is the fencer who exemplifies the ways in which language "always refers but never to the right referent," and the *Marionettentheater,* with its puppets turning on their lines, that exemplifies the formalized nature of textuality and the accompanying loss of reference.[7] In the famous reading of Rousseau's *Confessions,* the purloined ribbon is the epitome of a "free signifier" (*Allegories* 289). In these examples, language's potential for endless signification is identified with the body and its appurtenances. De Man's late essays assemble a kind of catalog, a collection of things that turn or spin or fold over; they collate a set of objects oddly similar to the Jamesian ones I have been describing and find in those objects properties that advance an argument of referential skepticism.

The body in Elaine Scarry's *The Body in Pain* has a far more stubborn, far denser materiality than the de Manian body seems to have; far from being a figure that reveals the undecidability of linguistic propositions, it is a substance that makes reference stick. In Scarry's account of wounding and warfare, the incontestable reality of the wounded body "anchors" the disputed issue that led to that wounding; abstract ideas and rhetorical structures become real and convincing when they are tied to bodies that have been damaged or destroyed, when they can be seen as reflected in a horrific view of a battlefield strewn with corpses, for instance.[8] But what is important to note here is that the wounded body itself is "nonreferential"; whatever reference it held to the culture that shaped and identified it has been undone by injury, and it will take on a new referential function only when it is tied to the outcome of a war, when its materiality is linked with an idea, a piece of language, a political position (119). The process of "making" works in precisely opposite fashion because it relieves persons of pain, makes of them something more than the burden of their embodiment, unlike wounding, which reduces persons to nothing but their corporeality. What it means to have a body is only knowable if it is externalized, projected into the made things around it that mime its structure, like a chair that mimes the backbone, the legs, the distribution of bodily weight (290–91). As poems and paintings do more overtly, ordinary things carry with them, on Scarry's account, a representation of the body; as William James says in a passage I quoted earlier, Scarry would say that the body is never known by itself, but always through the mediation of some other object (*PP*, 286).

In this entirely superficial survey, I have tried to emphasize a material grain in the rhetorical critic and to emphasize the referential and hence linguistic argument of the materialist one. This doubling of materialist and rhetorical techniques becomes even more pronounced when de Man and Scarry take up the same image. Early in *The Body in Pain,* Scarry analyzes the room, "the simplest form of shelter," as simultaneously an "enlargement of the body" and a "miniaturization of the world, of civilization" (38–39). The room's material attributes replicate yet "stand apart from and free of" the body's structure and functions. Walls, for example, mimic the body's potential to protect the self and so they externalize the need to keep something internal and private; at the same time, windows let in some of the outer world and so lead the room's inhabitant to internalize something exterior to herself. Although she does not say so, Scarry perceives the room as a lyric structure, endowing it with the hermetic permeability of a small poem in which a speaker simultaneously turns away from and speaks to—closes off from and opens up to—a social world.[9]

When de Man takes up the image of Marcel's room in Proust's *Du côté de chez Swann,* he takes up a passage that accords perfectly with the way Scarry would later conceive of the fluctuating privacy of the room: for Marcel, the room's "almost closed blinds" that admit just "a glimmer of daylight" permit him to grasp "the total spectacle of the summer" in a way he could not if he were taking a walk outside.[10] This passage is specifically about language—Marcel has retreated to his room to read—and its odd claim that one can comprehend a totality in a "glimmer," whereas immersing oneself in that totality means experiencing it "by fragments," becomes in de Man's reading a master-image for his account of figurative language as he goes over the passage not once but twice in *Allegories of Reading* (14). For de Man, the passage asserts the superiority of metaphor over metonymy but advances that claim by means of the metonymic structure it disavows. It hears in the sound of buzzing flies what Marcel calls a "necessary link" to the summer day, and so claims a metaphorical identity between them (A is B), yet it goes on to define that identity in images that depend for their sense not on identity, but on the adjacency of metonym, contingent associations like the "running brook" which, at the end of the passage, relays the cool darkness of the room and which depends not on a necessary connection, but on mere adjacency (13, 66). The room becomes for de Man a physicalization of how literary language undoes itself; it becomes the concrete image of deconstruction and the undecidabilities that are that method's indispensable foci.

The point I want to draw from this structure in de Man and its resemblance to Scarry's materialism is fairly simple. A material structure that might seem to stabilize historical criticism turns out to be a master image of cultural and rhetorical ambiguity, turns out to keep on turning inside into outside, keeps turning into each other a stubborn sense of the concrete and a slippery sense of rhetorical play. Turning to theory, we find it repeating at a higher level of abstraction the oscillations I have been describing in the first sections of this book: Scarry's and de Man's analyses of the room find it a space halfway between the actual and the imaginary (like Hawthorne's parlor in "The Custom-House"), halfway between outer and inner, halfway between a figure that epitomizes material shelter and a figure that epitomizes a linguistic activity like reading.

I want to argue that James and his culture understand this oscillation as itself a material process: the relation between rhetorical and bodily figure is in James's texts and milieu a matter of ceaseless "embellish[ment]" and "disfigur[ation]" (to adapt terms I quoted earlier from the preface to *Daisy Miller*), a matter of matter rubbing off on bodies, of artifact lending its material properties to the persons who handle or violate or merely look at it (*LC* 2:1277). Scarry and de Man present their rooms as endlessly generalizable images, transhistorical models for how culture and literature work; each theorist is completely frank about this claim, de Man writing that "there is absolutely no reason why analyses of the kind here suggested for Proust would not be applicable, with proper modifications of technique, to Milton or to Dante" (16–17), and Scarry generalizing her model of the room into a structure of the city and then to the process of "civilization" itself (39). But behind these images of the room hovers one more room that de Man and Scarry never mention but that nevertheless guides their interpretations; for this conception of domestic space as one that is simultaneously physical and "half-spiritualised," that seems "actually to . . . become a part of the texture of [the] mind," epitomizes late-nineteenth-century aestheticism, as the phrases I have just quoted from Walter Pater's "The Child in the House" suggest.[11] For Pater, the relation between the room and its inhabitant is one in which "inward and outward being" are "woven through and through each other into one inextricable texture— half, tint and trace and accident of homely colour and form, from the wood and the bricks; half, mere soul-stuff, floated thither from who knows how far."[12] This "inextricable texture" melds inner and outer, weaves together body and appurtenance so tightly the seams barely show.

My point in bringing forward this image from Pater, and in noting its similarities to the spatial images of Scarry and de Man, is to suggest that these critics partake of and come at the end of a historical movement toward the non-anxious identification of bodies and objects. The material relationships that are formed and re-formed in the rooms of Hawthorne and William and Henry James and Pater yield, in both the deconstructive and the materialist critic, an aesthetic that presents itself as endlessly generalizable and so detaches itself from the history of production and reproduction to which James himself is far more alert. In other words, both de Man and Scarry present as a philosophical argument something that, I have been indicating, is a historical formation. That history of bodies and things—a contingent, variable, microeconomic reshaping of matter— becomes in the work of these critics a conceptual, abstract way of organizing literary meaning. This abstraction is what makes their work powerful; it is also one that in Scarry is a source of some tension or conflictedness, while in de Man it becomes a formation that occludes his method's material foundations.

For while in *The Body in Pain*, Scarry developed a philosophy of making easily transported across different economies and different material worlds, ones separated by centuries, in the long essay "Work and the Body in Hardy and Other Nineteenth-Century Novelists," published the same year she examined that aesthetic within and showed it arising out of a late-nineteenth-century economy and a late-nineteenth-century cultural poetics. Much more specifically, as Scarry reads Hardy, Dickens, Zola, and George Eliot, it is those novelists' concrete micronarratives that generate what at the end of the essay she will frame as the diaphanous image of beauty, the epitome of the aesthetic image. The "many small moments" of material precision in nineteenth-century realism—the genre's ability to take in a touch of fresh paint that gives off on passers-by as they enter through a gate, or the intimate contact between an orchard-keeper's hands and the branches of his trees as the keeper prunes the branches and the branches scratch his hands—are what underwrite the much larger claims of *The Body in Pain*.[13] As Scarry puts it with characteristic recursiveness, the "human creature" is "forever rubbing up against and leaving traces of itself . . . on the world, as the world is forever rubbing up against and leaving traces of itself . . . on the human creature" (50).

Human creature/world/world/human creature: this chiasmus forms the very center of Scarry's aesthetic, as the reversal of *The Body in Pain*'s subtitle—*The Making and Unmaking of the World*—suggests. What the Hardy essay makes clear about this theoretical model is that it transforms into a general aesthetic a nineteenth-century philosophy of the body; alternatively, it translates and condenses into a rhetorical trope the ways in which in the nineteenth century real physical conditions were coded. This is true first of all because the trace is crucial to Scarry's thought: in focusing so microscopically and so insistently on Dickens's dirt or Hardy's smudges of paint or, in *The Body in Pain*, on Marx's conception of the commodity as "the materialized objectification of bodily labor" (247), Scarry imports into contemporary aesthetics a nineteenth-century conviction that events leave behind a material fragment as evidence that they have occurred, that actions leave residues, that nothing is ever lost.[14] It is true second of all because the hand and the sense of touch are crucial and privileged for Scarry's attempts to embody meaning. In *The Body in Pain*, Scarry explicitly follows Engels in his emphasis on the hand as "the direct agent of making" (253). But the Hardy essay reveals a less-obvious assumption that sustains the aesthetics at work in both texts: all the senses are reconceived according to the model of touch and reaching-out ("seeing" and "hearing" are "forms of reach," Scarry writes [74]). Hence the bodily experience and the acts of making that Scarry generalizes so broadly in her book take as their norm a tactile model, one that conceives of the body as interacting with a world that is very close to it, a world in which objects are handcrafted and in which things that are seen and heard are within the body's grasp; the large model at work here cannot readily assimilate the society of the spectacle, for example, or a culture in which much of the work is done by pushing buttons.[15] Accompanying this emphasis on the sense of touch is a third continuity between Scarry's work and nineteenth-century thought about the body—a conception arising out of Marx, but given greater specificity by sensation psychology—of the tool as a prosthesis, an extension of the physical senses. Citing the psychologist James Gibson's *The Senses Considered as Perceptual Systems*, Scarry writes in both the Hardy essay and in *The Body in Pain* of the fact that "a person can literally 'feel' at the end of a walking stick the grass and stones that are three feet away from his hand, just as a person holding the handle of a scissors actually feels the 'cutting action' of the blades a few inches away."[16] This knitting-together of human physiology with external implement is the continuity that Mark Seltzer has named "the body-machine complex"; it is a habit of thought that typifies both nineteenth-century realism's way of treating the world of objects, tools, and appurtenances and nineteenth-century psychology's focus on the sensorium.[17] As has been noticed in chapter 2, in the *Principles of Psychology* William James makes exactly the same observation as Gibson does about the walking-stick effect and other tools, such as a pencil or a knife, writing that sensations "migrate from their *original locality*" into the implements that link—and blur the difference between—the perceiving body and the perceived world (685). Hence when in *The Body in Pain* Scarry writes of the "reach of sentience, and the unity of sentience with the things it reaches," she transforms into a trope the metamorphic and mixed quality of the nineteenth-century body, the body whose edges blur into a material margin that surrounds them, one from which they cannot be easily distinguished (249).

A fourth way in which Scarry's chiastic figuring of the body and its habitat abstracts into a rhetorical pattern a nineteenth-century cultural poetics is more general and more all-encompassing: it lies in Scarry's focus on the body itself, her reduplication of the "intense somatic bias" of nineteenth-century thought (as Cynthia Eagle Russett has called it), her assumption that bodily shape and cultural change will be interrelated and that the latter will always somehow involve the former.[18] As Scarry concludes in the penultimate paragraph of the Hardy essay, "all human acts take place through and out of [the] body," a claim that may be true but that places no limits on the body as an explanatory device (82). In *The Body in Pain,* this body is almost breathtakingly generalized into a hermeneutically all-purpose body. One moment where this abstraction of the historically specific into a generally applicable and hence philosophical language becomes most apparent is when Scarry quite frankly detaches Marx's thought from its thorough critique of the inequities of nineteenth-century capitalism—Marx is too "often narrowly perceived in his capacity as critic of western economic structures," Scarry writes—and instead views his work as a widely valid theory of the nature of things, "our major philosoph[y] on the nature of material objects" (179). In this moment (and admittedly it is an unusually broad one, for there are other passages where Scarry does *not* suspend Marx's involvement with the specificities of factory labor and the workings of capital), Scarry simultaneously crosses out nineteenth-century contexts and adopts one of the nineteenth-century's precepts, the one that makes the body the explanation for everything or, more specifically, the one that holds that all compelling explanations must involve and appeal to the materiality of the body.

To grasp this move is to understand how the philosophical abstraction of the body is itself a product of specific historical processes; it is to understand that innumerable material processes underlie and keep current and shade the usage of a term that can seem to stand apart from history. In the *Grundrisse*, in a passage that Scarry does not consider, Marx theorizes abstraction in ways that can be used to analyze the logic and even the historical significance of her project. The passage is a powerful one because in it Marx seeks to historicize not any particular economic manifestation but the concepts of political economy itself. Alternately put, he seeks to reveal as particular manifestations of economic history the abstractions that govern his own discipline. Taking labor as his example, Marx argues that this abstraction, so basic to the thought processes of political economy, only appears in its most general form when the types of labor have arrived at the multiplicity of the kinds of work found in his own time: "As a rule, the most general abstractions arise only in the midst of the richest possible concrete development, where one thing appears as common to many, to all."[19] Crucial to Marx's explanation of how abstractions emerge is the teemingness, the variegated and specialized nature of nineteenth-century life, of "bourgeois society," which is "the most developed and the most complex historic organization of production"; labor becomes thinkable as a general concept when "individuals can with ease transfer from one labour to another" and "the specific kind is a matter of chance for them."[20] The abstract concepts of political economy thus reflect a culture of material flux, concrete change, and social randomness.

Applying Marx's precept to the matter at hand, we can say that the body in the nineteenth century becomes thinkable in abstract ways through the incessant material changes it undergoes and the stylistic variations it takes on. The freestanding body, susceptible to the generalizations of theoretical claims, is generated by contingency; Charlotte's scarf in *The Europeans,* Rose-Agathe's earrings and coiffures, Madame Merle's clothes, Mrs. Gereth's treasures, Mrs. Churchley's enormous red-feathered fan in "The Marriages," and Maria Gostrey's red ribbon in *The Ambassadors* all produce the body as a concept. These specific processes of adornment and personal stylization—specific in terms of their class, fairly specific in terms of gender, and materially specific in the kinds of things at work—are what Scarry renames "the body." In other words, when Scarry conceives of objects as "fragments of self-extension," when she posits the "artifact's inherent freedom of reference," when she speculates that "freestanding artifact[s] close to the body" are where invention begins, she generalizes on the fungible, pliable, mobile materials that nineteenth-century bourgeois culture first saturated with significance (196, 317, 321). Indeed, those objects' multiplicity and mobility are what made generalization possible in the first place. Rhetoric in this instance lifts the body out of history and transforms it into a philosophical entity: Scarry's chiasmus becomes a widely portable trope derived from the specific material conditions, and ways of thinking about those conditions, that it nonetheless leaves behind.[21]

I want to identify these conditions and their effects more precisely by turning back to de Man; I want to consider de Man in more detail because I wish to show that specific material models can shape critical practices that have no overt or announced interest in the material world. In a way, the point here is simpler than those made about Scarry, since de Man's project is far less multilayered; in large part, the power his writings once had came from his relentless focus on the figures of rhetoric. In a way, the point is more challenging, however, since it must ferret out the traces of bodily and material styles that in de Man's writings often (but not always) verge on disappearing. I will seek to show, however, that the air of philosophical abstraction in de Man turns out to be an allegation that renders nearly invisible his adherence—even his devotion—to a fairly specific material model. More particularly, the ambiguity of literary language is only conceivable for de Man in the material terms of the body, its accessories, and its domicile—only conceivable, that is, according to the contours of a material model specific to a certain (admittedly large) historical formation (the privatization of experience and the growth of commodity culture), a historical particularity de Man often takes pains to deny, as in the essay on lyric in *Blindness and Insight*.[22]

Indeed, the turn to problems of language in de Man's later work brings with it a turn to the body. In de Man's later work, the turn to rhetoric means that "we are no longer within a thematic context dominated by selfhood but in a figural representation of a structure of tropes" (*Allegories*, 186). The discursive centrality of the self, its (failed) function as a psychological principle of unity, is replaced by an economy, one that de Man identifies—and cannot imagine except by means of—the body, its extensions, its appendages, its shell. When de Man writes in the early 1960s of Montaigne, the issue is rather insistently or even obsessively one of "subjectivity"; when he writes of Montaigne in one of the late essays on Kant and materialism, the associations are with that strand of the essayist that imagines the body as severed parts, as "limbs, hands, toes, breasts, or what Montaigne so cheerfully referred to as 'Monsieur ma partie.'"[23] While it is probably true, as Terry Eagleton has observed, that "few critics have been more bleakly unenthused by bodiliness—by the whole prospect of a creative development of the sensuous, creaturely aspects of human existence" than de Man, it is also true that de Man *depends* on the body, its surrogates and doubles, its habitats and accessories, for making clear his most basic meanings.[24]

This dependence on and denial of physicality both emerge with extraordinary clarity in de Man's reading of Rousseau's *Pygmalion,* a reading that centers on—and attempts to cancel—the text's immoderate interest in the human body. On the one hand, material properties play a large role in the analysis: de Man quotes Rousseau's descriptions of the coldness of the marble and the trembling touches Pygmalion and Galathea exchange; he argues that "the intrinsic quality of the self is borrowed from the surface of its physical shape" when Pygmalion extols the beauty of Galathea's soul; indeed, he seems to move against any dematerialization of the signifier as he indicates that "the abstraction and the generality of a linguistic figure manifests itself necessarily in the most physical of modes" (*Allegories* 182). On the other hand, the materiality at work is explicitly denied: the coldness of the marble becomes a figure for the shock Pygmalion experiences at finding his own work of self-expression standing before him—"entirely alienated," as de Man puts it—and so neither exclusively himself nor exclusively other but bafflingly both. Indeed, de Man goes well out of his way to transform into a matter of rhetoric Rousseau's strongly sensory interests, to conceptualize the corporeality of this Pygmalion story: "this coldness [Pygmalion's emotional state] has nothing in common with the coldness of the original stone; Bachelard's thermodynamics of the material imagination would find nothing to feed on in *Pygmalion.* 'Hot' and 'cold' are not, in this text, derived from material properties but from a transference from the figural to the literal that stems from the ambivalent relationship between the work as an extension of the self and as a quasi-divine otherness" (178). Because he wants to maintain this reading of *Pygmalion* as a text in which "the deconstructive discourse of truth and falsehood . . . undoes selfhood . . . and replaces it by the knowledge of its figural and epistemologically unreliable structure" (187), de Man is forced to suppress Rousseau's climax: one would never know from *Allegories of Reading* that the moment when Pygmalion first feels Galathea's flesh coming alive is when he chisels away some of the draperies that hide the figure's breasts. This final touch needs to be suppressed because it would reveal the materiality of the reciprocity that de Man treats as purely rhetorical: it would be hard, in other words, to ignore the extraordinary abstraction of de Man's formulations if this moment were brought into play, hard not to instill in the reader a sense that something—too much—was lost in this critical allegory, or that the allegory de Man reveals brings to the foreground matters his method is ill-equipped to elucidate.

Examining de Man's reading of *Pygmalion* reveals a material basis within his method, a source of illustrations and examples without which that method's results would make little sense. This examination has revealed, as well, two sources of anxiety for that method's dematerializing materialism, two points that threaten to make the physical world very hard to abstract away. One, epitomized by Galathea's breasts, is the female body. The other, which makes its presence felt in the dismissal of Gaston Bachelard, is the phenomenological strain of twentieth-century French criticism. Although it may seem that these two entities are wholly unrelated, I will argue that in de Man's thinking they are tightly intertwined, not only because they both exert a kind of materialist pressure on his method but also because when, in the mid 1960s, de Man edited and revised a translation of Flaubert's *Madame Bovary,* he encountered them together. Since this phase of his career was also the moment in which de Man developed the viselike method of rhetorical analysis that became his most influential style, it is plausible to suggest that this encounter was a transformative one.

More specifically, in *Madame Bovary* and in the critical commentary on that novel, de Man finds a repertoire of images by which he will go on to organize literary meaning, a material economy that he will turn into a matter of rhetoric. The physical particularity of nineteenth-century French realism serves as an occulted source for his later work: he never writes about Stendhal or Balzac, and never writes about Flaubert again after editing the Norton Critical Edition, published in 1965, that I will focus on. Similarly, de Man's production of this edition is totally absent from critical commentary on his career, even from the two important book-length studies, those by Christopher Norris and Rodolphe Gasché.[25] Hence in several different ways, or rather at several different levels, de Man's career epitomizes the privilege accorded to general hermeneutics and the detachment of idealist aesthetics from the arts of everyday life: even as a material culture gets renamed as theory, so too is a text like *Blindness and Insight* accorded a prominence denied to a critical edition.

Against these powerful sublimations of the material world, *Madame Bovary* can serve as a powerful weapon; it can desublimate the physicality of the abstract critical methods that it itself helped to shape. Flaubert's representations of desire and consumption entail a scrupulous attention to bodily gesture, to nervous mannerism, to the tiny acts of use; no physical motion is too small, and so the novel takes in Emma ecstatically "scratching the velvet of the [theatre] box with her nails" at the melodrama in Rouen, or pricking her finger on the wire of her wedding bouquet as she rediscovers it shortly after the dance at Vaubyessard, or admiring the way "young beaux" so unlike her own Charles lean "the tight-drawn palm of their yellow gloves on the golden knobs of their canes."[26] Such processes of friction seem indispensable to the production of meaning in *Madame Bovary* because they are crucial both to the novel's account of material life and to its account of psychological life; in fact, they link these two levels of the text so tightly that they appear to merge together. One of Flaubert's terms for this chafing action is *frottement*—"rubbing," "friction," and, more figuratively, "contact," "interaction"—as when, after dancing, Emma finds that the ballroom floor's wax has left a residue on her shoes even as the experience has left its imprint on her desires: ". . . ses souliers de satin, dont la semelle s'était jaunie à la cire glissante du parquet. Son cœur était comme eux: au frottement de la richesse, il s'était placé dessus quelque chose qui ne s'effacerait pas" (". . . the satin shoes whose soles were yellowed with the slippery wax of the dancing floor. Her heart resembled them: in its contact with wealth, something had rubbed off on it that could not be removed," in de Man's translation).[27] Similarly, as Rodolphe contemplates his letter breaking off his affair with Emma, he looks at Emma's miniature as he recalls his memories of her, until memory and visual image somehow efface each other—"comme si la figure vivante et la figure peinte, se frottant l'une contre l'autre, se fussent réciproquement effacées" ("as if the living and painted face, rubbing one against the other, had erased each other").[28] Finally, a more abstract example comes when Emma grows tired of Léon and analyzes his faults; the narrator reflects that "le dénigrement de ceux que nous aimons toujours nous en détache quelque peu. Il ne faut pas toucher aux idoles: la dorure en reste aux mains" ("the picking apart of those we love always alienates us from them. One must not touch one's idols, a little of the gilt always comes off on one's fingers").[29]

As the progressive abstraction of these quotations suggests, a material process—one specific to the nineteenth-century body, as I have argued above—governs the text's sense of significance. The more figurative entities of Emma's "cœur," of Rodolphe's mental images, of an idealized Léon carry a materiality that, *Madame Bovary* insists, nothing can efface ("quelque chose qui ne s'effacerait pas," as the passage on the dancing shoes puts it). This strong sense of materiality is the focus for a strand of Flaubert criticism that begins with Charles du Bos in the 1920s and develops in the 1950s into a more sophisticated version with the work of two members of the Geneva School of phenomenological critics, Georges Poulet and Jean-Pierre Richard. While there are important differences among these critics and their accounts of *Madame Bovary,* three common characteristics need to be noted here. They all take the novel's material processes as images for how consciousness works in the physical world, treating the relation between subject and object as a *frottement,* a friction, a swapping of attributes, a "giving off on," as de Man sometimes translates it in Flaubert's text (the nearly oxymoronic English idiom of "off" plus "on" captures the sense of incessant, irresolvable quality of this back and forth movement fairly precisely).[30] Hence du Bos's early explanation of Flaubert's "genius for materiality" as the "power to identify himself with matter" becomes, in Poulet's account, "a deliberate confusion . . . between the subjective and the objective" "as if, by penetrating Emma's soul, the images of things had lost their objectivity and been transformed into feelings, or as if Emma, by becoming affected by material things, had become also somehow materi-al."[31] In Richard, this crisscross movement between subject and object is characterized as a blending of sensation and memory, a "*mélange*," a "*fusion*," as he calls it.[32]

Second, all these critics identify this material consciousness with the female figure. In Poulet's reading, Emma epitomizes Flaubert's own psychic disorientations by materializing her author's emotional vicissitudes; Flaubert's very conceptual-seeming vertiginous "whirl of ideas" becomes Emma's very physical-seeming fragmentation, dispersed as she is among the various objects of her desires.[33] In du Bos, this dispersal of male identity is associated—in ways du Bos does not quite rationalize—with both "a feminine scent" and with the "genius" for "materiality" du Bos so values in Flaubert.[34] In Richard, the reciprocity of matter and consciousness is figured as a process akin to touching—the one necessarily reciprocal physical sense—and specifically as the touch of a woman ("Woman attracts as if she were water, and water caresses like a woman," Richard writes as he characterizes a description of bathing in one of Flaubert's letters, a letter that becomes a point of orientation for the argument of Richard's *Littérature et Sensation*).[35] In ways that are neither directly acknowledged nor totally obscured, women give substance to the enterprise of phenomenological criticism; even when, as in du Bos, the substance at work is as amorphous as a scent, the female figure is a crucial physicalization for these critics, the figure that bestows definition upon the theme of consciousness, which might otherwise seem too amorphous to conceive clearly.

A third thing these three essays have in common is that they are all selected by de Man for the critical essays section of his edition of *Madame Bovary*. While an edition produced mainly for college courses might seem mere journeyman work, there are suggestions in the introduction that de Man thought of this book as something more than that: de Man writes that his "principle of . . . selection" for the essays has "very definitely been oriented towards problems of method that are important in the contemporary criticism of fiction" (xi). Inasmuch as the essays comment on each other and react to each others' claims, the selection "gives insight into the unified development of critical thought in the twentieth century" (xii).

Self-consciously producing a primer on literary criticism, then, de Man might also be seen here as constructing a lineage of his crucial predecessors, one that includes Saint-Beuve, Baudelaire, James (whose identification of "the real" in Flaubert with "the accessories" in the passage reprinted from *Notes on Novelists* merges the problem of bodily boundaries with the problem of literary significance as the phenomenologists would later do), Sartre, and Auerbach, as well as du Bos, Richard, and Poulet.[36] In commenting on these latter writers, de Man credits them with the ability to "recaptur[e] the creative consciousness of the writer," even as he suggests their limitations in their indifference to narrative structures (xii). But he is still quarreling with their legacy as late as the revised edition of *Blindness and Insight*, and still working through problems of materiality in what is virtually his last essay.[37] All of which suggests that de Man's deconstruction is in part produced by a phenomenological and materialist inheritance lost sight of in much commentary on that deconstruction itself, a sense of literary significance that cannot be fully abstracted from what de Man in his introduction to *Madame Bovary* calls the "material imagination" (xiii).

For if we turn to *Allegories of Reading,* we find that the fluctuations in meaning, which are what that book is really about, are conceived according to the material fluctuations in Flaubert, ones that de Man labored over as he revised Eleanor Marx Aveling's translation, ones that the phenomenologists had made their focal point. Indeed, these fluctuations—these rhetorical and grammatical ambiguities—are practically inconceivable apart from the physical objects and processes that, for Flaubert and many other nineteenth-century novelists, compose everyday life. This tight bond between meaning and a specific materiality is not so surprising in the chapter on Proust, where, as I argued above, linguistic structures and the architectural structure of the bourgeois home become in de Man's reading totally inextricable. It is more surprising—and so more revealing—to find the same material model at work in the chapter on Rilke, a writer whose work would seem far less invested in the physical matter of everyday life and whose favored genre of the lyric has so often seemed to preclude a strong concern with substance.[38] In de Man's reading, linguistic processes are described as physical ones; in reaching for specific and so sharable characterizations of the conceptual intricacies of language, de Man draws on a repertoire of metaphors that do their work almost unnoticeably in his text but that bespeak the presumption of a shared sense of the material world.

There are, first of all, some relatively unremarkable moments—but I am here trying to alienate somewhat our usual metaphors for what a text is— in which de Man draws on circulatory, knotted, and spatial figures in order to explain the workings of Rilke's lyrics. Poems' metaphors "do not connote objects, sensations, or qualities of objects"; instead, they "evoke" an "activity that circulates between" voice and poetic topic (*Alleegories* 29, 30). "There is . . . nothing in the poem that would entitle us to escape beyond its boundaries in search of evidence that would not be part of it" because the "interlacing" of theme and speaker "that constitutes the text" is "so tight that it leaves no room for any other system of relationships" (31). At some moments, the argument of Rilke's poems is carried by pure sound as each sound effect is "enclose[d]" into another, "as a larger box can enclose in its turn a smaller one" (31). In each of these instances, de Man explicitly cancels the material world and then reintroduces it as a characterization of language; purely rhetorical matters turn out to be a matter of small and private spaces, of worked and crafted (or corseted) ornament, of a transfer of properties between two things. If we are not explicitly in a world of Flaubertian *frottement* here, then we are in a material world nonetheless, one with some properties in keeping with Flaubert's very physicalized sense of how the literary text makes its meanings.

In the pivotal analysis of the chapter on Rilke, de Man's substitution of a general truth about language for a historically specific material formation emerges with even more clarity. The analysis—of "Am Rande der Nacht" ("At the borderline of the night")—is pivotal because it establishes the chiasmus as "the determining figure of Rilke's poetry," determining because it is "the crossing that reverses the attributes of words and of things" (38). As my preceding analysis of the chiasmus in Elaine Scarry's work might lead one to expect, at issue here are the exchanges of attributes between person and artifact that are central to a nineteenth-century aesthetic of everyday life. The poem is quite explicitly about the speaker's room ("*Meine Stube*") and about the status of personal objects ("*Die Dinge*"); as in his discussions of Proust, so here too, de Man formulates his theory not in terms of the machine—as other commentators have suggested—but in terms of domestic space.[39] Perceptively noting the dynamism of the objects in comparison to the flatness of the voice that describes them, de Man argues that the "inwardness that should belong, per definition, to the subject is located instead within things"; that the "usual structure has been reversed: the outside of things has become internalized" (36). Yet because these objects seem expressive without being fully assimilated to the poem's speaker, de Man characterizes the poem as representing "objects as containers of a subjectivity which is not that of the self that considers them," a paradox that, he asserts, is "difficult to comprehend . . . on the level of the themes" (37). This discrepancy is what opens the way for the interpretation of the poem as about "the coming into being of metaphor"; since the thematic reading of the poem makes no sense, the poem must be about "a potential inherent in language," in this case "the outside-directed turn that occurs in all metaphorical representations" (37).

I emphasize this moment in *Allegories of Reading* because it is one in which de Man almost straightforwardly renames a particular historical and material formation as an exclusively linguistic one. The reversals in Rilke's poem of inside and outside, in which "the outside of things has become internalized" while objects serve as "containers" of "subjectivity," are not unique discoveries of this poem, but instead constitute a definitive paradox of the discourse of decor (36, 37). An allegory of reading—for this chapter contains the broadest possible claims about "a paradox that is inherent in all literature"—is shaped by a specific sense of the objects of consumption, decor and personal ornament (50). In other words, the conundrum of the expressive power of objects, the *personality* of objects, is here not a purely philosophical point nor purely a question of rhetoric: it is Madame Merle's question much more particularly ("What shall we call our 'self'" when "we're each of us made up of some cluster of appurtenances"?), taking that moment from *Portrait of a Lady* as a summation of the cultural movements sketched in the previous chapters. At this moment in de Man's work, the very terms of literary criticism are formed by a specific material model—the hermeneutics of the accessory, the detailing of decor, the newly intimate sense of one's belongings.

So powerful are these material formations that they supply the terms when de Man seeks to cancel or circumvent the thematic criticism that could otherwise lead to an analysis of Rilke's place in the history of things, the history of personal property. Writing of Rilke's shortest and most opaque later lyrics, de Man argues that these poems "impl[y] a complete drying up of thematic possibilities." They are poems of "pure 'figure'" in which Rilke comes as close as any poet can to "the purity" of "semantic askesis":

> The figure stripped of any seduction besides that of its rhetorical elasticity can form, together with other figures, constellations of figures that are inaccessible to meaning and to the senses, located far beyond any concern for life or for death in the hollow space of an unreal sky. (48)

De Man asserts the complete abstraction of the rhetorical figure by means of a specific materiality; this exclusion of reference from the figure is itself figured through the historically particular physicality it is said to preclude. It is not just that the "elasticity" mentioned here links the passage to the pliable accessory of dress and ornament, an association that operates crucially as well in the later chapter in *Allegories of Reading* in the discussion of the purloined ribbon of Rousseau's *Confessions*. Nor is it only a matter of realizing that the passage practically defines real and rigorous reading as

the purging of those ornaments, the "stripping" away of obsfucatory layers—an implication that means that the sense this passage makes depends
on the material world the passage would deny. What really involves the
passage with a specific materiality is the figure—the bodily one—that
holds its own figures together.

For if positing the "elasticity" of a "stripped" and "seduct[ive]" "figure"
strikes one as a hopelessly mixed metaphor, then one must also acknowledge that women hold this catachresis together, and that the flexibility of
language and the flexibility of the nineteenth-century female body—particularly an adulterous one like Emma Bovary or Charlotte Stant or *A
London Life*'s Selina—have become impossible to distinguish. It is as if the
nearly-naked female body never mentioned in *Allegories of Reading*'s chapter on Rousseau's *Pygmalion* has migrated to another place in de Man's
book, where it serves as an account of rhetoric, serves to encapsulate and
substantiate the master terms of de Man's critical practice. Or it is as if all
rhetoric has taken on the properties of a stretchy and seductive falsifica-
tion that Flaubert imagines a laminating or embossing machine might
produce. Early in Part Three of *Madame Bovary*, when the reunited Emma
and Léon exchange exaggerated professions of their own passions,
Flaubert's narrator observes that "speech is like a rolling machine that
always stretches the sentiment it expresses" ("la parole est un laminoir qui
allonge toujours les sentiments").[40] The metaphor receives its literalization
as Léon fabricates a desire to be buried in a coverlet ("un couvre-pied")
given to him by Emma: the flexibility of rhetoric and the versatility of the
stuff that accessorizes the body are inseparable for Flaubert, an inseparability that de Man and other twentieth-century critics absorb, adopt,
inherit.

What is at stake for literary criticism in the study of material culture,
the surfaces of the everyday world, the most superficial layer of civilization? My answer has been that literary criticism's own logic has repeatedly and often unnoticeably incorporated within itself aspects of the material world by relying on those aspects for its sense of what language and literature are. Literary criticism has come to think of such all-encompassing
categories as textuality itself in terms derived from specific material models, ones that idealist aesthetics would sublimate to the point of invisibili-
ty. One could argue at this point that there has been very little materialist
literary criticism because, if we survey Anglo-American criticism of the last
100 years, we find very few studies that do not prefer and privilege the
conceptual over the concrete aesthetic practices that make the conceptual
legible and sharable. Or one could argue that all literary criticism has been
materialist and usually failed to recognize itself as such; as de Man so frequently does in the passages I have canvassed, criticism relies on a shared

model of the material world in order to make its meanings clear, in order to sustain its relation to its audience.

Attempting to achieve a truly superficial reading of Henry James, the preceding chapters have focused their attention on objects and surfaces crucial to the shaping of literary terms, concepts, and categories; they have uncovered the specific material forms that critical constructs both depend on and efface. By reading the world of decor back into the concept of consciousness, I have tried to show how much material history is embedded in an idea that has shaped Jamesian criticism for most of the last century; I have tried to show how thoroughly the contingent surfaces of the fin-de-siècle drawing room are interwoven with what counts as reading in depth.

CHAPTER EIGHT

THE COLOR OF AIR
New Materialism

W hat color is Balzac's air? That is the question James asks midway through his 1905 lecture "The Lesson of Balzac." The question springs from an extended meditation on "the individual strong tempera-ment in fiction," the special character that marks a novelist's work as rec-ognizably his or her own, a question on which, James notes, "there would be much to say" (*LC* 2:125). James is attempting to catch "the nature of the man himself . . . his very presence, his spiritual presence, in his work." Spirit proves elusive, however, so much so that eventually the long passage settles down into a litany of distinctive settings, some of which are archi-tectural spaces and some of which are landscapes, both of which are fur-ther specified by time of day or season of the year. Dickens's novels seem to James "always to go on in the morning . . . in a vast apartment that appears to have windows, large, uncurtained and rather unwashed win-dows, on all sides at once"; George Eliot's "general landscape" is that of an autumn sunset, with long shadows; Jane Austen's is that of "an arrested spring"; Thackeray evokes "the light . . . of rainy days in 'residential' streets" (*LC* 2:126). "The question of the color of Balzac's air," on the other hand, is less easily resolved: "rich and thick, the mixture of sun and shade diffused through the 'Comédie Humaine'" represents "an absolutely greater quantity of 'atmosphere,' than we shall find prevailing within the compass of any other suspended frame."

Thick and colored air, a great quantity of atmosphere: this book on James's preoccupation with the material world ends with matter that is mostly not matter, at least not the kind of matter susceptible to the sense of touch nor the economy of acquisition nor the aesthetics of adornment and personal ornament. This book ends, then, with a figure that seems beyond the reach of the analyses and arguments developed in the preceding pages. Inasmuch as this image serves for James as the cynosure of the aesthetic, it might lead to a very belated worry that materialism is not the mode in which James characteristically thinks and that the present project has exaggerated some minor moments in the fictions and a minor set of intellectual habits of those fictions' author.

I want to end with this image of air in order to show how the material can become, in James, a complex amalgam of physical qualities, visual impressions, representational practices, and signs of a larger political economy. More than that motive, however, what draws me to this figure is the resemblance between James's strategies and those of a strand of very recent critical works that read the material world back into literature's metaphors. Having argued in the previous chapter that the terms and methods of literary analysis typically presuppose an unacknowledged material model, I will close this book by examining the work of several scholars who strive to reattach literary studies to the world of things and the life of the senses.

The passage on the air, the atmosphere, of the novels of James's predecessors may seem a moment where impressionistic criticism has deployed an evanescent image to maintain the aesthetic as a wholly autonomous realm of experience, a world one cannot touch. And yet when we begin to examine the passages that lie behind the figure of colored air, we find that it is produced by a whole system of objects, indeed that it is *the* figure of the object system itself. The material nature of James's air becomes clear if we review several passages quoted in previous chapters. The "thick, coloured air" of Poynton is an effect of the reflected "light" of its "treasures" (10:146). Similarly, in *The Other House,* the "colour of the air" conveys a sense that the flowers and pictures, the florid, highly decorated effects of things, make the spaces between those objects material, themselves thick with decor.[1] In *A London Life,* the dowager Lady Davenant's drawing room has a "bright durable sociable air" that is the product of its homely, unfashionable appurtenances, which preserve the past at the expense of fashion (10:271). It is as if the air is itself a quasi-material medium that conveys the implications of objects, linking their physical qualities with the behavioral norms they connote, convey, even instill; the figure links a picturesque effect with a cultural code that is itself kept steadily present by the objects that make it real.

In *The Ambassadors,* James recurs to the figure so often that it seems he is consciously working out its implications as he uses air's quasi-physical nature to give a sense of material reality to nuances that cannot otherwise be named, as when "the air . . . thicken[s]" with "intimations" as Chad and Madame de Vionnet come into view when Strether is taking in the riverscape late in the novel, or when Strether, unable to capture the "something" that characterizes Madame de Vionnet's drawing room, "come[s] nearest to naming" it "in speaking of it as the air of supreme respectability," or when Strether sums up the Parisian morning (and somehow the French setting is crucial here) by reflecting that "the air had a taste as of something mixed with art" (22:256; 21:245, 79).

In that last usage, the passage elaborates its metaphor of taste by going on to imagine this "something" as the production of "a white-capped master-chef," so that the sensory immediacy of taste is bestowed upon atmospheric effects—they might almost be eaten—even as the figure also suggests the elusiveness of a complex blend of flavors. What is it, exactly, that leads James to endow the nebulous with a solidity here that seems to deny its definitive nature?

In *The American Scene,* in the chapter on Baltimore, the boughs of the trees "creat[e] in the upper air great classic serenities of shade" and "give breadth of style," an effect "borrowed . . . straight from far-away Claudes and Turners."[2] Earlier, at West Point, the interpretive questions and incessant study of the Jamesian analyst over how such a blank landscape could possibly offer "romantic effect" are rendered irrelevant by the fact that it *does:* such questions are "shivered . . . to mere silver atoms" by "the mere blinding radiance" because "the very powers of the air" "transcend all argument" as they present a "tone good enough for Claude or Turner."[3] The thing-like quality of the atmosphere takes precedence over analysis, as even the most hazy and shapeless ontology makes epistemology seem secondary, over-intellectualized, belated.

This materiality of the air, *The American Scene* suggests, is firmed up by, or even produced by, the medium of painting—the medium in which an atmospheric effect has little or no physical difference from more solid-seeming rocks or buildings, as both kinds of stuff consist of a thin layer of oil on canvas. But this smoky, shimmering haze is hardly a natural phenomenon occurring apart from a political economy and observed with an innocent eye that simply takes in what it sees; rather, it is the now-naturalized sign of industry generated by a host of paintings—particularly French Impressionist landscapes—in which smoke is a figure for production, as T. J. Clark observes in *The Painting of Modern Life.*[4] Commenting on Monet's seashores, Clark notes that these paintings are "absolute with industry" as "the play of paint . . . absorb[s] the factories and weekend villas" alike "with scarcely a ripple"; economic activity builds rather than mars the coherence of the picture.[5] Or, as James puts what is almost the same point in *The American Scene,* "in the splendid light, nature and science were joyously romping together" in the New York harbor; the harbor is blackened and smudged, but not so much so that "light of the picturesque" cannot "irradiate [such] fog and grime."[6] This passage from *The*

American Scene is unusual for James in that it makes explicit the link between his recurrent figure of air and the atmospheric effects that became a pictorial sign of industry. But even when his point of comparison is Claude, for example, we can speculate that the seventeenth-century haze of that painter is for James brought to newly heightened visibility by the painterly conventions governing the portrayal of nineteenth-century industry.

With his figure of "Balzac's air," then, James uses the concrete medium of one art to transform the material culture represented by another art into a critical concept: thinking of the air of a text as in some sense visible depends for its sense on one's having seen the atmospheric effects of painting, which are themselves a sign of a still larger economy rapidly expanding in James's time. This kind of largely dematerialized material character of each author—George Eliot's sinking sun, Austen's arrested spring, Thackeray's "light . . . of rainy days"—becomes James's way of telling them apart, becomes a critical tool for distinguishing their definitive attributes. Hence the figure of the air carries into the realm of the conceptual and the critical the matter of industrial production and the stuff of oil paint, as well as the perceptual habits reinforced by French landscape painting. Pushing back a little further in James's career, I want to suggest that the figure of the air in the late Balzac essay brings to bear upon the literary text the motif with which James had in his fictions attempted to capture the decor—the systems of taste—that made up his various settings: the "thicken[ed]" air of *The Ambassadors,* the "thick, coloured air" of *The Spoils of Poynton,* is in turn used to scrutinize *La Comédie Humaine.* Hence a construction of objects itself becomes a tool of literary analysis, critical commentary, and aesthetic judgment. But far from acting as a dematerializing figure, James's metaphor of the air draws lines of connection between industry, material culture, art, and novelistic discourse.

To grasp the nature of the Jamesian figure of air, then, is to understand that figure as definitively mixed, as maintained by a recursive movement between the material and the conceptual. This movement between the physical details of daily life and the metaphorical figures of theory and philosophy has guided this book from the beginning: *A Superficial Reading of Henry James* has attempted to uncover the material nature of such concepts as consciousness, portraiture, the text, and even culture. Perhaps the history of literary theory still needs a good deal of rewriting: perhaps the way we conceive of theory needs to be continually challenged, thinking of it, as we habitually do, as defined by the thinness of abstraction, as abstracted from the thickness of material life.

In her *Reading in Detail: Aesthetics and the Feminine* (1987), Naomi Schor critiqued what she called "idealist" aesthetics as a construct maintained at the expense of women, the ornament, and the decorative; the tradition of literary theory, stretching from the Greeks to Reynolds and Dr. Johnson to Hegel and beyond, monumentalized in huge textbooks like Walter Jackson Bate's *Criticism: The Major Texts* and Hazard Adams's *Critical Theory Since Plato*, attains much of its coherence by sublimating the concrete, the minute, and the quotidian.[7] When *Reading in Detail* appeared, it seemed far different from the new-historicist commitment to the anecdote and the new-historicist fascination with the workings of power that had come to dominate literary studies at that time. And in fact, Schor's book has never been fully assimilated within the discipline (the book is now out of print). Yet it brought together two related impulses in the humanities that I think will emerge as highly characteristic of our own fin de siècle and that will also emerge as having been genuinely useful and productive. One is a skepticism over the conceptual itself; the other is a new valuing of the physical matter of everyday life. When, in her book *Reinterpreting Property* (1993), the legal scholar Margaret Jane Radin defended a "thick theory of the self" that bestowed legal status upon the objects that are "so bound up with me that I would cease to be 'myself' if they were taken"; when the art historian Norman Bryson, in *Looking at the Overlooked* (1990), revalued the genre of still life by approaching it as a history of the table, a history of "the conditions of creaturality, of eating and drinking and domestic life"; when, in *On Longing* (1984), the literary critic and folklorist Susan Stewart wrested from the problem of literary form a material poetics, these scholars lowered the threshold of hermeneutic attention, coaxing into existence a new particularism that they poised against the abstractions of the foundational concepts of their disciplines—personhood, narrative, or even (in Bryson's case most explicitly, but all three writers just named do this in one way or another) subject matter.[8]

This thickening of the conceptual is how I would define the new materialism that emerges in the work of these and other scholars. Such work resists the disciplinary mandates that I spoke of in the beginning of this book, the ones that hold that the material world must be brought forward but not for too long before it is abstracted away by critique (of commodification, say) and by an agreed-upon level of necessary generalization, a commitment to the assumption that episodes in the history of artistic and material practices can always be usefully restated as higher-order claims that can then take their place in what Schor critiqued as idealist aesthetics.

As it happens, contemporary criticism has recently evolved an idiom that captures the view of meaning I am attempting to describe, a cluster of terms and connotations which do some of the same work as James's figure of air. That idiom is the various shades of meaning carried by the word "sense," as in the titles of Bill Brown's *A Sense of Things* (2003), Diana Fuss's *The Sense of an Interior* (2004), and Susan Stewart's *Poetry and the Fate of the Senses* (2002).[9] "Sense" and "the senses" might seem to pull in almost opposite directions, because they nominate on the one hand an understanding, an intelligence, even a wisdom and, on the other, one of the least rational, most immediate and physical zones of human experience. But it is crucial to the argument of these books that these senses of "sense" are not detachable from each other: these critics, so different from each other in many ways, nonetheless all oppose a decoupling of the literary figure from the world of sensory experience. Hence Brown characterizes his approach as exploring the "convergences of" "the sensation of thingness" and "the understanding" (17). Hence Fuss argues that the concrete domestic environment shapes the work of her chosen writers "in ways both intensely physical and deeply philosophical" (18). Hence Stewart seeks to demonstrate that "it is only by finding means of making sense impressions intelligible to others" that lyric poetry becomes readable in the first place (3).

As well as entailing a more concrete set of practices that I will detail in a moment, this continuum between sense and the senses is a view of meaning that may well represent a decisive shift in the critical understanding of the sign. Put most broadly, all of these critics suggest that the physical senses are what bind sign and signified. In Stewart's radically synesthetic rereading of the lyric tradition, the words of erotic poems become a highly corporeal event in the reader's experience: by evoking the senses of smell and taste—the senses of physical incorporation—language itself is identified with "the touch and feel of the object in the mouth," is identified with "the liquification of" the object. "The melting words of the lover, the manipulation of words in the mouth as an extension of erotic manipulation through hands and limbs" are crucial "resources for the poet of erotic poems," Stewart argues (32). This newly physicalized sense of language is also, I believe, what motivates Fuss to concentrate on Helen Keller in her study of writers and their rooms. For Fuss, it is crucial that Keller learned to read by touching raised letters printed on cardboard which were in turn placed on the objects they nominated. Hence, Fuss argues, "Keller's tactile linguistics never presupposes the alienation of subject and object that both Saussure and Lacan identify as the central feature of the birth of 'the speaking subject'" (112). In Brown's account of the role of material culture in late-nineteenth-century American fiction, what Brown calls "the logic of reference" becomes a specific set of rhetorical practices that represent the physical objects of a specific moment, a fairly particularized cultural milieu (17). The techniques of fiction become "imaginative technologies for lifting and redeeming" the "substratum" of "the material everyday" into a reader's awareness. In a complex reading of Sarah Orne Jewett's *The Country of the Pointed Firs,* Brown reconsiders that text's naturalism by emphasizing how the senses of taste, touch, and smell bridge the gap between characters and natural phenomena: the aromas, flavors, and textures of the herbs that are so crucial in Jewett's descriptions of coastal Maine are the means by which Jewett "establishes an overwhelming intimacy between natural and human matter" (90). Unlike sight, which distances perceiving subject and the object of attention, "*smell* . . . depends on proximity, on chemical contact, on physical infiltration." This immediacy of sensation, on Brown's reading, is what underwrites *The Country of the Pointed Firs*'s brand of naturalism, which assumes a continuity between people and natural objects, which figures characters as grasshoppers or trees. As Brown explains, "the metaphorization of the . . . villagers themselves as both flora and fauna seems so artless," so inevitable, because "it simply reads like the rhetorical effect of the narrated fact of the intimacy between people and place" (90). That is "the way that objects become figures of thought and of speech," to use the terms with which *A Sense of Things* explains its purpose as a whole (16).

I am struck by two intertwined aspects of Brown's analysis of *The Country of the Pointed Firs* that are important for the working definition of new materialism I am developing here. One is the central role of the senses, which on this account do a lot of the work of Jewett's text and which are considered explicitly, considered as topics in themselves. (You can write a lot about a text's visual imagery, say, without considering the senses at all, without considering, as Brown does, that "the *sight* of objects always depends on sufficient distance" [90].) Indeed, if one looks at the prominent discussions of Jewett published a decade before Brown's, one finds that the physical senses play no role in these analyses.[10] Another crucial feature of Brown's reading is the tight bind it discovers between the role of the senses and the working of language, between material culture and linguistic matters. The "logic of reference" is not, on this account, susceptible to the kind of homogenizing ahistoricism I analyzed in the preceding chapter; rather, language's workings depend on a particular array of objects and on particular ways of being involved with those objects. In other words (and at the risk of exaggerating Brown's position), an analysis of language in *The Country of the Pointed Firs* would have to work differently if that novel were about the proprietor of a general store rather than an herb-gatherer.

That is how a new concern for the physical senses reshapes the sense of the sign in the critics I am discussing here. There are some other shared intellectual habits, shared predilections, and shared aversions I want to name here, ones that have a lot to do with the way these critics do their work from one page to the next. Continuing the emphasis on practical aesthetics I have adopted in this book, I will bring my project to a close by itemizing three habits of reading that together characterize the approach here nominated as new materialism.

First is a *newly intimate conception both of subject matter and of the task of interpretation.* Thus Brown indicates that one goal of *A Sense of Things* is that of achieving a "grittier, materialist phenomenology of everyday life" (3), while Fuss thinks of her topic as "the everyday friction between people and things" (Fuss, 15). In practice, that topic leads Fuss to an extended discussion of the myriad treatments Proust kept on hand for his allergies, to the way the couch in Freud's consulting room positions the patient's body, to the precise dimensions of Emily Dickinson's bedroom (191–92 , 90–91, 55). As in Brown's attention to the sense of smell in Jewett, "close reading" in these instances means a reading that stays close to the body. Arguing that "every literary figure has a literal base," Fuss takes up the thematics that their several critical traditions have assigned to these authors—Proust's shrinking from the world, Freud's erotic conception of the interpersonal, Dickinson's emphasis on confinement and liberation—and drives those themes back into their physical origins (7). Declining the diagrammatic clarity of previous work on the body and its habitats, such an approach seeks to discover a messy corporeality underlying the abstractions of critical truisms. Hence Fuss notes that while Georges Poulet was among the first to emphasize the significance of space in Proust's time-obsessed novel, "Poulet's investigation of Proustian space . . . remains curiously intangible and indefinite," wholly focused on "metaphorical space" and wholly uninterested in "the space of the domestic interior"—an interior Fuss herself goes on to detail with extraordinary specificity (152).

Another example—another "sense" book I have not yet mentioned— will make clearer the kind of hermeneutic shift I am describing here. In *Common Scents: Comparative Encounters in High-Victorian Fiction* (2004), Janice Carlisle reconsiders nineteenth-century British codifications of class by analyzing how the sense of smell is used to create, convey, and sustain those distinctions. "Repeatedly in the fiction of the 1860s," Carlisle observes, "encounters" between members of different classes "are depicted in terms of an inodorate perceiver of smells and his or her smelly other."[11] Like the other books on "sense," Carlisle's work shuttles between what she calls "the material and the immaterial," "matter and spirit": "Recognizing an odor, registering its effects, comparing what smells to what does not—all such perceptual activities when recorded in a novel of the 1860s provide access to the common sense of that decade, the rarely articulated, taken-for-granted result of experiences supposedly shared by all one's fellows, if not by all humankind" (21, 5). Hence something as complex and mediated as what a culture believes goes without saying is sustained by innumerable, involuntary, *im*mediate bodily responses. Sometimes the matter that Carlisle finds Victorian culture inspiriting is pleasant, like the rose leaves that scent the corridors of the best country homes, according to the olfactory imagination of Rosamond Vincy in *Middlemarch* (153). But often these smells are "gross," as Carlisle says, evidence of messy bodies ("habiliments, impregnated with . . . the dirt of a life," as one of the 1860s novels quoted puts it) that one cannot shut out (32).

That messy body leads to a second distinguishing characteristic of the new materialism, which is that *it admits more concrete details than can be contained by any neatly defined cultural logic.* In the titles I am considering, "sense" is the word that blurs the boundaries established by the more schematic studies that precede these books; that word, in other words, takes the place that "logic" would have occupied if these studies had appeared fifteen years previously, as in Walter Benn Michaels's *The Gold Standard and the Logic of Naturalism* (1987), or Fredric Jameson's *Postmodernism, or, The Cultural Logic of Late Capitalism* (1991).[12] Brown is explicit about his interest in what "the cultural logic of capitalism" cannot explain, arguing "that the human interaction with the nonhuman world of objects, however mediated by the advance of consumer culture, must be recognized as irreducible to that culture" (5–6, 13). This resistance to the reduction of culture to a "logic" helps to explain the extraordinarily sudden eclipse of Michel Foucault in many recent literary studies: he appears in the text of only one of these four "sense" books, in a moment where Brown distinguishes the taxonomic scheme Foucault theorized in *The Order of Things* from Jewett's far more sensuous take on natural history (90). This "sacrifice" of schematic "clarity," as Brown calls it (5), makes for a certain shift in the diction of criticism, away from the "logistics" and "relays" with which Mark Seltzer systematized the material world in *Bodies and Machines* (1992), and toward a language of material particularity and emotional affect.[13] If part of the challenge of writing criticism at the end of the twentieth century was to reduce the multiplicity of culture to a set of "logistics," the challenge now seems to be to lower the threshold of perception and, at least on occasion, to give up a tone of steely detachment. Hence Brown shifts his tone in the introduction of his book from language that posits the "limit of modernism" to ask, "why do you find yourself talking to things? . . . is it simply because you're lonely?" (12). Similarly, Fuss details with extraordinarily minute particularity Proust's "passionate attachment to the somber and seemingly lifeless furniture of his parents," arguing that this "object-love" for his mother's Boulle worktable and his father's armchair "operates . . . as the antidote to lost time" by bestowing upon the mourned figures a physical presence (164–65). The point is not merely that Fuss reports such details, but that by specifying such material practices so carefully, Fuss implicitly identifies her project with the emotions that led her subject to maintain this furniture in the first place. Even such simple moments as Carlisle's words "smelly" and "gross" suggest a new relation to subject matter when matter is indeed the critic's subject.

Here a comparison to Stewart will further clarify the point, since *Poetry and the Fate of the Senses* concerns a different genre than the other texts I am considering, and since that focus on lyric carries with it less of a burden to work against commodification-driven or Foucauldian, discipline-centered analyses. In the introduction to her book, Stewart writes, "Aesthetic activity viewed in the light of the history of ideological ends is no longer aesthetic; it erases the free activity of pleasure and knowledge that the aesthetic brings to human life" (40). This position could easily, but wrongly, be critiqued as itself an instance of an aesthetic ideology, if one did not take into account the sense in which Stewart means "ideology," and if one did not understand the claim in relation to the poetic analyses Stewart performs throughout this book. In *The Pleasure of the Text,* Roland Barthes usefully defines "ideology" as "the idea *insofar as it dominates:* ideology can only be dominant."[14] Stewart's strategy can be understood, then, as one of dilating and particularizing sensory experiences associated with poetry until they reach the point that no ideology can easily contain them. She is not saying that the senses *cannot* be rendered the object of ideology; indeed, the sentence I quote above comes in the midst of her discussion on the history of attempts to regulate and hierarchize those senses. But she is suggesting that the senses can be cultivated to resist ideology, that sensory experiences have the potential for generating experiences and pleasures that are not easy to keep within any political program. This is why *Poetry and the Fate of the Senses* pauses so long over the "variegated chalcedony" of the agate named in an H. D. poem, why it goes on at such length over the way smell shapes and disorients readerly understanding in Jonathan Swift's lyrics, why it seeks to relate such varied uses of the senses as speaking, listening, smelling, and touching to the workings of poetry (36, 30–32). For it is only through the force of accumulated examples in this long (447-page) book that enough variety can be detailed to keep the aesthetic open, beyond the reach of any reductive scheme.

The intimacy of the interpretations in question here and their resistance to schematics virtually entail a third characteristic of the criticism I am talking about, which is that it resists adopting the subject/object dichotomy as an explanatory device. Indeed, these critics argue—sometimes through the way they handle their materials and sometimes by direct statement—that *the distinction between subject and object cannot be a guiding principle of cultural history or literary studies.* Fuss states the point directly, asserting that the subject/object distinction is a "binary yet to be adequately challenged in cultural criticism" (15). She makes this assertion in part because the sense of sight, which is so frequently inseparable from subject/object thinking, proves to get at only a small part of her topic: as William James intuited in the *Principles of Psychology*, inhabiting the physical world is an activity that engages hearing, smell, taste, and touch as much as it does sight. Hence a new interest emerges in the books under discussion in what Carlisle labels "the chemical" senses of taste and smell (4) and in what Stewart identifies as the "autocentric" senses (smell, taste, and some forms of touch), the senses that are "physically localized on or in the body" (37).[15] Though their topics would seem to differ tremendously, both Stewart and Carlisle write about these senses, so often coded as inferior ones, as ones that involve "fusion" or "exchange" between perceiver and perceived rather than involving distance and objectification (Stewart, 38; Carlisle, 10). This new sense of the exchange—whether psychological or material—of properties between subject and object is basic as well to Brown's approach, which posits at the outset that the relation between human beings and things happens as an "indeterminate ontology where things seem slightly human and humans seem slightly thing-like" (13).

As that word "indeterminate" suggests, the language used to capture this fusion of human bodies and subjectivities with the material world is loosely deconstructive in its origin, as is the impulse to undermine a binary opposition like subject and object. Hence the sensual resistance to the subject/object dichotomy could be seen as a strictly philosophical argument, carrying with it the abstraction I have sought to identify in de Man and Scarry. That possibility makes it important to recognize the ways in which the large ambiguity I am discussing has a history, one these books seek to trace. One way in which that tracing happens is through a new attention to the nineteenth-century sciences that mixed matter and spirit, bodies and objects, as in Carlisle's discussions of psychophysiologists, who tried "to merge philosophic conceptions of the mind . . . with research on the anatomy and physiology of nerves and brain" (6), or Brown's attention to the late-nineteenth-century school of physiological aesthetics (26). In the epistemology posited by these sciences, it is hard to know where objects stop and human beings begin, as is the case with Bernard Berenson and Vernon Lee, theorists of empathy I have discussed in preceding chapters. Another way in which the "the join between mind and matter" becomes a historical phenomenon is through the placement of the room, that privileged trope of explication, within larger political economies (Fuss, 16). Hence Fuss rereads the Proustian interior within the context of the Haussmannization of Paris, the violent process by which the old facades and shops were standardized into a uniform architecture that largely obliterated visual remnants of the past; Proustian longing, the "searching for the lost object," emerges on this reading not (or not only) as a general human emotion, but as a set of feelings that emerges in response to the work of the wrecking ball and the aesthetic-political program it imposed (156).

This understanding of the senses as the merging of subject and object becomes a historical narrative in Stewart as well, for Stewart's whole book is an attempt to take literally Marx's pronouncement that "the forming of the five senses is a labour of the entire history of the world down to the present" (40).[16] Hence Stewart might be said to have rewritten the history of poetry according to the concerns I have been outlining in this chapter, concerns for the particularization of the senses. As in her chapter on the history of the romantic nocturne, poetic influence is re-understood as successive expansions of consciousness, so that the reception of a poem yields a broadening or fine-tuning of subsequent sensory experience: the atmospheric qualities of night, the way that human beings rely on kinesthetic perception in the darkness, the qualities of the colors when glimpsed in faint illumination, and the synesthesia that leads the senses to merge with each other all become knowledge that is inherited by Wordsworth from Anne Finch, and by Keats from Wordsworth (259). In this way, "new modes of moving and attending, of using touch, sight, smell, and hearing, are the consequences as well as the source" of innovations in poetic form (291). That is how the history of poetry, on Stewart's account, reflects Marx's awareness that the senses themselves are historical artifacts.

I have marshaled together these recent critical studies in an attempt to capture something of the special quality of our own moment in the history of literary studies: my purpose here at the end has been to catch this shift in a way that others may find inspiring or in need of correction or (I hope) both. In his essay on "The Plates of the *Encyclopedia*," Barthes began by reflecting on the fact that "Our literature has taken a long time to discover the object; we must wait till Balzac for the novel to be the space not only of pure human relations but also of substances and usages called upon to play their part in the story of passions."[17] At least in the English-speaking world, it seems criticism has taken a similarly long time even to begin to find terms adequate for the lives we lead in the material world. Resisting the imperative to abstract, efface, or ignore that realm of experience, I have taken Henry James as the focus of my attention because his texts have the power to unsettle preferences for the conceptual (over the material), the essential (over the ornamental), the theoretical (over the practical). Perhaps the criticism that emerges from the recent materialist turn will be radically recursive in its handling of those oppositions, accepting the ironies of a discipline that is definitively miscellaneous, sundry, itself a catachresis. Perhaps the dispensation in literary studies we are now entering will be an eccentric hybrid of rhetorical analysis and material culture; it will do its work by means of swatches and samples of matter in conjunction with the linguistic, imaginative works that think their meanings, their aesthetic principles, their rhetorical structures, through those substances.

Notes

Notes to Introduction

1. H. G. Wells, *Boon, The Mind of the Race, The Wild Asses of the Devil, and the Last Trump* (London: Fisher Unwin, 1915), 106–7.
2. Maxwell Geismar, *Henry James and the Jacobites* (New York: Hill and Wang, 1962), 5, 10.
3. Laurence B. Holland, *The Expense of Vision: Essays on the Craft of Henry James* (Princeton: Princeton University Press, 1964), 112.
4. Jean-Christophe Agnew, "The Consuming Vision of Henry James," in *The Culture of Consumption: Critical Essays in American History, 1880–1980,* ed. Richard Wightman Fox and T. J. Jackson Lears (New York: Pantheon, 1983), 73, 84, 100.
5. Martha Banta, *Taylored Lives: Narrative Productions in the Age of Taylor, Veblen, and Ford* (Chicago: University of Chicago Press, 1993), 75.
6. Mark Seltzer, *Bodies and Machines* (New York: Routledge, 1992), 90.
7. Seltzer, *Bodies and Machines,* 49, 4.
8. Jonathan Freedman, *Professions of Taste: Henry James, British Aestheticism, and Commodity Culture* (Stanford: Stanford University Press, 1990), 105–10, 84–58, 81.
9. Freedman, *Professions of Taste,* 160.
10. Henry James, *The Europeans,* ed. Tony Tanner and P. Crick (London: Penguin, 1984), 163. Further references appear parenthetically within the text.
11. Henry James, *The Bostonians,* ed. Charles R. Anderson (Harmondsworth: Penguin, 1984), 45–46.
12. Susan Stewart, *On Longing: Narratives of the Miniature, the Gigantic, the Souvenir, the Collection* (Baltimore: Johns Hopkins University Press, 1984); Naomi Schor, *Reading in Detail: Aesthetics and the Feminine* (New York: Methuen, 1987), 3; Raymond Williams, *Marxism and Literature* (Oxford: Oxford University Press, 1977), 19.
13. Williams, *Marxism and Literature,* 61.
14. Judith Butler, *Bodies That Matter: On the Discursive Limits of "Sex"* (New York: Routledge, 1993), ix.

Notes to Chapter 1

1. Henry James, "Rose-Agathe," in *The Complete Tales of Henry James,* ed. Leon Edel, vol. 4 (Philadelphia: Lippincot, 1962), 125. Further references appear parenthetically within the text.
2. Herman Melville, *The Confidence-Man: His Masquerade,* ed. Hershel Parker (New York: Norton, 1971), 199.

3. Sigmund Freud, "'The Uncanny,'" in *An Infantile Neurosis and Other Works, The Standard Edition of the Complete Psychological Works of Sigmund Freud,* vol. 17, trans. James Strachey et al. (London: Hogarth Press, 1955), 229.

4. Mark Seltzer, "Physical Capital: The Romance of the Market in Machine Culture," in *Bodies and Machines* (New York: Routledge, 1992), 45–90. Seltzer's observation that the plate-glass windows of urban scenes of consumption almost inevitably become mirrors in which the consuming subject sees himself or herself very usefully glosses the way James depicts the coiffeur's window in "Rose-Agathe" (*Bodies and Machines,* 52). For further discussion of late-nineteenth-century America as a "society radically confused about what people are," and about "what is imitation and what is real," see Susan Gillman, *Dark Twins: Imposture and Identity in Mark Twain's America* (Chicago: University of Chicago Press, 1989), quotation on 78.

5. For a superb analysis of the manikin and how it incites mimetic desire, see Stuart Culver, "What Manikins Want: *The Wonderful World of Oz* and *The Art of Decorating Dry Goods Windows,*" *Representations* 21 (1988): 97–116. Culver's analysis makes clear how late-nineteenth-century marketing experts like L. Frank Baum assume that the live model or manikin's perpetual motion will incite endless longings in consumers (106–10).

6. For an early effort to question this presupposition that consciousness stays centered, see Leo Bersani, "The Narrator as Center in *The Wings of the Dove,*" *Modern Fiction Studies* 6 (1960): 131–44; for a recent, full-scale dismantling of the principle and of its applicability to the fiction it supposedly describes, see Sharon Cameron, *Thinking in Henry James* (Chicago: University of Chicago Press, 1989). My own concern here is much less with whether the figure of the center of consciousness can be maintained as a reliable and coherent reflection of James's texts when those texts are read rigorously—Bersani and Cameron convincingly argue that it cannot—than with the way in which the figure carries with it and simultaneously effaces the presence of the body and its objects. In chapter 2, I will return to this issue in order to make a historical critique of Cameron by detailing the unacknowledged materialist assumptions that underlie her study.

7. For a deconstructive reading, see John Carlos Rowe, *The Theoretical Dimensions of Henry James* (Madison: University of Wisconsin Press, 1984), 4–24; for a historicist one, see Jean-Christophe Agnew, "A House of Fiction: Domestic Interiors and the Commodity Aesthetic," in *Consuming Visions: Accumulation and Display of Goods in America, 1880–1920,* ed. Simon J. Bronner (New York: Norton, 1989), 133–56.

8. Even renunciation would be understood in late-nineteenth-century aesthetic culture as retaining a material edge because of the organic traces the renounced object leaves behind in the body. This trace and the theories behind it will become important later in this book's historical revision of seeing in James and his culture, especially in the brief discussion of empathy at the end of chapter 3 and then in the longer analysis of Bernard Berenson's career in chapter 4.

9. Three studies of defacement and creation have influenced strands of this one: Philip Fisher, *Making and Effacing Art: Modern American Art in a Culture of Museums* (New York: Oxford University Press, 1991); Michael Fried, *Realism, Writing, Disfiguration: On Thomas Eakins and Stephen Crane* (Chicago: University of Chicago Press, 1987); David Freedberg, *The Power of Images: Studies in the History and Theory of Response* (Chicago: University of Chicago Press, 1989).

Notes to Chapter 2

1. This kind of passage has seemed to some critics to authorize a conservatively humanist interpretation of the material world, an interpretation like that of Charles R. Anderson in *Person, Place, and Thing in Henry James's Novels* (Durham: Duke University Press, 1977). In singling out from the novels' profusion of material things one object for each character—a thing which serves as a "symbol" of the character's personality—Anderson both imposes an artificial stability on the material world as James represents it and wrongly insists on the priority of character to material things (4). Even the passage from *The Spoils* quoted above undermines Anderson's approach, with the ambiguity that hovers around its use of the word "make": there is a strong implication operating that Mrs. Gereth's house *makes* her, shapes her consciousness and habits, an implication that participates in the turn-of-the-century cultural poetics of art and the senses (a claim worked out at length in chapter 3).

2. Henry James, *The Other House*, ed. Tony Tanner (London: Dent, 1996), 10. Further references appear parenthetically within the text.

3. I want to acknowledge at the outset that taking James's exaggerated attention to ornament as an inversion of values—those of essence and accident, say—and as a study in the cultural poetics of embodiment are not the only ways to read this strand of James's fiction. In *The Science of Sacrifice: American Literature and Modern Social Theory* (Princeton: Princeton University Press, 1998), Susan L. Mizruchi reads the ribbons and feathers that so frequently festoon the Jamesian heroine in terms of the adornment of the sacrificial victim, the scapegoat (202–3); the ornaments that I label "accessories" can thus be understood as evidence of the crucial role that the metaphor of religious ritual plays in James's imagination and in the works of historical theology and social theory that James read. Mizruchi's analysis focuses on the adornment of Nanda in *The Awkward Age*, a moment where accessories take on a "a unique gravity" in James's fiction, as Mizruchi notes (203), but the point helps to make sense as well of the way in which *Daisy Miller* and *The Portrait of a Lady* combine an interest in ancient religious settings with an interest in clothing and personal ornament. For the purposes of my own work, what is most valuable about Mizruchi's argument is that it provides an additional explanation for why the Jamesian accessory is so unstable and hence so productive of meaning: "all sacrificial objects . . . are sacred and profane," combining in a single process what a community most values and what it needs to exclude (81).

4. Northrop Frye, *Anatomy of Criticism: Four Essays* (Princeton: Princeton University Press, 1957), 263. For Frye, prose is a "transparent medium" comparable to the "plate glass in a shop window," a remark which reinforces my suggestion that prose is often conceived as a medium that displays objects, a suggestion also borne out by Frye's characterization of the long sentences of James's late style as "*containing* sentences" (265, 267).

5. Susan Stewart, *On Longing: Narratives of the Miniature, the Gigantic, the Souvenir, the Collection* (Baltimore: Johns Hopkins University Press, 1984), 125.

6. Henry James, "The Papers," in *The Better Sort* (New York: Scribner's, 1903), 378.

7. For my knowledge of the Renaissance cabinet, I have relied on Lorraine J. Daston, "The Factual Sensibility," *Isis* 79 (1988): 452–70; for Daston's analysis of

the Ovidian poetics which governed the assemblage of cabinets (a taste that led to the acquisition of objects such as "corals arranged in scenes of mountains or forests, or fragments of marble . . . incorporated into paintings as clouds or water"), see 456–57.

8. In England, the Married Women's Property Act of 1870 rendered the term legally obsolete because it allowed married women the right to earn money and hold property apart from their husbands—with many loopholes and caveats. The act did not resolve issues such as the disinheritance of a widow from her house, an unresolved issue central to *The Spoils of Poynton,* and while legally dead the concept of paraphernalia is still alive in the late-Victorian cultural imagination, hovering along the margins of *The Golden Bowl,* for example, which begins with Charlotte's attempt to find a wedding gift for Maggie. On paraphernalia as a legal entity and women's property more generally, see Lee Holcombe, *Wives and Property: Reform of the Married Women's Property Law in Nineteenth-Century England* (Toronto: University of Toronto Press, 1983), 23, 41.

9. Commentaries that abstract this passage both from a world of concrete making and from the gendered (and gendering) labor which that making implies include R. P. Blackmur, "Introduction," in Henry James, *The Art of the Novel* (New York: Scribner's, 1934), xxvii; J. Hillis Miller, *The Ethics of Reading: Kant, de Man, Eliot, Trollope, James, and Benjamin* (New York: Columbia University Press, 1987), 103; Sharon Cameron, *Thinking in Henry James* (Chicago: University of Chicago Press, 1989), 47–50.

10. Here it is revealing to note the material metaphors that Georges Poulet uses in characterizing the Jamesian circle of consciousness: a spider web, a silken iridescence, a sea wave. All of these hover on the edge of material concreteness, as if Poulet needs to give the metaphor concrete shape and keep it immaterial at the same time (Poulet, *The Metamorphoses of the Circle,* trans. Carley Dawson and Elliott Coleman [Baltimore: Johns Hopkins University Press, 1966], 307). In an essay that partially anticipates my own attempt to demonstrate that the general aesthetic which emerges out of James's work is generated by a practical aesthetics of everyday life, Sara Blair identifies some of the substances and economies that compose the kind of immaterial materiality I am discussing here. Blair compellingly argues that James resembles "that emerging modern persona, the lady of the house," whose hidden labor yields the "finished products" of "beauty, leisure, or in James's case, literary mastery" ("In the House of Fiction: Henry James and the Engendering of Literary Mastery," in David McWhirter, ed., *Henry James's New York Edition: The Construction of Authorship* [Stanford: Stanford University Press, 1995], 64).

11. In arguing for a James who identifies bodily ambiguity with rhetorical ambiguity—or even rhetorical play—my critical terms fall in line with those of other recent critics who treat James's sense of gender and sexuality as matters of playful irony, parody, experiment, and performativity. See especially Leland S. Person, *Henry James and the Suspense of Masculinity* (Philadelphia: University of Pennsylvania Press, 2003); Eric Haralson, *Henry James and Queer Modernity* (Cambridge: Cambridge University Press, 2003); and Eric Savoy, "Embarrassments: Figure in the Closet," *Henry James Review* 20 (Fall 1999): 227–36. Like my own work, these studies owe a general debt to Ross Posnock's revisionary emphasis on a James who treats identity itself as fluid, who "submit-

ted his own selfhood, and the very concept of selfhood, to an extended ordeal of vulnerability," experiment, and risk (Posnock, *The Trial of Curiosity: Henry James, William James, and the Challenge of Modernity* [New York: Oxford University Press, 1991] 19).

12. Rebecca Harding Davis, *Life in the Iron-Mills,* ed. Cecelia Tichi (Boston: Bedford Books, 1998), 52–53.

13. Edgar Allan Poe, "The Man That Was Used Up," in *Poetry and Tales,* ed. Patrick F. Quinn (New York: Library of America, 1984), 307, 315–15.

14. Nathaniel Hawthorne, *Tales and Sketches,* ed. Roy Harvey Pearce (New York: Library of America, 1982), 940, 409.

15. This stage of my argument partially reprises what has become more or less a consensus in studies of nineteenth-century American literature: that the intertwining of persons and things takes on a new intimacy and inextricability. Gillian Brown finds in the "personalization" of objects the confluence of true womanhood and possessive individualism, an argument that forges an illuminating link between the political assumptions that govern antebellum culture and the material texture of that culture's novels and lady's books. Mark Seltzer outlines the logic of "the aestheticization of the natural body that market culture promises." Lori Merish argues that "sentimental discourses of consumption . . . instated a particular form" of subjectivity so that "personal possessions are endowed with characterological import." Bill Brown characterizes the cultural logic of the 1890s as operating in and creating an "indeterminate ontology where things seem slightly human and humans seem slightly thing-like." My own contribution in this chapter lies in linking a prose style—a textual effect—and a minute sensory experience to the large cultural shift discussed by those whose works have preceded my own. See Gillian Brown, *Domestic Individualism: Imagining Self in Nineteenth-Century America* (Berkeley: University of California Press, 1990), 42–43; Mark Seltzer, *Bodies and Machines* (New York: Routledge, 1992), 125; Lori Merish, *Sentimental Materialism: Gender, Commodity Culture, and Nineteenth-Century American Literature* (Durham: Duke University Press, 2000), 2; Bill Brown, *A Sense of Things: The Object Matter of American Literature* (Chicago: University of Chicago Press, 2003), 13.

16. Nathaniel Hawthorne, *The Scarlet Letter,* ed. Nina Baym (New York: Penguin, 1983), 35. Further references appear parenthetically within the text.

17. Walter Benn Michaels analyzes the American Renaissance romance in terms of the fluctuations of the market—including the slave market—in "Romance and Real Estate," *The Gold Standard and the Logic of Naturalism: American Literature at the Turn of the Century* (Berkeley: University of California Press, 1987), 85–112. My own interest is more in the vicissitudes of the middle-class body than in the markets upon which Michaels centers, but my sense of the instabilities of romance as intertwined with the alienability of property is certainly indebted to him, and as a reading of Hawthorne or Poe (for example) makes clear, the market and the body cannot be held as discrete realms in the period under discussion.

18. Nathaniel Hawthorne, *The Marble Faun,* ed. Richard H. Brodhead (New York: Penguin, 1990), 467.

19. Nathaniel Hawthorne, *The Blithedale Romance,* ed. Seymour Gross and Rosalie Murphy (New York: Norton, 1978), 106. Further references appear parenthetically within the text.

20. Sharon Cameron, *The Corporeal Self: Allegories of the Body in Melville and Hawthorne* (Baltimore: Johns Hopkins University Press, 1981), esp. 1–3, 11–13.

21. Herman Melville, *Moby-Dick,* ed. Harrison Hayford and Hershel Parker (New York: Norton, 1967), 430. Further references appear parenthetically within the text.

22. Samuel Otter, *Melville's Anatomies* (Berkeley: University of California Press, 1999), 5, 4.

23. For information on Henry, Sr.'s, injury, I have relied on Alfred Habegger, *The Father: A Life of Henry James, Sr.* (New York: Farrar Straus Giroux, 1994), 66–82.

24. Oliver Wendell Holmes, "The Human Wheel, Its Spokes and Felloes," *Atlantic Monthly* 11 (May 1863): 578, 574. Further references appear parenthetically in the text.

25. William James, "The Consciousness of Lost Limbs," in *Essays in Psychology,* ed. Frederick H. Burkhardt et al. (Cambridge: Harvard University Press, 1983), 207.

26. William James, "The Consciousness of Lost Limbs," 208–9n5.

27. My characterization of still life painting here is much indebted to Norman Bryson, *Looking at the Overlooked: Four Essays on Still Life Painting* (Cambridge: Harvard University Press, 1990), esp. 60–95; and to Richard Shiff, "Cézanne's Physicality: The Politics of Touch," in *The Language of Art History,* ed. Salim Kemal and Ivan Gaskell (Cambridge: Cambridge University Press, 1991), 129–80.

28. Michel de Certeau, *The Practice of Everyday Life,* trans. Steven Rendall (Berkeley: University of California Press, 1984), xii, xvii.

29. Henry James, *Notes of a Son and Brother,* in *Autobiography,* ed. Frederick W. Dupee (New York: Criterion, 1956), 415. Further references appear parenthetically within the text.

30. For an example of a psycho-sexual reading of the obscure hurt—the kind of reading I am not pursuing here—see Carol Holly, *Intensely Family: The Inheritance of Family Shame and the Autobiographies of Henry James* (Madison: University of Wisconsin Press, 1995), 119–36. For a view that complements my own approach by seeing the Jamesian wound not as a gap in the body that participation in a consumer economy might fill but instead as the visible sign of masculinity, see Susan M. Griffin, "Scar Texts: Tracing the Marks of Jamesian Masculinity," *Arizona Quarterly* 53:4 (Winter 1997): 61–82. Griffin's essay is unusually attentive to the prevalence of the "torn, marked, scarred body" in James, tracing that body from the first published stories to the late fictions "The Jolly Corner and "The Beast in the Jungle" (61).

31. *The Correspondence of William James,* vol. 1, *William and Henry: 1861–1884,* ed. Ignas K. Skrupskelis and Elizabeth M. Berkeley (Charlottesville: University Press of Virginia, 1992), 142–43.

32. *The Correspondence of William James,* 1:113–14.

33. *The Correspondence of William James,* 1:114.

34. Henry James, *The Europeans: A Sketch,* ed. Tony Tanner and Patricia Crick (London: Penguin, 1984), 79. Further references appear parenthetically within the text.

35. Melville, *Moby-Dick,* 436; Davis, *Life in the Iron-Mills,* 69–70.

36. Poe, "The Man That Was Used Up," 316.

37. Frederick Douglass, *Narrative of the Life of Frederick Douglass, An American Slave,* ed. Houston A. Baker, Jr. (New York: Penguin, 1982), 107.

38. Harriet Beecher Stowe, *Uncle Tom's Cabin; or, Life Among the Lowly,* ed. Ann Douglas (New York: Penguin, 1981), 81, 175; chapters 5, 11.

39. See Michaels, *Gold Standard,* 101–5, 117–31; Seltzer, *Bodies and Machines,* 47–48, 72–73, 80–81, 137–10; Merish, *Sentimental Materialism,* chapters 3–5.

40. Toni Morrison's statement in *Playing in the Dark: Whiteness and the Literary Imagination* (Cambridge: Harvard University Press, 1992) that "[i]t is possible . . . to read Henry James scholarship exhaustively and never arrive at a nodding mention . . . of the black woman who lubricates the turn of the plot and becomes the agency of moral choice and meaning in *What Maisie Knew*" succeeded impressively in bringing this issue to the center of subsequent scholarship (13). Kenneth Warren identifies the Jamesian technique of point of view—and its emphasis on the demarcation of individual perspective—with the separate-but-equal politics that became the social norm and eventually the legal doctrine of postbellum America (*Black and White Strangers: Race and American Literary Realism* [Chicago: University of Chicago Press, 1993], 18–47). Michaels, in a rejoinder to Morrison and Warren, argues that what repulses James is not dark-skinned people (which would be true if his politics were the same as Thomas Dixon's) but vulgar people instead ("Jim Crow Henry James?" *Henry James Review* 16 [1995]: 286–91). For Rowe's precise delineation of the different impulses that shape James's representation of dark-skinned people, and for an excellent overview of the critical debate, see his *The Other Henry James* (Durham: Duke University Press, 1998), 120–54.

Notes to Chapter 3

1. Thorstein Veblen, *The Theory of the Leisure Class* (New York: Penguin, 1979), 111, 135.

2. Karl Marx, *Capital: A Critique of Political Economy,* vol. 1, trans. Ben Fowkes (New York: Vintage, 1977), 138. Michel de Certeau makes the point even more succinctly than I do, referring to the critical term "consumers" as "euphemistic" because it begs the question of how individuals deploy what they consume (*The Practice of Everyday Life,* trans. Steven Rendall [Berkeley: University of California Press, 1984], xii). In making this argument, I mean to question the model of visual and vicarious consumption that Jean-Christophe Agnew establishes in his important essay, "The Consuming Vision of Henry James" (in *The Culture of Consumption: Critical Essays in American History, 1880–1980,* ed. Richard Wightman Fox and T. J. Jackson Lears [New York: Pantheon, 1983], 65–100). While my emphasis in this chapter on what Agnew calls the "internalization" of commodities is clearly in the spirit of his approach, I argue that there is much to be gained by closely detailed analysis of the world of things and, further, that there are reasons to distrust the emphasis on vision and detachment that all Jamesian commentators—beginning with James himself—have maintained.

3. Mary Poovey, "The Social Constitution of 'Class': Toward a History of Classificatory Thinking," in *Rethinking Class: Literary Studies and Social Formations,* ed. Wai Chee Dimock and Michael T. Gilmore (New York: Columbia University Press, 1994), 15.

4. Poovey, "The Social Constitution of 'Class,'" 20.

5. Philip Fisher, "A Humanism of Objects," in *Making and Effacing Art: Modern American Art in a Culture of Museums* (New York: Oxford University Press, 1991), 233. Here I would also like to acknowledge a general debt to Norman Bryson, *Looking at the Overlooked: Four Essays on Still Life Painting* (Cambridge: Harvard University Press, 1990).

6. Fisher, "A Humanism of Objects," 243–44.

7. For a much fuller account of this link, see Elaine Scarry, *The Body in Pain: The Making and Unmaking of the World* (New York: Oxford University Press, 1985), 243–326. Scarry argues that "the act of human creating includes both the creating of the object and the object's recreating of the human being" who uses it (310). In what follows, I extend Scarry's argument by showing how this process of recreation realizes class distinctions. This recursive movement between bodies and things, highly characteristic of James's thinking about the object world in *The Spoils,* means that objects are understood as made present by bodies even when those things are not explicitly present. This sublimated presence is the reason I disagree with the important and very interesting reading of the novel Bill Brown develops in *A Sense of Things: The Object Matter of American Literature* (Chicago: University of Chicago Press, 2003). Brown rightly observes that *The Spoils* specifically refers to only two objects at Poynton—the Italian cabinet in the red room and the Maltese cross—but wrongly argues that the novel's account of the material world is ultimately concerned with that world on a metaphysical level (147, 155). The body and the psyche are the physical entities that Brown's account leaves out, entities that would have been understood as continuous—with objects and with each other—in the highly somatic idiom of Gilded-Age thought, as this chapter will show.

8. Edith Wharton and Ogden Codman, Jr., *The Decoration of Houses* (New York: Scribner's, 1897), 186. Further references appear parenthetically within the text.

9. Just as Veblen notes with horror the "endless variety of architectural distress" that typifies the modern house (154), so too do Wharton and Codman note the economics of emulation—the "tendency to want things because other people have them, rather than to have things because they are wanted" (17)—that distort contemporary tastes. Veblen's belief that "the simple and unadorned article is aesthetically the best" places him on the cutting edge of design and makes *The Theory of the Leisure Class* a surprisingly reliable guide for the aesthetically inclined (152). For a valuable discussion of the relation between James and Veblen, see Ross Posnock, *The Trial of Curiosity: Henry James, William James, and the Challenge of Modernity* (New York: Oxford University Press, 1991), 259–61; and for a discussion of how critiques of commodity culture were themselves commodified, see Jonathan Freedman, *Professions of Taste: Henry James, British Aestheticism, and Commodity Culture* (Stanford: Stanford University Press, 1990), 81–82, 102–11.

10. H. B. H., "Successful Houses," *House Beautiful,* December 1896, 1–2.

11. Clarence Cook, *The House Beautiful: Essays on Beds and Tables, Stools and Candlesticks* (New York: Scribner's, 1878).

12. For one example, see Alice Morse Earle, *China Collecting in America* (New York: Scribner's, 1892), which refers to collectables as "spoils" (3).

13. Arthur Russell, "Grueby Pottery," *House Beautiful,* December 1898, 3.

14. Russell, "Grueby Pottery," 6, 7–8, 4, 8.

15. Amalie Busck, "Beaten Metal-Work," *House and Garden*, November 1902, 572.

16. Samuel Swift, "American Garden Pottery," *House and Garden*, January 1903, 33, 34.

17. Oscar Wilde, "Art and the Handicraftsman," in *Miscellanies*, ed. Robert Ross (London: Methuen, 1908), 299, 302.

18. Russell, "Grueby Pottery," 6.

19. Swift, "American Garden Pottery," 33, 34.

20. A. W. B., "Notes and Reviews," *House and Garden*, November 1903, 251–52.

21. Catharine E. Beecher and Harriet Beecher Stowe, *The American Woman's Home* (1869; rpt., Hartford, Conn.: Stowe-Day Foundation, 1987), 108.

22. Edgar Allan Poe, "The Fall of the House of Usher," in *Poetry and Tales*, ed. Patrick F. Quinn (New York: Library of America, 1984), 327, 328; Harriet Beecher Stowe, *Pink and White Tyranny: A Society Novel* (Boston: Roberts Brothers, 1871), 147; Charlotte Perkins Gilman, *"The Yellow Wall-Paper" and Other Stories*, ed. Robert Shulman (New York: Oxford University Press, 1995), 5, 9.

23. On Froebel and his influence on education, see Michael Steven Shapiro, *Child's Garden: The Kindergarten Movement from Froebel to Dewey* (University Park: Pennsylvania State University Press, 1983), 20–23.

24. Maria Montessori, *The Montessori Method*, trans. Ann E. George (1912; rpt., New York: Schocken, 1964), 185, 145, 163. See also John Dewey, *The School and Society*, in *"The Child and the Curriculum" and "The School and Society"* (Chicago: University of Chicago Press, 1956), 12–18, 40–47, 127–28.

25. William James, *Talks to Teachers on Psychology and to Students on Some of Life's Ideals*, ed. Frederick H. Burkhardt et al. (Cambridge: Harvard University Press, 1983), 31, 43–44, 31.

26. Mary Abbott, "Individuality in Homes," *House Beautiful*, March 1898, 93.

27. *The Decoration of Houses'* rendering of individuality as imitation links the design book to Wharton's later fiction, particularly to the careers of Undine Spragg in *The Custom of the Country* (who invariably "want[s] what the others want") and Newland Archer in *The Age of Innocence* (who invariably finds himself "saying all the things that young men" in his "situation were expected to say") (*The Custom of the Country*, ed. Stephen Orgel [New York: Oxford University Press, 1995], 64; *The Age of Innocence*, ed. R. W. B. Lewis [New York: Collier, 1986], 82). For an earlier important reading of *The Decoration of Houses* in the context of Wharton's fiction, see Amy Kaplan, *The Social Construction of American Realism* (Chicago: University of Chicago Press, 1988), 77–80. Kaplan treats *Decoration* as part of "Wharton's effort to write herself out of the private domestic sphere and to inscribe a public identity in the marketplace" (67).

28. *Decoration of Houses*, 132; Havelock Ellis, *Man and Woman: A Study of Human Secondary Sexual Characters*, 4th ed. (London: Walter Scott, 1904), 124. On the physiology of the female touch, see Cynthia Eagle Russett, *Sexual Science: The Victorian Construction of Womanhood* (Cambridge: Harvard University Press, 1989), 42–46; Russett points out that this is an area of contention, with some scientists finding that men possess the sharper sense of touch. On the traditional refining office of the female hand, see Lori Merish, "'The Hand of Refined Taste'

in the Frontier Landscape: Caroline Kirkland's *A New Home, Who'll Follow?* and the Feminization of American Consumerism," *American Quarterly* 45 (December 1993): 485–523.

29. Abbott, "Individuality in Homes," 91–92. Consider James's comment on Lamb House, which he leased the same year *The Spoils* appeared in book form (a lease that the novel's royalties presumably helped to pay): "I have lived into my little old house and garden so thoroughly that they have become a kind of domiciliary skin, that can't be peeled off without pain" (quoted in Leon Edel, *Henry James: A Life* [New York: Harper & Row, 1985], 643).

30. Charles L. Eastlake, *Hints on Household Taste,* 4th ed. (1878; rpt., New York: Dover, 1969), 83–84.

31. On this tradition, see Marc Bloch, *The Royal Touch: Sacred Monarchy and Scrofula in England and France,* trans. J. E. Anderson (London: Routledge & Kegan Paul, 1973). Bloch notes that objects touched by the monarch were also thought to possess healing power and that vestiges of the myth survived in England into the end of the nineteenth century (222–23).

32. Frank Podmore, *Studies in Psychical Research* (London: Kegan Paul, 1897), 67. James's own account of a piece of haunted furniture—in this case a writing desk—is the story "Sir Dominick Ferrand" (1892).

33. Gustave Flaubert, *Bouvard and Pécuchet,* trans. A. J. Krailsheimer (Harmondsworth: Penguin, 1976), 144.

34. Scarry, *The Body in Pain,* 125.

35. William James, *The Principles of Psychology,* ed. Frederick Burkhardt et al. (Cambridge: Harvard University Press, 1983), 113. Further references appear parenthetically within the text. *The Principles'* chapter on habit draws heavily on the language and imagery of work by the physiologist William Benjamin Carpenter and other neuroscientists. Such borrowings are easily traced and I have not noted them when they occur; their plentifulness suggests the extent to which James's chapter crystallizes a widely shared set of assumptions about how the body becomes acculturated.

36. Wai Chee Dimock, "Class, Gender, and a History of Metonymy," in *Rethinking Class: Literary Studies and Social Formations,* 59.

37. Francis Galton, *Finger Prints* (London: Macmillan, 1892), 63. Further references appear parenthetically within the text.

38. Francis Galton, "Identification by Finger-tips," *Nineteenth Century* 30 (August 1891): 303–4. See also *Finger Prints:* "Is this upstart claimant to property the true heir, who was believed to have died in foreign lands?" (149). Galton's use of the word "claimant" here would have conjured up images of the celebrated Tichborne Claimant, Arthur Orton, who appeared in England in 1866, claiming to be the long-lost heir to a large fortune.

39. Anthony Giddens, *The Class Structure of the Advanced Societies* (London: Hutchinson, 1973), 105. This is the place to mention what may seem to be an obvious problem with *The Spoils,* one that F. O. Matthiessen raised fifty years ago. Matthiessen complained of a mismatch between Fleda's origins and her refinement, of a "lack of congruity between the environment which would have produced [such] a character and the traits the author has imputed to" her (*Henry James: The Major Phase* [London: Oxford University Press, 1944], 90). To argue in this way is to fault the novel for not holding class together and, ulti-

mately, to fault class itself for not holding together. One of my points in this chapter is that class is indeed incoherent but that its incoherence makes it a most resilient concept.

40. My point here is indebted to Susan Stewart, *On Longing: Narratives of the Miniature, the Gigantic, the Souvenir, the Collection* (Baltimore: Johns Hopkins University Press, 1984).

41. Vernon Lee and C. Anstruther-Thomson, "Beauty and Ugliness," *Contemporary Review* 72 (1897): 567. For more on the aesthetics of empathy, see the essays collected in *Empathy, Form, and Space: Problems in German Aesthetics, 1873–1893*, introd. and trans. Harry Francis Mallgrave and Eleftherios Ikonomou (Santa Monica, CA: Getty Center for the History of Art and the Humanities, 1994); Robert Vischer's "On the Optical Sense of Form" (1873) is especially pertinent here.

42. Bernhard Berenson, *Florentine Painters of the Renaissance* (New York: Putnam's, 1896), 14, 50.

43. Berenson, *Florentine Painters*, 10.

44. My argument here bears similarities to Jeff Nunokawa's account of the vicissitudes of property in the Victorian novel, especially to his claim that novel economies achieve an ultimate stability by transforming property into objects of the female imagination; see *The Afterlife of Property: Domestic Security and the Victorian Novel* (Princeton: Princeton University Press, 1994), 13–15.

Notes to Chapter 4

1. "Academy Outrage," *The Times*, 5 May, 1914.

2. When they treat this incident, James's biographers strain to make it mean something and to fill in its alluring vacancies. Hence Leon Edel asserts that Mary Wood "said she had never heard of Henry James"—a claim totally unsupported by any cited source—and then notes that James received an avalanche of condolences over the incident: "The suffragette had only caused him to receive, hardly a year after his seventieth birthday, still another ovation." Edel's narration of the incident falls in line with his emphasis on seeing the end of James's life as a series of crowning achievements and insulates the Master from the more unruly aspects of Edwardian culture (Leon Edel, *Henry James: A Life* [New York: Harper & Row, 1985], 686). Fred Kaplan treats the incident as "a bizarre prelude to the violence to come," a summation that simultaneously consigns the incident to the realm of the impossibly weird and makes it a harbinger of World War I (Fred Kaplan, *Henry James, The Imagination of Genius: A Biography* [New York: William Morrow, 1992], 551).

3. David Freedberg, *The Power of Images: Studies in the History and Theory of Response* (Chicago: University of Chicago Press, 1989), 378–428.

4. For Jamesian criticism that understands painting as a static and relatively atemporal medium within the Jamesian text, see Laurence B. Holland, *The Expense of Vision: Essays on the Craft of Henry James* (Princeton: Princeton University Press, 1964), esp. 43–49, with its emphasis on painting as a metaphor for "completion" (50); John Carlos Rowe, *The Theoretical Dimensions of Henry James* (Madison: University of Wisconsin Press, 1984), which finds a disquieting "formalism" in

Lambert Strether's habit of seeing scenes in terms of pictures and which sustains its argument according to an opposition between "pure impression" and "complex social action" (199, 201); Jonathan Freedman, *Professions of Taste: Henry James, British Aestheticism, and Commodity Culture* (Stanford: Stanford University Press, 1990), which equates portraiture with reification (e.g., 158). For a discussion of James's representation of painting that does *not* see painting as static but sees it instead as crucial to the endless reproduction of persons in capitalism, see Mark Seltzer, *Bodies and Machines* (New York: Routledge, 1992), esp. 66–69.

5. Norman Bryson, *Vision and Painting: The Logic of the Gaze* (New Haven: Yale University Press, 1983), 164.

6. "Another Academy Outrage," *The Times*, 13 May 1914.

7. Quoted in Dario Gamboni, *The Destruction of Art: Iconoclasm and Vandalism since the French Revolution* (New Haven: Yale University Press, 1997), 95. This is a highly rigorous study of its seemingly eccentric topic; I am much indebted to it.

8. "National Gallery Outrage," *The Times*, 11 March, 1914.

9. "National Gallery Outrage." Here I develop comments made by Gamboni, *The Destruction of Art*, 96, and Freedberg, *The Power of Images*, 412, on economic value and the vandalism of paintings. For an excellent study of the symbolic aspect of the forms of suffragist protest, see Cheryl R. Jorgenson-Earp, *"The Transfiguring Sword": The Just War of the Women's Social and Political Union* (Tuscaloosa: University of Alabama Press, 1997).

10. "The Damaged Venus," *The Times*, 13 March, 1914.

11. Oscar Wilde, *The Picture of Dorian Gray*, ed. Isobel Murray (Oxford: Oxford University Press, 1981), 223. Further references appear parenthetically within the text.

12. Pliny the Elder, *Natural History*, trans. H. Rackham (Cambridge: Harvard University Press, 1938–63), 35, 64–66. For recent discussions of this story, see Bryson, *Vision and Painting*, 1–3; Stephen Bann, *The True Vine: On Visual Representation and the Western Tradition* (Cambridge: Cambridge University Press, 1989), 27–40.

13. On this large matter of Wilde's decentering poetics, see Eve Kosofsky Sedgwick, *Epistemology of the Closet* (Berkeley: University of California Press, 1990), 131–76. For another discussion of the economy of Wilde's novel, see Jeff Nunokawa, "The Importance of Being Bored: The Dividends of Ennui in *The Picture of Dorian Gray*," in *Novel Gazing: Queer Readings in Fiction*, ed. Eve Kosofsky Sedgwick (Durham, NC: Duke University Press, 1997), 151–66. From Sedgwick, I take a deeper understanding of how strange and crucial the Wildean surface is; from Nunokawa, I take a stronger sense of how endless and crucial circulation is in Wilde.

14. Georg Simmel, "The Picture Frame: An Aesthetic Study," trans. Mark Ritter, *Theory, Culture, and Society* 11 (1994): 12.

15. On the relation between portraiture and narrative, see Françoise Meltzer, *Salome and the Dance of Writing: Portraits of Mimesis in Literature* (Chicago: University of Chicago Press, 1987), and Wendy Steiner, *Pictures of Romance: Form against Context in Painting and Literature* (Chicago: University of Chicago Press, 1988). Some of this paragraph's phrasing also owes a general debt to Susan Stewart, *Crimes of Writing: Problems in the Containment of Representation* (New York: Oxford University Press, 1991).

16. I know of no compelling evidence that Wilde read James's "Liar"; nor, of course, do I know of any compelling evidence that he did not. Freedman, who writes about James's more general relation to *Dorian* (*Professions of Taste*, 41–46, 192–96), and Christopher Lane, who writes about the two texts together, make no mention of any direct influence ("Framing Fears, Reading Designs: The Homosexual Art of Painting in James, Wilde, and Beerbohm," *ELH* 61 [1994]: 923–54). My sense is that slashing a painting is one of those metaphors Wilde and James uncomfortably shared, one of those metaphors that their similar interests led them to adopt more or less simultaneously.

17. This paragraph bears a general debt to Richard Brilliant, *Portraiture* (Cambridge: Harvard University Press, 1991), and a more specific debt to Maurice Grosser's definition of the portrait as "a picture painted at a distance of four to eight feet of a person who is not paid to sit" (Grosser, *The Painter's Eye* [New York: Rinehart, 1951], 15–16; cited in Brilliant, *Portraiture*, 71).

18. See *The Portrait of a Lady* (3:287) and "Honoré de Balzac" (1875) in Henry James, *Literary Criticism: French Writers, Other European Writers, The Prefaces*, ed. Leon Edel and Mark Wilson (New York: Library of America, 1984), 48.

19. The Colonel's lies are endlessly interpretable; for a canny homosocial reading see Lane, "Framing Fears," 928–36.

20. Henry James, "John S. Sargent," in *The Painter's Eye: Notes and Essays on the Pictorial Arts*, ed. John L. Sweeney (1956; Madison: University of Wisconsin Press, 1989), 227. Further references appear parenthetically within the text.

21. See the reproductions in Richard Ormond and Elaine Kilmurray, *John Singer Sargent: The Early Portraits*, vol. 1 of *Complete Paintings* (New Haven: Yale University Press, 1998), 113–18, figures 50–60. On this point, the passages of revision and overpainting evident in a portrait such as *Mrs. Charles Inches* also indicate that James's theoretical model of the quick impression overrides his ability to see some of the material particulars of the paintings he writes about (Ormond and Kilmurray, *Sargent: The Early Portraits*, plate 198, p. 203, and enlarged detail, p. 194).

22. *Henry James and Edith Wharton: Letters, 1900–1915*, ed. Lyall H. Powers (New York: Scribner's, 1990), 212.

23. On touch and the marks of identity in James and Galton, see chapter 3.

24. Giovanni Morelli, *Italian Painters: Critical Studies of Their Works*, trans. Constance Jocelyn Ffoulkes, 2 vols. (London: John Murray, 1900), 1: 74, 37.

25. Morelli, *Italian Painters*, 1:75.

26. Richard Wollheim, "Giovanni Morelli and the Origins of Scientific Connoisseurship," in *On Art and the Mind* (Cambridge: Harvard University Press, 1974), 197.

27. Bernhard Berenson, *Lorenzo Lotto: An Essay in Constructive Art Criticism* (New York: Putnam's, 1895), 78; Berenson, "Rudiments of Connoisseurship," in *The Study and Criticism of Italian Art* (London: George Bell, 1902), 143, 145. James would not meet Berenson until sometime in the beginning of the new century, but he would have heard of him from their mutual friends Isabella Stewart Gardner and Hendrik Andersen, as well as from his brother William, who taught Berenson at Harvard and later wrote a noncommittal review of *Florentine Painters* (William James, untitled review, in *Essays, Comments, and Reviews*, ed. Frederick H. Burkhardt et al. [Cambridge: Harvard University Press, 1987], 523–24). A

long review of Berenson's *Florentine Painters of the Renaissance* appeared in the *Atlantic Monthly* while that journal was publishing serial installments of *The Spoils of Poynton* ("The Philosophy of Enjoyment of Art," *Atlantic Monthly* 77 [1896]: 844–48). Much later, in *The Outcry*, which was first a play (1909) and then a novel (1911), James would draw on Berenson for his character Breckenridge Bender, an American art dealer bent on raiding Europe for masterpieces.

28. Berenson, "Rudiments," 145.

29. Nikolai Lange as quoted in William James, *Principles of Psychology*, ed. Frederick H. Burkhardt et al. (Cambridge: Harvard University Press, 1983), 421. See also the discussion of vision and touch in James's chapter on "The Perception of Space," esp. 818, 821.

30. Bernhard Berenson, *Florentine Painters of the Renaissance* (New York: Putnam's, 1896), 27.

31. Robert Vischer, *On the Optical Sense of Form* (1873), in *Empathy, Form, and Space: Problems in German Aesthetics, 1873–1893*, ed. and trans. Harry Francis Mallgrave and Eleftherios Ikonomou (Santa Monica, CA: Getty Center for the History of Art and the Humanities, 1994), 104.

32. Vernon Lee and C. Anstruther-Thomson, "Beauty and Ugliness," *Contemporary Review* 72 (1897): 550.

33. Lee and Anstruther-Thomson, "Beauty and Ugliness," 554, 561.

34. Bernhard Berenson, *Central Italian Painters of the Renaissance* (New York: Putnam's, 1897), 74.

35. Berenson, *Florentine Painters*, 39.

36. Here it should be made clear that I am following Regenia Gagnier's discrimination of the varieties of aestheticism between Wilde's "socially-oriented aestheticism," which is "public, erotic, active," and "the properly decadent aestheticism" of Joris-Karl Huysmans's Des Esseintes in *À Rebours*, which is "solitary, neurotic, reactive" (Gagnier, "A Critique of Practical Aesthetics," in *Aesthetics and Ideology*, ed. George Levine (New Brunswick, NJ: Rutgers University Press, 1994), 270. On these terms, Nash is a decadent aesthete, while the other disciples of art in *The Tragic Muse* struggle toward a devotion to making. Freedman makes this discrimination more implicitly (*Professions of Taste*, 190).

37. Ludwig Wittgenstein, *Philosophical Investigations*, trans. G. E. M. Anscombe, 3rd ed. (New York: Macmillan, 1968), 48.

Notes to Chapter 5

1. Samuel D. Warren and Louis D. Brandeis, "The Right to Privacy," *Harvard Law Review* 4 (1890): 195, 207. Further references appear parenthetically in the text. There is no shortage of commentary on Warren and Brandeis—often called the most influential journal essay in American law—but there is not much material that analyzes the article in the context of nineteenth-century American culture. Three useful exceptions are James H. Barron, "Warren and Brandeis, *The Right to Privacy*, 4 Harv. L. Rev. 193 (1890): Demystifying a Landmark Citation," *Suffolk University Law Review* 13 (1979): 875–922; [Unsigned note], "The Right to Privacy in Nineteenth-Century America," *Harvard Law Review* 94 (1981): 1892–1910; Robert E. Mensel, "'Kodakers Lying

in Wait'": Photography and the Right to Privacy in New York, 1885–1915,"
American Quarterly 43 (1991): 24–45.

2. On the tendency of Americans of the period to characterize their own time
as one of publicity and self-display, see Philip Fisher, "Appearing and Disappearing
in Public: Social Space in Late-Nineteenth-Century Literature and Culture," in
Reconstructing American Literary History, ed. Sacvan Bercovitch (Cambridge:
Harvard University Press, 1986), 155–88.

3. For earlier arguments that link James's fiction with the origins of the legal
right to privacy, see Alexander Welsh, "Threatening Publicity," in *George Eliot and
Blackmail* (Cambridge: Harvard University Press, 1985), 61–64; Brook Thomas,
"The Construction of Privacy in and around *The Bostonians*," *American Literature*
64 (1992): 719–47.

4. *The Complete Notebooks of Henry James*, ed. Leon Edel and Lyall H. Powers
(New York: Oxford University Press, 1987), 40.

5. *Boyd v. United States*, 116 U.S. 628, 630 (1886). This is not to say that the
majority decision in *Boyd* is a straightforward discovery of a right to privacy in the
fourth amendment or that *Boyd* is explicitly concerned with the right to one's own
body. Though the decision does affirm the protection of one's papers, its affirma-
tion of that right rests much more heavily on property rights than on privacy
rights.

6. Stephen Greenblatt, *Renaissance Self-Fashioning: From More to Shakespeare*
(Chicago: University of Chicago Press, 1980), 179.

7. Jonathan Goldberg, *Writing Matter: From the Hands of the English
Renaissance* (Stanford: Stanford University Press, 1990), 100. As the source of the
quotation perhaps suggests, the Renaissance is another point at which these relations acquire a high degree of visibility and urgency, and it is hardly coincidental
that the nineteenth-century literary commentary I will consider below devotes
itself almost entirely to certain Renaissance texts. Nor is it coincidental that one
point at which the body has emerged most visibly in the criticism of our own time
is Renaissance studies; there is a whole anthology made up of essays devoted to
individual organs and members (the leg, the tongue, joints, the anus) (see *The
Body in Parts: Fantasies of Corporeality in Early Modern Europe*, ed. David Hillman
and Carla Mazzio [New York: Routledge, 1997]). For work on the relations
between writing and the body in late-nineteenth-century American culture, see
especially Walter Benn Michaels, *The Gold Standard and the Logic of Naturalism:
American Literature at the Turn of the Century* (Berkeley: University of California
Press, 1987), and Michael Fried, *Realism, Writing, Disfiguration: On Thomas
Eakins and Stephen Crane* (Chicago: University of Chicago Press, 1987); both discover a strong tendency in the Gilded Age to associate the materiality of writing
with the physicality of the self.

8. Meyer Schapiro, *Words, Script, and Pictures: Semiotics of Visual Language*
(New York: George Braziller, 1996), 173.

9. Henry James, *The Princess Casamassima*, ed. Derek Brewer and Patricia
Crick (Harmondsworth: Penguin, 1986), 302–3. Here I use the 1886 edition,
since its registration of the effects of writing is in this instance more concrete than
the New York Edition's version of the passage.

10. *Complete Notebooks*, 195.

11. Fritz Machlup defines knowledge occupations as ones "that are designed

chiefly to aid in the generation, transmission, or reception of knowledge of any type, sort, or quality, including giving, directly or through instruments, visual, aural, or otherwise sensible signals, and ranging from carrying new messages to creating new knowledge" (*Knowledge and Knowledge Production* [Princeton: Princeton University Press, 1980], 228–29). Machlup's term seems a useful one to bear in mind here because it sees telegraph clerks, literary reviewers, paper manufacturers, bookbinders, and so forth, as part of the same developing economy of information production and distribution—a perception which, I am suggesting, Machlup shares with James. The term also seems to me useful for any attempt to develop a more materially and historically specific understanding of the famous Jamesian concern with knowledge. For more on James's interest in scriptive professions, see Mark Seltzer, *Bodies and Machines* (New York: Routledge, 1992), 77–80, 195–97.

12. Susan Stewart, *On Longing: Narratives of the Miniature, the Gigantic, the Souvenir, the Collection* (Baltimore: Johns Hopkins University Press, 1984), 44.

13. Gaston Bachelard, *The Poetics of Space,* trans. Maria Jolas (Boston: Beacon Press, 1969), 78.

14. On the construction of grave-robbing as a violation of privacy, see Catherine Gallagher, "The Duplicity of Doubling in *A Tale of Two Cities,*" *Dickens Studies Annual* 12 (1984): 125–45.

15. *Complete Notebooks,* 33–34. The literary history here is actually even more intertwined, since Hawthorne knew Silsbee when both were living in England; it is not clear whether or not James knew this. On Hawthorne's acquaintance with Silsbee, see James R. Mellow, *Nathaniel Hawthorne in His . Times* (Boston: Houghton Mifflin, 1980), 479–80. See also Richard H. Brodhead's incisive discussion of the uses that James makes in developing *The Aspern Papers* of Hawthorne's characteristic motifs (*The School of Hawthorne* [New York: Oxford University Press, 1986], 106–7).

16. Laurence B. Holland, *The Expense of Vision: Essays on the Craft of Henry James,* 2nd ed. (Baltimore: Johns Hopkins University Press, 1982), 130–38, 144–45.

17. Walter Bagehot, *Literary Essays,* ed. Norman St. John-Stevas (London: The Economist, 1965), 195.

18. Virginia Woolf, *Mrs. Dalloway* (New York: Harcourt, Brace, 1925), 113.

19. Edward Dowden, ed., *The Sonnets of William Shakespeare* (London: Kegan Paul, 1881), 6. On nineteenth-century constructions of Shakespeare see S. Schoenbaum's fairly exhaustive *Shakespeare's Lives* (Oxford: Clarendon Press, 1970), 251–613. On the sonnets' critical history, see also Hyder Edward Rollins, ed., *A New Variorum Edition of Shakespeare: The Sonnets* (Philadelphia: Lippincott, 1944).

20. Robert Browning, *The Poems,* ed. John Pettigrew (New Haven: Yale University Press, 1981), 2: 438. Further references by line number appear parenthetically within the text.

21. Bachelard, *Poetics of Space,* 82. A longer analysis here might well pay attention to the further associations of sonnets and privacy in Browning's representations of Shakespeare, as well as to the intertwining of portraits and poetry in both Renaissance poetics and in *The Aspern Papers.* Briefly: in Browning's well-known essay on Shelley, Shakespeare stands as the prime example of the objective poet,

an example that returns in "At the 'Mermaid,'" another poem about Shakespeare and the one that immediately precedes "House" in Browning's 1876 collection, *Pacchiarotto and How He Worked in Distemper.* "At the 'Mermaid'" takes as its epigraph an adaptation of the first line of Ben Jonson's "To the Reader," a poem about Shakespeare's portrait which was printed opposite the portrait in the First Folio. Jonson's concluding lines—"Reader, look / Not on his Picture, but his Book"— seem ironically echoed in the editor's fixation on Juliana's miniature portrait of Aspern and on the sexual experience (or even just the lived experience) that Aspern's poems imply without really revealing.

Furthermore, sonnets and miniature portraits were sometimes seen in the Renaissance as analogous forms which, as Patricia Fumerton argues, simultaneously revealed and concealed the true self. Fumerton demonstrates that both sonnets and miniatures were strategically coded as private, revealed to others only in scenes of stagy intimacy; both establish and test the boundaries between public and private realms ("'Secret' Arts: Elizabethan Miniatures and Sonnets," *Representations* 15 [1986], 57–97).

Finally, Susan Stewart suggests that the miniature offers a world that we can know only through visual experience, a world that, since it is enclosed and contained, we can never touch (*On Longing*, 57–70). In these respects, viewing the miniature is an experience very close to the editor's experience with Aspern's poems and nineteenth-century readers' experiences with Shakespeare's sonnets as I have summarized them. For a rich analysis of James's relation to Browning's aesthetics and public image, see Ross Posnock, *Henry James and the Problem of Robert Browning* (Athens: University of Georgia Press, 1985).

22. Oscar Wilde, *The Portrait of Mr. W. H.,* in *Complete Shorter Fiction,* ed. Isobel Murray (Oxford: Oxford University Press, 1979), 154.

23. Samuel Butler, *Shakespeare's Sonnets Reconsidered, and in Part Rearranged* (London: Longmans, 1899), 119, 87.

24. Marjorie Garber, *Shakespeare's Ghost Writers: Literature as Uncanny Causality* (New York: Methuen, 1987), 1–12.

25. Michel Foucault, *The History of Sexuality,* vol. 1, *An Introduction,* trans. Robert Hurley (New York: Vintage, 1980), 107.

26. Eve Kosofsky Sedwick, *Between Men: English Literature and Male Homosocial Desire* (New York: Columbia University Press, 1985), 28.

27. William A. Cohen, *Sex Scandal: The Private Parts of Victorian Fiction* (Durham: Duke University Press, 1996), 196.

28. C. M. Ingleby, *Shakespeare's Bones* (London: Trubner, 1883), 28–29.

29. Ingleby, *Shakespeare's Bones,* 18–21.

30. Henry James, "In Warwickshire," in *English Hours,* ed. Leon Edel (Oxford: Oxford University Press, 1981), 122–23.

31. Letter to Violet Hunt, 26 August 1903, quoted in Leon Edel, *Henry James, The Master: 1901–1916* (Philadelphia: Lippincott, 1972), 145.

32. Letter to Harry James, April 1914, quoted in Edel, *Henry James, The Master,* 142.

33. E. L. Godkin, "The Rights of the Citizen. IV.—To His Own Reputation," *Scribner's Magazine* 8 (July 1890): 65, 66. Warren and Brandeis cite Godkin at the beginning of their article, noting that "the evil of the invasion of privacy by the newspapers, long keenly felt, has been but recently discussed by an able writer" (195).

34. Henry James, "The Papers," *The Better Sort* (New York: Scribner's, 1903), 336. Further references appear parenthetically in the text. James's most explicit critique of what he sees as the American "mistrust of privacy" comes in *The American Scene* (1907; rpt., ed. Leon Edel [Bloomington: Indiana University Press, 1968], 62; see also 9–11, 166–68). For an important discussion of the roles played by gender and the body in the dissemination of cultural values like privacy, see Lynn Wardley, "Woman's Voice, Democracy's Body, and *The Bostonians,*" *ELH* 56 (1989): 639–65.

35. For my discussion of the story, see chapter 2.

36. Henry James, *The Bostonians,* ed. Charles R. Anderson (Harmondsworth: Penguin, 1984), 123.

37. Golderg, *Writing Matter,* 97.

38. In addition to the preface, see the notebook entry that led to "The Private Life" (*Complete Notebooks,* 60–61).

39. For the suggestion that we imagine ghosts as only partially disembodied, I am indebted to Georges Rey, "Survival," in *The Identities of Persons,* ed. Amélie Oksenberg Rorty (Berkeley: University of California Press, 1976), 57–61. Rey notes that most pictures of "ghosts are pictures of familiar physical bodies, just paler" (58). In *Shakespeare's Ghost Writers,* Marjorie Garber provides a somewhat different account from mine of the author as ghost, but she, too, emphasizes this sense of the ghostly as the partially disembodied.

40. W. H. Auden, "Shakespeare's Sonnets," in *Forewords and Afterwords,* ed. Edward Mendelson (New York: Random House, 1973), 89; originally published as Introduction to William Shakespeare, *Sonnets* (New York: New American Library, 1964). All further references are to the Random House collection and appear parenthetically within the text.

41. Eve Kosofsky Sedgwick, *Epistemology of the Closet* (Berkeley: University of California Press, 1990), 72.

Notes to Chapter 6

1. Henry James, *The Sacred Fount,* ed. Leon Edel (London: Rupert Hart-Davis, 1959), 30. Further references appear parenthetically within the text. On James and the breakdown of evidential reasoning, see Alexander Welsh, *Strong Representations: Narrative and Circumstantial Evidence in England* (Baltimore: Johns Hopkins University Press, 1992), 237–56.

2. William Dean Howells, *Questionable Shapes* (New York: Harper's, 1903). In thinking about the late fiction, I have learned from the deconstructive tradition in general and in particular from Julie Rivkin's analysis of deferred and substituted meaning in *The Ambassadors.* Obviously, I believe that Rivkin's approach runs the risk of restating a particular political economy as if it were a general condition of language, but I will not deny that her argument has been instructive. See Julie Rivkin, *False Positions: The Representational Logics of Henry James's Fiction* (Stanford: Stanford University Press, 1996), 57–81.

3. Charles Dickens, *David Copperfield,* ed. Nina Burgis (Oxford: Oxford University Press, 1983), 195, 199. On Emma Bovary's taste for fashion as a taste for adultery, see Tony Tanner, *Adultery in the Novel: Contract and Transgression* (Baltimore: Johns Hopkins University Press, 1979), 254–65, 284–91.

4. My argument here is much indebted to Michael Trask, "Chance, Choice, and *The Wings of the Dove,*" in *Cruising Modernism: Class and Sexuality in American Literature and Social Thought* (Ithaca: Cornell University Press, 2003), 44–73. Trask's argument associates the material properties of objects in the late Jamesian text—especially slipperiness and stickiness—with James's sense of how early-twentieth-century social flux destabilizes referential security in his fiction. My argument here bears similarities as well to Tony Tanner's observation that adultery in the novel is linked with the mixing of material things and the destabilization of property (*Adultery in the Novel,* 284–91). But my argument differs hugely from Tanner's because where he insists that adultery causes the "collapse" of culture, I argue that adulterous matters *are* culture, that they epitomize the ways in which culture promulgates itself, or at least they do for James in the late fiction (65). Tanner has a strong need to understand adultery as the pathological case, even when his readings, especially in the case of *Madame Bovary,* blur beyond recognition the line between the pathological and the healthy.

Finally, for a canny discussion of the amorphous, ambient material qualities I have been discussing as the never-to-be-pinned down marks of homosexual desire, see Leland Monk's analysis of James's story "The Author of *Beltraffio*" ("A Terrible Beauty Is Born: Henry James, Aestheticism, and Homosexual Panic," in *Bodies of Writing, Bodies in Performance,* ed. Thomas Foster, Carol Siegel, and Ellen E. Berry [New York: New York University Press, 1996], 247–65).

5. Jean-Paul Sartre, *Baudelaire,* trans. Martin Turnell (New York: New Directions, 1950), 174.

6. John Locke, *Two Treatises of Government,* ed. Peter Laslett (Cambridge: Cambridge University Press, 1988), 288.

7. Locke, *Two Treatises,* 287.

8. See, for example, in the *Principles of Psychology* the characterization of thoughts as *"owned"* (221), of the objects of consciousness as things that we "appropriate" (304), of the successive "pulse[s] of thought" as analogous to a herd of branded cattle, marked with the sign of ownership (319), and of the self as a "proprietor" (322).

9. John Locke, *An Essay Concerning Human Understanding,* ed. Peter H. Nidditch (Oxford: Oxford University Press, 1979), 104, 117, 316, 150. Further references appear parenthetically within the text. Here I have been guided by Neal Wood's argument that Locke's conception of humans as acquisitive creatures shapes his metaphors for knowledge (Wood, *The Politics of Locke's Philosophy: A Social Study of "An Essay Concerning Human Understanding,"* [Berkeley: University of California Press, 1983], 159).

10. On this shifting relation between private collection and public museum, see Lorraine J. Daston, "The Factual Sensibility," *Isis* 79 (1988): 459–60, and then the work she cites by Giuseppe Olmi, "Science—Honour—Metaphor: Italian Cabinets of the Sixteenth and Seventeenth Centuries," in *The Origins of Museums: The Cabinet of Curiosities in Sixteenth- and Seventeenth-Century Europe,* ed. Oliver Impey and Arthur MacGregor (Oxford: Oxford University Press, 1985), 5–16.

11. For criticism that identifies in various ways the implication in James that consciousness can be externalized, see Sharon Cameron, *Thinking in Henry James* (Chicago: University of Chicago Press, 1989), who shows in her chapter on *The Wings of the Dove* how thought is "objectified," "made material" (122–68); Ruth

Bernard Yeazell, *Language and Knowledge in the Late Novels of Henry James* (Chicago: University of Chicago Press, 1976), who argues that characters' consciousnesses in the late novels "create the terms of" their worlds (12); Mark Seltzer, *Henry James and the Art of Power* (Ithaca: Cornell University Press, 1984), who shows how in the late fiction that "the desire to know is also a will to power" (77).

12. Karl Marx, *Capital: A Critique of Political Economy*, vol. 1, trans. Ben Fowkes (New York: Vintage, 1977), 493–94n4.

13. Donald Preziosi, *Rethinking Art History: Meditations on a Coy Science* (New Haven: Yale University Press, 1989), 69.

14. For my knowledge of Soane and his museum, I have relied on the Museum handbook roughly contemporary with James's novel: *General Description of Sir John Soane's Museum*, 8th ed. (Oxford: Hart, 1905). I have also consulted Gillian Darley, *John Soane, An Accidental Romantic* (New Haven: Yale University Press, 1999), and John Elsner, "A Collector's Model of Desire: The House and Museum of Sir John Soane," in *The Cultures of Collecting*, ed. John Elsner and Roger Cardinal (London: Reaktion, 1994), 155–76. Elsner's essay strains the evidence very hard in order to maintain his conception of the museum as the image of rationalized totality, and I have implicitly argued against this essay in my own discussion.

15. Ovid, *Metamorphoses*, trans. Mary M. Innes (Harmondsworth: Penguin, 1955), Book 8, lines 165–67, p. 183.

16. On this malleability, see Leo Bersani's argument, in "The Jamesian Lie," that James's novels of falsehood "propose a language responsive almost exclusively to the inspirations of its own surfaces" (Bersani, *A Future for Astyanax: Character and Desire in Literature* [Boston: Little, Brown, 1976], 146).

17. David Murray, *Museums, Their History and Their Use*, 3 vols. (Glasgow: MacLehose, 1904), 1:264. Further references are to volume 1 and appear parenthetically within the text by page number only.

18. For a study of the structuring of the archive in Britain at the end of the nineteenth century, see Thomas Richards, *The Imperial Archive: Knowledge and the Fantasy of Empire* (London: Verso, 1993).

19. On the shift toward a separation of vision and touch in nineteenth-century thought, see Jonathan Crary, *Techniques of the Observer: On Vision and Modernity in the Nineteenth Century* (Cambridge: MIT Press, 1990). I largely agree with Crary's hypothesis, but the texts I have examined in this book indicate that the assimilation of looking and touching had a much longer half-life than Crary suggests; Crary locates the separation of the senses in the 1850s, long before the association had ceased to do its work in pedagogical theory or ideas about craft (124).

20. Benjamin Ives Gilman, *Museum Ideals of Purpose and Method* (Cambridge: Harvard University Press, 1918), 388, 289.

21. Cameron, *Thinking in Henry James*, 159–60.

22. For other interpretations of *The Sacred Fount* as a novel about thinking, interpreting, and observing, see Paul B. Armstrong, *The Challenge of Bewilderment: Understanding and Representation in James, Conrad, and Ford* (Ithaca: Cornell University Press, 1987), who approaches the novel as a study in "the possibilities and pitfalls that beckon to and threaten the composing powers of consciousness," a rad-

ical study in "Jamesian hermeneutics" (29, 31); and Allon White, *The Uses of Obscurity: The Fiction of Early Modernism* (London: Routledge, 1981), who takes "the central anxiety of the novel" as the question of whether the narrator is "an obsessed voyeur indulging a vulgar fantasy, or an urbane observer who skillfully unravels all the minute signals given out by" the other guests (144). Peter Brooks brings forward the matter of the body in *The Sacred Fount* before letting it slip away into the spectral realm of epistemological conundrum (Brooks, *Body Work: Objects of Desire in Modern Narrative* [Cambridge: Harvard University Press, 1993], 107).

23. Yeazell, *Language and Knowledge*, 1–15.

24. Walter Pater, *The Renaissance: Studies in Art and Poetry*, ed. Donald L. Hill (Berkeley: University of California Press, 1980), 189. Jonathan Freedman also notes the use of Pater here and wittily characterizes the reversal as James's transformation "of Pater's hard, gemlike flame [into] a hard, flamelike gem" (Jonathan Freedman, *Professions of Taste: Henry James, British Aestheticism, and Commodity Culture* [Stanford: Stanford University Press, 1990], 197).

25. George Santayana, *The Sense of Beauty* (1896; rpt. New York: Dover, 1955), 83.

Notes to Chapter 7

1. Brown, *The Material Unconscious: American Amusement, Stephen Crane, and the Economies of Play* (Cambridge: Harvard University Press, 1996), 4.

2. John Guillory, *Cultural Capital: The Problem of Literary Canon Formation* (Chicago: University of Chicago Press, 1993), 229. Guillory's specific reference is to the end of Paul de Man's essay "Phenomenality and Materiality in Kant" (de Man, *Aesthetic Ideology*, ed. Andrzej Warminski [Minneapolis: University of Minnesota Press, 1996], 90.

3. Pierre Bourdieu, *Distinction: A Social Critique of the Judgement of Taste*, trans. Richard Nice (Cambridge: Harvard University Press, 1984), 170.

4. Catherine Gallagher, "Blindness and Hindsight," in *Responses: On Paul de Man's Wartime Journalism*, ed. Werner Hamacher et al. (Lincoln: University of Nebraska Press, 1989), 207.

5. Avital Ronell, *Stupidity* (Urbana: University of Illinois Press, 2002), 105.

6. Paul de Man, "Semiology and Rhetoric," *Allegories of Reading* (New Haven: Yale University Press, 1979), 10. Further references to this book appear parenthetically within the text; I have included the shortened title *Allegories* when context alone does not make clear the source of the quotation.

7. Paul de Man, "Aesthetic Formalization: Kleist's *Über das Marionettentheater*," *The Rhetoric of Romanticism* (New York: Columbia University Press, 1984), 285–86.

8. Elaine Scarry, *The Body in Pain: The Making and Unmaking of the World* (New York: Oxford University Press, 1985), 285–86. Further references appear parenthetically within the text; I have included the title when context alone does not make clear the source of the quotation.

9. Here I follow the analysis of lyric in Theodor W. Adorno, "On Lyric Poetry and Society," in *Notes to Literature*, vol. 1, ed. Rolf Tiedemann, trans. Shierry Weber Nicholsen (New York: Columbia University Press, 1991), 37–54.

10. I quote the passage in de Man's translation (*Allegories of Reading,* 13–14).

11. Walter Pater, "The Child in the House," *Imaginary Portraits,* in *Walter Pater: Three Major Texts,* ed. William E. Buckler (New York: New York University Press, 1986), 223, 225.

12. Pater, "The Child in the House," 224.

13. Elaine Scarry, "Work and the Body in Hardy and Other Nineteenth-Century Novelists," *Resisting Representation* (New York: Oxford University Press, 1994), 66. This essay originally appeared in *Representations* 3 (1983): 90–123; my citations are from *Resisting Representation,* where the essay appears under the heading "Participial Acts: Working." Further references appear parenthetically within the text; I have included the shortened title "Work and the Body" when context alone does not make clear the source of the quotation.

14. On the nineteenth-century belief that nothing is ever lost, see Alexander Welsh, *George Eliot and Blackmail* (Cambridge: Harvard University Press, 1985), 98–109; Gillian Beer, *Darwin's Plots: Evolutionary Narrative in Darwin, George Eliot and Nineteenth-Century Fiction* (London: Routledge, 1983), 19–26.

15. On the importance of touch in nineteenth-century thought, see Jonathan Crary, *Techniques of the Observer* (Cambridge: MIT Press, 1990), 19.

16. *The Body in Pain,* 248. The idea is restated in almost exactly the same language in "Work and the Body," 85n11.

17. Mark Seltzer, *Bodies and Machines* (New York: Routledge, 1992), 4.

18. Cynthia Eagle Russett, *Sexual Science: The Victorian Construction of Womanhood* (Cambridge: Harvard University Press, 1989), 48.

19. Karl Marx, *Grundrisse: Foundations of the Critique of Political Economy,* trans. Martin Nicolaus (London: Penguin, 1973), 104.

20. Marx, *Grundrisse,* 105, 104.

21. In the passage on abstraction in the *Grundrisse,* Marx does not quite ban such philosophizing, such application to widely varying historical moments of concepts made conceivable only by present-day economic life; he writes that one can understand with a new rigor such feudal economic practices as tribute money if one is acquainted with the modern system of rents. But to "identify" such widely separated moments, Marx warns, is to "smudge over all historical differences" (Grundrisse 105); likewise, to write about the body can easily yield work that is deeply involved with a contingent construction of physicality but that does not understand itself as such.

22. See the once-famous passage at the end of this essay where, having transformed modernity into an ambivalence of poetic language, de Man proceeds to sweep away what he disparages as "genetic historicism" on the basis that an *un*ambivalent poetic language is inconceivable (de Man, "Lyric and Modernity," *Blindness and Insight: Essays in the Rhetoric of Contemporary Criticism,* 2nd ed. [Minneapolis: University of Minnesota Press, 1983], 185).

23. See the discussion of Montaigne as "subjectivist, the chronicler of pure immanence" in the 1953 essay "Montaigne and Transcendence" (Paul de Man, *Critical Writings, 1953–1978,* ed. Lindsay Waters [Minneapolis: University of Minnesota Press, 1989], 3) as compared to the later mention of Montaigne in "Phenomenality and Materiality in Kant" quoted in my text (*Aesthetic Ideology,* 88).

24. Terry Eagleton, *The Ideology of the Aesthetic* (Oxford: Basil Blackwell, 1990), 10.

25. Christopher Norris, *Paul de Man: Deconstruction and the Critique of Aesthetic Ideology* (New York: Routledge, 1988); Rodolphe Gasché, *The Wild Card of Reading: On Paul de Man* (Cambridge: Harvard University Press, 1998).

26. Gustave Flaubert, *Madame Bovary*, ed. and rev. trans. Paul de Man (New York: Norton, 1966), 162, 48, 160. References to de Man's preface appear parenthetically within the text.

27. Gustave Flaubert, *Madame Bovary*, ed. Bernard Ajac (Paris: Flammarion, 1986), 116–17; Flaubert, *Madame Bovary* (Norton), 40.

28. *Madame Bovary* (Flammarion), 269; *Madame Bovary* (Norton), 145.

29. *Madame Bovary* (Flammarion), 355; *Madame Bovary* (Norton), 205.

30. James also uses this expression on occasion, as in *The Bostonians,* where the narrator sums up Selah Tarrant's influence on his wife by noting, "Her husband's tastes [had] rubbed off on her soft, moist moral surface" (*The Bostonians,* ed. Charles R. Anderson [Harmondsworth: Penguin, 1984], 94); or in "The Author of *Beltraffio*," when Mark Ambient's wife fears her husband's "influence" might "rub off on" the "tender sensibility" of their child like "a subtle poison or a contagion" (16:38); or, as previously noted, in *The Aspern Papers,* where the editor supposes that some "esoteric knowledge had rubbed off on" Miss Tina because she has "handled" the "mementoes" of her aunt's affair with Jeffrey Aspern (12:44).

31. Charles du Bos, "On the 'Inner Environment' in the Work of Flaubert," in *Madame Bovary,* ed. de Man, 363; Georges Poulet, "The Circle and the Center: Reality and *Madame Bovary*," in *Madame Bovary,* ed. de Man, 394.

32. Jean-Pierre Richard, *Littérature et Sensation* (Paris: Éditions du Seuil, 1954), 145, 127.

33. Poulet, "Circle and Center," in *Madame Bovary,* ed. de Man, 403.

34. du Bos, "'Inner Environment' in Flaubert," in *Madame Bovary,* ed. de Man, 363.

35. Jean Pierre Richard, "Love and Memory in *Madame Bovary,*" in *Madame Bovary,* ed. de Man, 427.

36. Henry James, "Gustave Flaubert," *Notes on Novelists,* rpt. in *Madame Bovary,* ed. de Man, 345.

37. See the end of the essay "The Dead-End of Formalist Criticism" in *Blindness and Insight* (245) and the essay "Phenomenality and Materiality in Kant" in *Aesthetic Ideology* (70–90).

38. The materialism of lyric is itself becoming the stuff of critical revision; for arguments that lyric is profoundly engaged with questions of physical things, see Daniel Tiffany, *Toy Medium: Materialism and Modern Lyric* (Berkeley: University of California Press, 2000); Carrie Noland, *Poetry at Stake: Lyric Aesthetics and the Challenge of Technology* (Princeton: Princeton University Press, 1999); Thomas J. Otten, "Jorie Graham's _____s," *PMLA* 118 (2003): 239–53.

39. For the point that de Man's writings adopt the perspective of "an eighteenth-century mechanical materialist," see Fredric Jameson, *Postmodernism, or, The Cultural Logic of Late Capitalism* (Durham: Duke University Press, 1991), 246. Jameson's argument helps to account for de Man's seeming strangeness—and hence his allure—to many of his readers in the 1970s and 80s; Jameson suggests that "much that strikes the postcontemporary reader as peculiar and idiosyncratic about his work will be clarified by juxtaposition with the cultural politics of the great Enlightenment philosophes: their horror of religion, their campaign against

superstition and error (or 'metaphysics')." While I agree with this subtle observation, I also argue that these eighteenth-century constructions of materiality are themselves filtered through a nineteenth-century construction of the body as protean and of the relation between the body and its spaces as one of the transfer of properties, of *frottement,* as I explain above.

40. *Madame Bovary* (Norton), 169; *Madame Bovary* (Flammarion), 307.

Notes to Chapter 8

1. Henry James, *The Other House,* ed. Tony Tanner (London: Dent, 1996), 10.

2. James, *The American Scene,* ed. Leon Edel (Bloomington: Indiana University Press, 1968), 328–29.

3. James, *The American Scene,* 149–50.

4. T. J. Clark, *The Painting of Modern Life: Paris in the Art of Manet and his Followers,* rev. ed. (1984; Princeton: Princeton University Press, 1999), 182.

5. Clark, *The Painting of Modern Life,* 180–81.

6. James, *The American Scene,* 73, 76.

7. Naomi Schor, *Reading in Detail: Aesthetics and the Feminine* (New York: Methuen, 1987), 3–4, 11–22.

8. Margaret Jane Radin, *Reinterpreting Property* (Chicago: University of Chicago Press, 1993), 65, 26; Norman Bryson, *Looking at the Overlooked: Four Essays on Still Life Painting* (Cambridge: Harvard University Press, 1990), 13–14; Susan Stewart, *On Longing: Narratives of the Miniature, the Gigantic, the Souvenir, the Collection* (Baltimore: Johns Hopkins University Press, 1984).

9. Bill Brown, *A Sense of Things: The Object Matter of American Literature* (Chicago: University of Chicago Press, 2003); Diana Fuss, *The Sense of an Interior: Four Writers and the Rooms That Shaped Them* (New York: Routledge, 2004); Susan Stewart, *Poetry and the Fate of the Senses* (Chicago: University of Chicago Press, 2002). Further references appear parenthetically within the text accompanied by the author's name when context alone does not make the source apparent.

10. Here I am thinking of the chapter on Jewett and the literary market in Richard H. Brodhead, *Cultures of Letters: Scenes of Reading and Writing in Nineteenth-Century America* (Chicago: University of Chicago Press, 1993), 142–76; and the essays collected in June Howard, ed., *New Essays on "The Country of the Pointed Firs"* (Cambridge: Cambridge University Press, 1994). This is not to say that these books are not valuable, just that the way we read has changed.

11. Janice Carlisle, *Common Scents: Comparative Encounters in High-Victorian Fiction* (New York: Oxford University Press, 2004), 29. Further references appear parenthetically within the text.

12. Walter Benn Michaels, *The Gold Standard and the Logic of Naturalism* (Berkeley: University of California Press, 1987); Fredric Jameson, *Postmodernism, or, The Cultural Logic of Late Capitalism* (Durham: Duke University Press, 1991).

13. Mark Seltzer, *Bodies and Machines* (New York: Routledge, 1992), 3.

14. Roland Barthes, *The Pleasure of the Text,* trans. Richard Miller (New York: Farrar, Strauss, 1975), 32.

15. Stewart follows, and somewhat reworks, the analysis provided in Ernest G.

Schachtel, *Metamorphosis: On the Development of Affect, Perception, Attention, and Memory* (New York: Basic Books, 1959).

16. The source of this quotation is Marx, *Economic and Philosophic Manuscripts of 1844,* in *Karl Marx, Frederick Engels, Collected Works,* ed. James Allen et al. (New York: International, 1975), 3:302.

17. Roland Barthes, "The Plates of the *Encyclopedia,*" in *A Barthes Reader,* ed. Susan Sontag (New York: Hill and Wang, 1982), 218.

INDEX

accessories, as duplicitous, 118–20, 137; as promiscuous properties, 110–12; as the Jamesian real, 23–24, 149; and self-maintenance, 32–33; and wounded body, 33
Adorno, Theodor, 187n9
adultery, as characterization of the material world, 110–32
aestheticism, 45; reflexiveness of, 66–73
The Age of Innocence (Wharton), 175n27
Agnew, Jean-Christophe, xviii, 168n7, 173n2
The Ambassadors (James), 59, 92, 111–13, 129–32, 155–56
ambiguity, as bodily matter in James, 8–10, 18–20
The American (James), xviii
The American Scene (James), 156–57, 184n34
The American Woman's Home (Beecher and Stowe), 46
Anderson, Charles R., 169n1
Anstruther-Thomson, Clementine, 58, 81
Armstrong, Paul B., 186n22
The Aspern Papers (James), 88–89, 93–98, 189n30
Atlantic Monthly (periodical), 78
Auden, W. H., 108–9
"The Author of *Beltraffio*" (James), 185n4, 189n30
The Awkward Age (James), 76–77

Bachelard, Gaston, 95, 146
Bagehot, Walter, 99
Balzac, Honoré de, 9, 72, 154, 157
Bann, Stephen, 178n12
Banta, Martha, xviii

Barron, James H., 180n1
Barthes, Roland, 163, 165
"Beauty and Ugliness" (Lee and Anstruther-Thomson), 58, 81
Beecher, Catharine, 46
Beer, Gillian, 188n14
Berenson, Bernard, 58–59, 78, 80–81
Bersani, Leo, 168n6, 186n16
"The Birthplace" (James), 92, 104–5
Blackmur, R. P., 170n9
Blair, Sara, 170n10
The Blithedale Romance (Hawthorne), 22–25
Bloch, Marc, 176n31
Boon (Wells), xv
The Bostonians (James), xx, 106, 189n30
Bourdieu, Pierre, 136
Bouvard and Pécuchet (Flaubert), 52
Boyd v. United States (Supreme Court case), 89–90,
Brandeis, Louis D., 87–89, 97, 105
The Breakfast Table (Sargent), 77–79
Brilliant, Richard, 179n17
Brodhead, Richard H., 182n15, 190n10
Brooks, Peter, 186n22
Brown, Bill, 136, 158–62, 163–64, 171n15, 174n7
Brown, Gillian, 171n15
Browning, Robert, 99, 107, 182n21
Bryson, Norman, 63, 158, 172n27, 174n5, 178n12
Butler, Judith, xxiii
Butler, Samuel, 100

Cameron, Sharon, 25, 125, 168n6, 170n9, 185n11
Capital (Marx), 40, 117
Carlisle, Janice, 161–62, 164